Raising Our Athletic Daughters

RAISING OUR ATHLETIC DAUGHTERS

How Sports Can Build Self-Esteem and Save Girls' Lives

JEAN ZIMMERMAN
AND GIL REAVILL

DOUBLEDAY

New York   London   Toronto   Sydney   Auckland

PUBLISHED BY DOUBLEDAY
a division of Bantam Doubleday Dell Publishing Group, Inc.
1540 Broadway, New York, New York 10036

DOUBLEDAY and the portrayal of an anchor with a dolphin
are trademarks of Doubleday, a division of
Bantam Doubleday Dell Publishing Group, Inc.

Library of Congress Cataloging-in-Publication Data

Zimmerman, Jean.
Raising our athletic daughters: how sports can build self-esteem
and save girls' lives / Jean Zimmerman and Gil Reavill. — 1st ed.
p.   cm.
Includes bibliographical references (p.   ).
1. Sports for women—Social aspects—United States. 2. Women
athletes—United States—Social conditions. 3. Sex discrimination
in sports—United States. 4. Self-esteem in adolescence—United
States. I. Reavill, Gil, 1953–   . II. Title.
GV709.18.U6Z55   1998
796′.082—dc21   98-7639
CIP

ISBN 0-385-48959-5

1   3   5   7   9   10   8   6   4   2

For Maud

Contents

Preface

As parents, as educators, as a society we are searching for answers in the late 1990s, when the cultural environment we provide for our children, and especially for our daughters, seems increasingly threatening and malignant. We've been troubled by a picture painted of adolescent girls today which indicates that our daughters lose something of themselves as they cross the threshold to adulthood, an essential part of the self that a leading theorist of female adolescence, Carol Gilligan, has labeled "voice."

A wake-up call for many parents came with the widespread dissemination of a survey report by the American Association of University Women (AAUW) in 1992. "Shortchanging Girls, Shortchanging America" is only one of a series of studies that have painted a dark picture of the way our society treats its daughters. The survey found a troubling downward arc to related aspects of girls' lives as they continue through secondary school. They experience a larger drop in self-esteem than do boys, and as a result are "more likely to lose interest in activities that challenge them, less likely to believe in their own abilities, and less likely to question teachers even when they believe the teachers are wrong."

Other research has reinforced the findings of the AAUW report. Most recently, the Commonwealth Fund's Survey of the

Health of Adolescent Girls, conducted in 1996–97 by Louis Harris and associates, recorded the responses of 6,748 boys and girls in grades five through twelve. Two of the survey's key findings were that girls are at a significantly higher risk than boys for suffering depressive symptoms and that girls lose their self-confidence as they mature, in contrast to boys, who gain in self-confidence as they grow older.

Clearly, there is a pronounced difference in the way young girls and young boys respond to modern life. The life choices of too many of our daughters are compromised by drug and alcohol abuse, early pregnancy, sexually transmitted diseases, eating disorders, self-mutilation, depression, and suicide. For many, concerns about body image become almost an obsession. We give radically different messages to our daughters and our sons, with often tragic results. We are raising a nation of Ophelias, to use a metaphor made popular by clinical psychologist and author Mary Pipher, who describes our culture as "girl poisoning."

But one source of optimism registers against this bleak background. Our daughters are pouring onto the playing fields of this country in unprecedented numbers. There is a growing awareness that girls enjoy sports and that sports are good for girls. New evidence is developing which indicates that girls who play sports tend to avoid the physical, psychological, and social pitfalls of modern adolescence. For a number of reasons, playing sports empowers girls.

But something is still not right. For girls today, the desire and the readiness to play are there, but the way is often blocked. Raising an athletic daughter—even in this era of ferocious WNBA court pounders and the triumph of female athletes at both the 1996 Atlanta and 1998 Nagano Olympic Games—parents may experience and observe situations that are disconcerting, if not disturbing. Twenty-five years after the passage of Title

IX, the law that mandates equal resources for girls' and boys' athletic programs, stubborn disparities still exist. It can be as simple as the number of sports available for girls in your area, either in the school system or outside of school. Boys might be able to participate in soccer, baseball, football, basketball, swimming, hockey, martial arts, while for girls there may be only basketball, gymnastics, swimming, and soccer. Girls' locker rooms always seem to be smaller, their practice times less convenient, and their games likely to be scheduled on school nights, when attendance is sparse, rather than on crowd-friendly weekends. The girls' teams carpool, the boys' teams get the hired bus.

The national media offer only minimal news coverage of our daughters' sports heroines or of the women's teams they follow. Studies reveal that more than 95 percent of national sports coverage pertains to male athletes. Athletic girls lack female role models. Even if your daughter loves sports and gets a chance to play, her coaches might be all men.

Our daughters drop out of sports at much higher rates than our sons, and it tends to happen right on the cusp of adolescence, when girls most need the benefits athletics can provide. Too many parents have the experience of seeing their child get involved with some kind of activity—soccer, say, or gymnastics—when she is in elementary school, only to have her announce her intention to quit when she reaches junior high. While a third of high school freshman girls play sports, that percentage drops to 17 percent in their senior year.

Some parents may be surprised by the characterization of American girls today as eager to play sports. They might see their daughters spending much more time loafing around the house watching TV than engaging in any kind of physical exertion. This is the source of a contemporary paradox: at a time of spiraling interest in sports for girls and women, physical activity among our children is dropping precipitously. Since 1982, there has been a 21 percent plunge in the number of teenagers who exercise regularly. It's as if our society is made up of two cultures, playing-field culture and television-watching culture, and the two of them are drifting inexorably apart.

This book represents the fruit of our efforts to talk to those people most intimately involved with these concerns—girls who play sports. We spoke to athletes all over the country who are participating in a wide range of sports, as well as some girls who have dropped out of sports entirely. We also interviewed professional athletes, parents, educators, coaches, trainers, program directors, and academics. We talked with girls in grade school, high school, and college, with their friends and relatives. Our own friends and family members gave us opportunity for interviews. The community we live in furnished a rich ground for investigation. We sifted through studies and reports and delved into the "secret history" of the female athlete.

We were looking for ways in which the world of sports can benefit our daughters as well as ways to open that world as much as possible for them.

We found considerable cause for optimism. The girls we met impressed us with their energy, poise, and confidence. These are young women who actively and intelligently make their own choices and shape their own lives. They help communicate the message that sports, at their best, can be an expression of the human yearning for excellence. And they provide reason for us to believe that in raising our athletic daughters, we are raising girls to be strong, self-determined women.

Raising Our Athletic Daughters

1

Leveling the Field

Girls Are Ready for Sports—Are Sports Ready for Girls?

"Go."

Kate Greathead launches into the first of six 800-yard training laps she will do this afternoon. Although she is its youngest
member, Greathead is one of the standouts on Hastings High
School's cross-country team. She tested up for varsity the previous year, during eighth grade. In three days she will head to the
New York State Cross-Country Championships in Westbury, on
Long Island, the only one of her team to qualify, a rare feat for a
freshman. Bruce Crandall, her coach, a man not given to over-
statement, says simply that Greathead has "some native talent."

"Thirty-eight, thirty-nine, forty . . . good!" Crandall calls
out the seconds as, across the quarter-mile track, Kate hits the
halfway mark. Her long strides eat up the yardage, and as she

kicks up her running shoes she shows her whole sole to anyone trailing behind. At four o'clock the dusk is just beginning to settle on the quick-closing late-October day. The beeches that ring the track at Reynolds Field, across the street and down a concrete walkway from the high school, hold the slanting rays of the sun and shower down yellow leaves. Half the track lies in shadow. Kate hits her rhythm. Even though it's chilly, she runs bare-legged, wearing light green shorts and a gray sweatshirt emblazoned with a Hastings *H* cut diagonally into green and gold halves.

At the state championships, she will be up against the most talented teenage runners in New York, close to two hundred of them. Kate is dreading it. She always dreads it, just as, after a race, she always feels good to have run it. Part of her struggle is with herself, with her own thoughts. During a race an image will sometimes flash through her head. She sees herself dropping to the ground, disqualifying herself, quitting. "The adrenaline is used up after the first two minutes, and then you're in pain," she says ruefully. The second-guessing begins. "Why do I do this sport?" she will ask herself. "It's so painful—what do I get out of it?" The only way out of self-doubt, for Kate, is to run through it.

Her mother sent her to camp for tennis, a more "social" sport, less of a grind on the body. Her parents try, but they cannot really understand the attraction running cross-country holds for her. They are more likely to see the pain than the gain. Neither of them had ever been jocks themselves. The family never watched sports together on television, not even the Olympics. They waited too long, Kate thinks, to get her into organized sports programs. She lived in New York City before she moved to Westchester County. Kate and her father used to circle the Central Park reservoir together. They gave that up when she got so much faster than her dad ("He jogs," she says. "I run"). There have been a lot of upheavals in her life recently. Her parents divorced. The split was amicable, but it was something for her to deal with all the same. She and her mother and two younger sisters had moved twice in as many years. This year, she had made the transition from middle school to high school.

Her heart hammers in her chest; each footfall is a mini-jolt that will wind up, over her running career, putting thousands of tiny stress fractures into the bones of her legs. Yet she manages to push away all thought of pain and focus on her strategy for the upcoming race. Avoid going out too fast. Save some strength in reserve for the last kick. Know which girls fade on the hills, and take advantage of that. Pace is the race.

She is the only member of the team still out on the track, still training, as dinnertime comes on. At fifteen, Kate is tall, narrow-shouldered, a bit gangly. Her scrubbed face and ponytail give her an updated girl-next-door look. Kate Greathead has actually stood in for Everygirl, U.S.A., in a filmed documentary based on Britain's celebrated *28-Up* series, which traces the progress of a select group of children every seven years as they grow up. Kate has now done two segments, at age seven and fourteen, the latter featuring her working out at the track.

Kate laps the quarter-mile, skimming by a pair of huffing adults, passing them easily with her half-graceful, half-gawky stride. She normally thinks of herself as uncoordinated but never feels that way when she runs. "I like to feel stronger" is the way she articulates what running does for her. In the physical sense, it's true. Running will condition her cardiovascular system, strengthen her immune system, build her muscles. The poundings that her legs withstand will add bone mass to them and actually make her healthier and tougher as an athlete.

But emotionally? Kate Greathead is poised at a threshold. Manifold pressures will come to bear on her over the next few years. How will she handle the challenges of being an adolescent girl in our complicated modern world? What will it take for her to grow from a healthy child into a strong woman?

The coach calls out the time. The lone girl runs in and out of the afternoon sun.

Everygirl is a fiction, just as Anytown, U.S.A., is a fiction. But they are useful ones. Hastings-on-Hudson, New York, where Kate Greathead lives, is a small community half an hour north from the busy hive of Manhattan. In its daily rhythms and suburban atmosphere, it represents the way much of America lives at the end of the 1990s. The town provides a window to what has changed for girls over the past three decades, in sports and in other realms as well.

In some ways, Hastings appears a throwback to a simpler time. Its residents pride themselves on the village's parks and green spaces. The community is relatively crime-free. Its population of eight thousand and small size (just over two square miles) give it an old-fashioned small-town feeling, and yet its proximity to New York City makes cultural amenities like theater, music, and art easily accessible for residents. After spending her childhood on Manhattan's Upper East Side, where she attended private schools, Kate moved with her family first to Chappaqua, also in Westchester County, and then a year later to Hastings. The schools in Hastings have for many years been a magnet for families with young children. They were part of the draw for Kate's mother, Christina Pennoyer, when she decided to move the family to Hastings.

But even in a relatively safe and peaceful place such as this, the harsh realities of the modern world can intrude. Parents in town worry about the same things that worry parents all across the country. In many families, both mother and father hold full-time jobs. Single-parent households in Hastings are stretched the way they are all over America. The result is a substantial amount of time when many young people lack adult supervision. In the nation as a whole, there are between 5 and 7 million "latchkey children"—an old-fashioned term in a day when many houses require a digital security code for entry. Roughly a third of all twelve-year-olds in this country are routinely left to fend for themselves while their parents are at work.

The hours between 3 and 8 P.M. have been labeled the "witching hours" by child professionals. While the common belief holds that Friday and Saturday late-night partying is when most kids get into trouble, the truth is that unsupervised afternoons and early evenings present the most danger. In the hour after the school bell rings, the teenage crime rate triples. "When we send millions of young people out on the streets after school with no responsible supervision or constructive activities, we reap a massive dose of juvenile crime," states a report prepared for the U.S. Attorney General's Office. When communities, desperate to address the rise in youth crime, initiate late-night curfews, they are missing the real problem.

Recreational sports—even pickup games around the neighborhood—used to provide a refuge for many children. But that situation has shifted with the "professionalization" of children's sports, whereby the emphasis in athletic programs is placed on elite players with highly competitive skills. "What's happened is that as parks and recreation funds have dried up, kids who are not looking at sports as an alternative are choosing negative alternatives," says Women's Sports Foundation Executive Director Donna Lopiano. "We have got to realize the stakes in terms of what we are going to pay for in crimes and teenage pregnancies. There needs to be a national movement to really bring public attention to the importance of after-school activities for kids during this high-risk period of time."

Crime, drugs, pregnancy, and unprotected sex inevitably become attached to questions about morality, especially when we talk about their incidence among children and teenagers. But they are more dispassionately seen as health concerns. A study released in July 1995 by the National Center for Health Statistics cited a whole array of "risk-taking behaviors" that kids in this country regularly engage in, from smoking tobacco to carrying a gun. Of the 10,645 kids age twelve to twenty-one surveyed, a quarter had within the previous month driven with a driver who had been drinking. Forty-five percent had taken a drink themselves and a quarter had engaged in binge drinking (five or more drinks in a row). Almost 30 percent of those surveyed had used an illegal drug at one point in their lives, and 60 percent reported they had sexual intercourse at least once. Once again, it is during the witching hours that most at-risk behavior occurs. That is also when most teenage pregnancies are conceived.

Jim Davis has been the director of the Hastings Youth Council for over two decades. "Drug and alcohol use hasn't changed much over the years," Davis says, "but the consequence of the same behavior is more deadly than it ever was. Drinking and drugs lead to lower impulse control, which can lead to unprotected sex. I don't care about legislating morality, but unprotected sex leads to AIDS."

Other local professionals share his concern. Sharon Farber is a Hastings psychotherapist who specializes in treating eating disorders. She has presented workshops for parents on "Surviving Your Child's Preadolescence." Parents who came of age in the 1960s, she says, are "raising their children as if their home is and should be a democracy, as if everyone should have a voice in major decision-making." Farber is one of those who worries that there might be stubborn problems hidden beneath the town's smooth veneer. Many parents "really don't know anything about what should be appropriate boundaries between themselves as parents and their children. They don't understand the tremendous risk that their children are at in this environment. Parents are not nearly protective enough of children. There's a lot of denial." Farber believes girls face particular difficulties. "One of the biggest problems in this town and probably all over the country is that girls are maturing physically earlier than ever before, so their bodies are ready for things before their minds and their hearts are." She concurs with the analysis of Mary Pipher, Carol Gilligan, and others: "Despite the feminist revolution, girls have been raised, especially at [adolescence], to go quiet and go stupid."

Like other adults who work with kids in Hastings, both Jim Davis and Sharon Farber grapple with disturbing trends. While some kids in Hastings find plenty to do, others appear at loose ends. There have been repeated instances of underage drinking. In the last few years, the town has been hit twice by teen suicide, the latest in February 1997, when a high school senior drove fifteen minutes south to the George Washington Bridge, parked, and leaped over the rail. In a tightly knit community, events such as these rip through the social fabric and leave parents wondering what they can do to protect their children.

Kate Greathead recalls being in her new school in her new town for all of five months when news of the more recent suicide broke. "It was hard, but it wasn't as hard as for the people in high school who knew the girl," Kate recalls. Closer to home was a slashing incident on the Old Croton Aqueduct Trail, a dirt-track right-of-way that runs through town and is used by hikers and joggers. A runner was cut across the face in what was characterized by police as a possible gang initiation. Kate realized that

she had been running at the same spot an hour after the incident happened. Though such circumstances are not enough to
disturb her equanimity (or at least, she will not admit that they
do), they reinforce something that we instinctively know to be
true: modern life can be frighteningly random, complex, dangerous.

Parents, to use Benjamin Spock's memorable phrase, are
"terrified optimists." We want to believe we can shield our
daughters from all that would harm them. The enduring answer,
of course, is to transform society so that it is less harmful to girls.
But there is not much a parent can do, in the short run, to
change TV programming, or fashion advertising, or the level of
violence in the world. In the face of such a tall order, it is easy to
feel powerless. Many of us don't know where to begin.

While we've been worrying about the pressures facing our
daughters, another force has been building, a dramatic shift in
how girls approach their lives, their bodies, their selves. From
cradle to college, more and more girls now consider participation in sports their birthright. That in itself is astonishing, given
the barriers erected over the years to keep athletics "for boys
only." What is even more compelling is that this is largely a children's crusade, spearheaded by our daughters themselves. Today, a star on the girls' high school basketball team can be voted
homecoming queen, a combination that would have been excep-
tional even a generation ago, when the Baby Boomers were in
their teens.

Until recently, the sweat and hard physical work required for
most sports weren't considered compatible with growing up female. Even today many adults carry this baggage. Mothers as well
as fathers may feel a bit discomfited when they see their daughters competing aggressively, especially in tough sports such as

wrestling, football, or boxing. Through the experience of parenting, a whole generation raised amid the egalitarian ideals of the women's movement has confronted its own uncertainty about sex roles. Becoming a parent tends to traditionalize a relationship. Responsibilities once shared are suddenly divided into "women's work" and "men's work." And our increasing conformity to tradition comes at the same time we begin to raise our children. We may feel ambivalence about this, but we fall back on biology as some sort of immutable constant, a force that cannot be resisted or swayed. "I know I shouldn't say this," begins the nominally enlightened mother or father, before confessing, "but boys and girls are different—they just are."

Yes, we should accept and celebrate the difference. But where does biology end and acculturation begin? What kind of messages, subtle and otherwise, do we send our children from birth? What do our daughters learn when they detect our discomfort if they come home dirty, or with their clothes torn, or with a scrape on the knee? How about the pinprick of discomfort we might feel when they triumph over a boy in an athletic contest, or become fanatical about baseball, or start to lift weights? There might be a rare parent who can answer truthfully that girls as much as boys own the athletic experience, but the rest of us have a way to go.

Luckily, our discomfort hasn't stopped many of our daughters. "The public," says Anna Seaton Huntington, Olympic rower and America's Cup sailor, "accustomed to a diet of simple sweethearts and ever ambivalent about aggressive women, may initially balk at the knowledge that most female athletes don't care what they look like, sound like, or smell like as long as they are crossing the finish line first." Girls aren't waiting for a blessing on what is "suitable" activity for young ladies. Jettisoning such stereotypes as "girls don't sweat" and "girls don't get dirty," they are jumping headlong into all sorts of activities that have long been the exclusive domain of boys, as well as some new sports their mothers might not have heard of, much less considered appropriate. They are engaging in strenuous games of soccer, softball, basketball, and volleyball. Today's girls snowboard and pile into rugby scrums and race mountain bikes. They throw unhittable fastballs and run blistering sprints.

Over the last two decades the whole culture of American school sports has been transformed, and many of the changes have to do with the way we approach sports for girls and women. In 1970, only 1 in 27 girls participated in high school sports. Today that ratio is 1 in 3. The hard numbers are that fewer than 300,000 high school girls were on a school sports team in 1971, while they were 2,367,936 strong in 1995. More than 16,000 high schools (out of a nationwide total of 20,000) now have a girls' basketball team. All this during a period when the athletic participation of boys remained fairly flat, at around 3 million. According to one survey, a healthy majority of parents (87 percent) now agree with the proposition that sports are equally important for girls and boys. Here is an enormous change, a fundamental change, in what girls do. And it has led to changes in how girls view themselves.

Recognition of women's athletics gained tremendous momentum in the wake of the 1996 Olympic Summer Games in Atlanta. In an unprecedented hat trick, American women swept the three most popular team sports, gaining gold medals in softball, basketball, and soccer. Only a bronze in volleyball prevented a gold medal grand slam. NBC declared the Atlanta Olympics "The Year of the Woman." The network delivered a whole pantheon of female athletes using richly textured profiles. America responded, with female viewership soaring to record levels. It wasn't the first time women athletes became hugely popular stars, but that summer there were more of them and in a greater variety of sports. Our daughters witnessed the tough, in-the-dirt play of Dot Richardson, who although the oldest member of the U.S. women's softball team stood out as its leader. Legions of new fans cheered as charismatic soccer star Mia Hamm and her teammates utterly dominated the sport. Sheryl Swoopes and Lisa Leslie gave girls a basketball Dream Team all their own. Never has there been an Olympics that has burned so many female names into the popular memory.

It happened again at Nagano in 1998, when the spoils of the Winter Olympics also seemed to belong to the women. Women's figure skating was once more the most popular sport in the games, and the battle between Michelle Kwan and Tara Lipinski was front-page news around the world. Perennial crowd favorite Picabo Street skied to a dramatic hundredth-of-a-second gold in downhill. That she did so months after recovering from knee surgery and just weeks after a serious headlong collision sent a powerful message about her physical toughness and female athletes' perseverance in the face of adversity. The American women's ice hockey team played impeccably in its march to the gold medal, besting Canada in a final game marked by a fierce— and highly entertaining—rivalry. The men's hockey team, on the other hand, could muster only a seventeenth-place finish and was disgraced by a room-trashing incident that left behind an image of churlishness and lack of good sportsmanship. Commentators suggested that here was the contrast between men's and women's sports in a nutshell: the women playing a good, clean, highly competitive game, and the men behaving as if they were spoiled babies. It was one of those moments when our vision of what women can do in sports was significantly expanded. The Olympic Commission voted just before Nagano that no new sport would be added to the official Olympic roster unless it was played by both female and male athletes.

The success of the female Olympians helped pave the way for something that had been tried repeatedly in decades past, but never with success: professional women's sports leagues. During the year leading up to the 1996 Summer Olympics, the sponsorship muscle of the National Basketball Association had been put in the service of the women's USA team. NBA commissioner David Stern had closely monitored the unprecedented year-long undefeated streak of the gold medalists as they played in tournaments all around the country, against college teams, and all around the world, against other national teams.

In April 1996 Stern announced the formation of the Women's National Basketball Association. It was only one of two new leagues for women created that year. The American Basketball League was formed as well, with a different season (fall/winter instead of summer) and a different philosophy (concentrating on cities where women's college ball was traditionally popular rather than on larger NBA markets) than the WNBA. Both leagues featured players who previously had been forced to make their professional money in women's leagues overseas, as well as college-fresh stars such as Jennifer Azzi, Rebecca Lobo, and Lisa Leslie.

Once again, as it had with the Olympics, the public, particularly the female public, responded. The WNBA forecast an audience of four thousand per game, but instead averaged three times that number. The league quickly succeeded in "moving the fabric"—to accommodate the larger crowds, arenas had to move back the curtain they used to mask empty seats. With their husbands, with their sons, with sisters and friends, but most especially with their daughters, women showed up to scream and shout and go wild. It was a phenomenon waiting to happen. NBA superstar and NBC commentator Reggie Miller suddenly became "Cheryl Miller's brother," a reference to the Phoenix Mercury coach and former UCLA standout. Spike Lee, a courtside fixture at NBA games, brought a new fan to New York Liberty games, his four-year-old daughter. *USA Today,* after ignoring the season's initial games, was forced to bow to readers' demands that it provide more extensive coverage. The success of the WNBA and the ABL spawned plans for a host of new professional leagues for women, including soccer, ice hockey, and fastpitch softball.

In the midst of the WNBA's inaugural season, Title IX had a birthday. (Officially, the legislation is termed Amendment IX of the Civil Rights Act, but today it is universally known as Title IX.) It had been twenty-five years since the federal government mandated that all educational institutions receiving taxpayers' money must provide equal opportunity to both sexes in all programs. The occasion allowed for broad-stroke assessments of the state of women's sports in America. Originally designed to get more women onto university faculties, Title IX had a largely unforeseen collateral effect on athletic programs. Title IX worked to get girls the uniforms, locker room space, playing fields, practice times, and program offerings that they needed to compete in athletics.

For such wide-ranging legislation, the act had an uncertain gestation. In 1970, Oregon Congresswoman Edith Green had proposed amending the federal Civil Rights Act of 1964, adding a prohibition against sex discrimination to statutes that already prohibited discrimination on the basis of race, religion, or national origin. During the debate over the amendment in Congress in the summer of 1970, testimony focused not on athletics but on horror stories presented by female academics, mostly professors and graduate students shut out of programs or denied tenure because they were women. Sports programs figured in the debate only tangentially. In August 1971, Indiana Senator Birch Bayh introduced a similar amendment in the U.S. Senate. Congress officially enacted Title IX on June 23, 1972, as part of the Omnibus Education Act. It was only later, after the law was put on the books, that the NCAA, the administering authority for collegiate athletics, realized its impact, with one NCAA commissioner labeling the statute "the death of college sports."

By far the most visible effect of the law has been on athletics. It is what the words "title nine" have come to mean—the effort to give girls equal access to school athletic programs. In that sense, at least, Title IX is a model of effective legislation. The year it was enacted, 1972, remains the demarcation line for the phenomenal growth of women's sports. On its twenty-fifth anniversary in the summer of 1997, the still-somewhat-obscure federal statute was topic of the week. Instead of an unbroken expanse of column inches describing male athletes' achievements and concerns, suddenly readers of the sports pages—so overwhelmingly male that newspapers often place advertisements for strip clubs there—confronted unfamiliar terrain. Here were the children of Title IX, a parade of female mountain bikers, soccer strikers, volleyball spikers. For a brief moment, the (men's) sports pages became, simply and more expansively, the sports pages. The celebration of Title IX's anniversary was an education for many Americans. Women and girls were dead-set serious about sports.

During this time, sports commentators talked about an "explosion" in women's athletics. "It's not an explosion but the tide coming in," Donna Lopiano of the Women's Sports Foundation told reporters. "It's been building over a long time. You add all of the things up—Title IX, gender equity, television and corporate interest—and you've reached critical mass. This is not an accident in history. This is a major cultural change that I don't see going back."

As *Business Week* put it, "It's the girls' turn to score, and Corporate America is taking notice." Accordingly, in October 1996, AT&T Wireless Services spent $3 million to become the title sponsor for the newborn Women's Professional Fastpitch League. Evian, Nissan, Coors Light, and other companies announced that they would underwrite Women's Professional Volleyball Association to the tune of more than $5 million. The ABL and the WNBA also garnered hefty sponsorship, the ABL with Reebok and McDonald's, the WNBA with Nike, Spalding, Champion, and Lee Jeans. A major female athlete such as Florence Griffith-Joyner could now count on lucrative endorsement contracts from a wide spectrum of sponsors: "Flo-Jo" has appeared in ads for Agfa (film), Proxy (shoes), Mizuno (sporting goods), Mitsubishi (appliances), Toshiba (copiers), and LNJ (toys).

The past two years have seen the start-up of five magazines that target women athletes, published by some of the most powerful media companies, including *Sports Illustrated for Women, Condé Nast Sports for Women,* and *Jump.* Television reflects corporate confidence in the trend, with Lifetime carrying WNBA games and a series of specials on women in sports. (Of course, there is still a huge differential between the average pay of male and female sports stars: Rebecca Lobo earned $250,000 in 1997, compared with Patrick Ewing's estimated salary of $17 million. Michael Jordan earns $33 million per year, eleven times the total annual payroll of the WNBA.) Advertising campaigns by the biggest sports apparel companies, such as Nike and Reebok, feature the new female superstars of basketball, soccer, and swimming and highlight women's mental and physical fortitude and their desire to get in the game. Nike's "If You Let Me Play Sports" ad campaign cites a litany of benefits for girls who play sports.

Manufacturers have finally begun to offer athletic gear specifically designed for women. At first, this meant only cosmetic changes, such as a wider color choice. But recently there has been concentrated research on just how the female anatomy functions in athletic performance. The sporting goods industry woke up to the reality that women make 80 percent of all athletic-gear purchasing decisions and responded with cycling seats, climbing harnesses, boxing chest protectors, backpacks, wet suits, softball bats, and pole-vault poles newly designed to fit a woman's frame. "The 'p'-word we are looking for is not 'pink,' it's 'performance,' " says Anne Flannery, manager of the women's athletic division at Spalding. As a result, female ballplayers no longer have to hunt to find a baseball glove contoured for a woman's hand. Julie Smith, a top softball player, consulted with Spalding to develop its women's glove—intended, according to company literature, "for the serious woman athlete."

To gauge how far we've come in how short a time, consider that the sports bra was developed only in the late 1970s (the first one was made by sewing two jockstraps together). There is also that ultimate barometer of the public mood, the message T-shirt, bearing such attitude-intensive slogans as these: "Don't Think of It as Losing to a Girl, but Getting Beat by the Better Athlete (Girls Dominate)," "Basketball Is a Boy's Sport—As If!" and "I'd Play Boys' Sports If There Were Some Competition."

Over the course of the last two decades, the Hastings school system gradually reoriented itself to accommodate the rising number of girls interested in sports and the changes dictated by Title IX. Taking 1972, the year Title IX was enacted, as a base year, there are now twenty-four athletic programs for girls in Hastings High School where before there were nine. This is in the context of other changes, some of them rooted in the demographics of a small town. In the early seventies high school enrollment could support a full football squad. Football was to some extent the focal point of the town's fall weekends. Games were well attended by people from all over the community, not just the parents of players, and the cheerleading squads of those years were full strength. But as the baby boom subsided into a baby bust, the pool of players shrank to the point that a village team was no longer viable. "They were only fielding eighteen, twenty boys," recalls Joe DeGennaro, the current athletic director and a Hastings High alumnus. "Some of them were going to have to play both offense and defense, and when that happens the kids get tired, and there were going to be injuries."

Apocalypse came to Hastings football in the early 1990s, when the team was forced to merge with its archrival, Dobbs Ferry. "There was a lot of pain," says Thomas Fazio, the Hastings High principal, recalling rancorous town meetings and arguments over which colors the team would wear. The Hastings Yellow Jackets and the Dobbs Ferry Eagles became, in a compromise that epitomizes the sometimes risible outcome of decision by committee, the Eagle Jackets. Hastings's green and gold and Dobbs's blue and white became blue and gold. All in all, seven sports are now combined between the two schools, but football was the one which hurt the most. The pool of available talent has been decimated not just by small class size but by a shift in interest as well. The combined teams can field only twenty-eight boys, and the future looks to be not much brighter. Just one Hastings boy participates in the local Pop Warner football league for kids under seventh grade. There are currently two Hastings cheerleaders in the combined Hastings–Dobbs Ferry squad.

Football's declining popularity in Hastings does not reflect a lack of interest in youth sports overall. Fazio, the high school principal, currently estimates that 70 percent of the school body is involved in sports programs, both boys and girls alike. This is a ratio that is considerably higher than the national average (37 percent for high school girls and 51 percent for boys). But different sports are now attracting Hastings kids. The struggle to field a single varsity football team and one modified (junior high) team contrasts with six well-rostered soccer teams, three for girls and three for boys. "Our fields are jammed up with AYSO [American Youth Soccer Organization] soccer on the weekends," DeGennaro says. Parents and kids alike are eschewing high-impact, injury-prone football for kinder, gentler—but just as competitive—sports. In the country as a whole between 1985 and 1995, high school students' soccer participation rose by 81 percent, while their involvement in football shrank by 5 percent. "There are year-round opportunities in soccer," DeGennaro points out. "Football is a one-season sport."

Hastings has a carefully articulated scholar-athlete philosophy. Coaches attempt a no-cut policy whenever possible (boys' basketball is usually the one exception), and there are academic requirements for all sports. "My first responsibility will be my classes," reads the "contract" all Hastings athletes sign. "My second responsibility will be the team." The win-at-all-costs philosophy has been officially jettisoned. "Sports," says DeGennaro, "fits into the whole perspective of life. You're not always going to win."

In 1988, when Thomas Fazio was appointed principal, one of his mandates was to expand the girls' sports programs. Panels of parents, teachers, and students who interviewed him complained, Fazio recalls, "that there wasn't equity, that the girls were getting shortchanged." The parents he spoke to were "quite explicit" in their expectations, and the issue was not just a minor theme of Fazio's hiring process. "I heard about it repeatedly," he recalls. In 1991, when a longtime athletic director retired, Fazio elected to fill the position with a woman, Nancy Kalafus, the former women's basketball coach at Columbia University. In the five years of her tenure, Kalafus beefed up the girls' programming at the school virtually across the board. She increased the number of basketball teams for girls, and in 1996 and 1997 the girls' varsity won scholar-athlete team awards. The girls' softball team won the league championship in 1996.

Title IX compliance is only part of the reason for this shift. The Hastings athletic budget balances down to the penny all monies spent on boys' and girls' programs. But numbers and trophies can't convey the full breadth of the attitudinal change that DeGennaro, for one, has seen firsthand, from his time as a student athlete at Hastings in the 1980s to his current tenure as athletic director at the school. When he lettered in baseball and basketball, he remembers, "people looked down at certain sports girls played." So extreme was the difference in treatment of girls' and boys' sports that DeGennaro finds himself wondering "how we got away with some of the things we got away with," a perspective sharpened by his experience as the father of a two-year-old daughter. Currently, he reports that "the gym is packed" for girls' volleyball matches: "Everybody comes; it's a happening." The male athletes treat their female peers with "a certain respect," DeGennaro says, adding that when he restored a tradition of girls' and boys' doubleheaders in basketball, "our guys loved it."

In the spring of 1997, Donna Shalala, secretary of Health and Human Services, convened a press conference just prior to the starting buzzer at the NCAA Women's Final Four tournament in Cincinnati. The timing and setting were carefully chosen. Shalala wanted to capitalize on the big audience for women's college basketball that had developed over the previous decade. Final Four games were now selling out a year in advance. Shalala knew there were a lot of eyes trained on Cincinnati that day, the eyes of many young female basketball fans, the attention of many parents. She had a point to drive home, and these were the people she wanted to reach. Shalala smiled at the image she presented as she delivered her message. The five-feet-tall secretary stood on a chair positioned between two professional basketball players, representatives from the ABL. Both women easily dwarfed her. But if the image was comic, Shalala's words were in earnest. "There are still too many people who think getting fit isn't feminine," Secretary Shalala told the assembled crowd. "There are not enough opportunities for girls to participate in sports at every level."

Shalala then officially announced the completion of a report by the President's Council on Physical Fitness and Sports, "Physical Activity and Sport in the Lives of Girls." Sports and fitness experts, primarily from academia, had come together under the aegis of Shalala's department and under the direction of the Tucker Center for Research on Girls and Women in Sport, a four-year-old think tank based at the University of Minnesota. The council's charge was to examine the entire question of girls and sports, to ask whether girls benefited from participation in athletics, in what ways, and whether there might be drawbacks or dangers to our daughters getting involved in sports. The end report was perhaps the first comprehensive look at the topic, certainly the first interdisciplinary look, in that the council synthesized the work of experts from fields as disparate as nutritional studies and field hockey, motivational psychology and teenage sexuality.

Scholars and advocates who had made women in sports their life's work—people like Linda Bunker, the associate dean of academics and student affairs at the University of Virginia; Judy Mahle Lutter, president of the Melpomene Institute in St. Paul, Minnesota; Don Sabo, a professor of sociology at D'Youville College in Buffalo, New York, who focuses on questions of gender in athletics—took a holistic approach to their subject. They sought to determine the effects of sports participation on the "complete girl." Their report corroborates the basic premise that sports and physical activities are great for girls, that they offer a whole panoply of physiological, psychological, sociological, and mental health benefits. Further, the report successfully establishes the question of girls' participation in sports as a public health issue. The benefits are so measurable, and the protection provided against at-risk behaviors so marked, that any barriers preventing our daughters from participating in sports may be seen as barriers to their lifelong health and happiness.

The President's Council report brought together the growing body of research that confirms the benefits of athletics for girls of all ages. High school girls who are athletes do better in school than girls who don't play sports, earning higher grades and getting better standardized test scores. They are also less likely to drop out of high school and more likely to go on to college than their nonathletic counterparts. Many student athletes confirm that the demands of their sports involvement help them establish their academic priorities. The large time commitment which sports require—one study showed that serious, varsity-level athletic training at the high school level consumes twenty-eight hours per week—seems to enhance rather than detract from their school performance, the same principle behind the old saw "If you want a job done, give it to a busy person." Since athletes have a set amount of time in which to complete homework assignments, they must learn to manage their time effectively. At some schools, athletes avail themselves of time between the end of the school day and practice to complete assignments that other students might put off until late in the evening. Students who play on a team also often must maintain a certain grade point average, a strong incentive to study, perform, and, on a more basic level, simply to show up. One varsity senior says her love of basketball gets her up and dressed and to school on time in the morning, because she knows it is a game day and she doesn't want to miss out.

The confidence that girls gain through sports and the comfortable attitude many develop in relation to competition are often directly translatable to the classroom. Researchers have noted a specific dynamic, for example, that may explain the traditional gap between girls' and boys' scores in mathematics. Because of complex social conditioning, when boys fail at a math problem, they tend to blame outside factors—the problem was too difficult, or it was not explained properly. When girls fail, they are more likely to blame themselves. Their anxiety over failure leads to more failure. Female athletes, on the other hand, grow accustomed to risk, to failure, to the possibility of improving their performance through sustained effort—confidence-building experiences invaluable for academic success. A 1996 research paper confirmed a relationship between girls' involvement in high school athletics and higher science grades and test scores.

There is ample research to show that sports participation is good for the physical health of all kids. The strenuous exercise involved in playing sports strengthens the immune system, increasing resistance to colds and viruses. It helps kids develop the appropriate motor skills for each stage of their development. Girls who engage in regular physical activity are less likely to be overweight and more likely to have lower levels of blood sugar, cholesterol, and triglycerides and lower blood pressure than non-exercising girls.

Researchers have also found that young athletes carry many of these physiological benefits with them into adulthood. Physical activity during adolescence also helps young female athletes develop stronger, denser bones. It's an early preventive measure against osteoporosis later in life. In general, female high school athletes develop fewer chronic health problems as they age, compared with their nonactive peers, including prime killers such as heart disease and breast cancer. The correlation between lower breast cancer rates and physical activity has not been conclusively determined, but evidence is accumulating that such a relationship exists. One to three hours of exercise a week from menarche to menopause correlates to a 20 to 30 percent reduction in breast cancer risk. Four or more hours of exercise per week can reduce a woman's risk by almost 60 percent.

"Not to have confidence in one's body is to lose confidence in oneself," writes Simone de Beauvoir. In our appearance-oriented culture, girls experience this loss of confidence at epidemic levels—what historian and *The Body Project* author Joan Jacobs Brumberg calls "bad body fever." Researchers in one study found girls as young as third grade professing they were "on a diet." In another study, 82 percent of the adolescent girls who indicated that they were trying to lose weight were in fact well within current medical guidelines for healthy weight.

While research on the link between sports participation and body image is just getting started, it seems clear that girls who engage in athletics are less troubled by issues concerning their weight, both when they are young and later in life. There are two elements here—the degree to which kids are overweight and the degree to which they obsess over the way they look. Involvement in athletics addresses both problems. Kids who play sports tend to be leaner than those who are sedentary. In addition, "playing on a higher number of school sports teams was indicative of better body image," reports *The Melpomene Journal* about a study of girls in YWCA summer programs in 1995. "Body image became increasingly positive with an increase in participation on sports teams.''

We are still in an era when adolescent girls idolize Cindy Crawford and other supermodels. This can have disastrous impact on girls who feel they can't measure up to this ideal—one study indicates that girls with low body image are more likely to compare themselves to models. But even the iconography of the supermodel is changing to include more athletic imagery. Cindy Crawford's fitness videos have sold millions of copies. Rachel Hunter is a kick boxer. Elle McPherson, a former synchronized swimmer in school, has climbed Kilimanjaro and is a competitive sailor. Athlete-model hyphenates such as the volleyballer Gabrielle Reece and WNBA's Lisa Leslie have helped establish sports accomplishment as part of the feminine ideal. "I'm passionate about both," says Leslie about modeling and playing basketball. "We have to stop feeling that we've got to choose one thing and cut off our other options."

The revolution slices both ways: if models can be athletes, athletes can embody feminine ideals. Many people still recall the moment they first saw Jackie Joyner-Kersee, "the greatest female athlete," lined up at the blocks, her long nails varnished a bright red. This was a direct challenge to the bias that held that sports would necessarily masculinize a woman, and it made almost as much of a statement as her world-record heptathlon score. "I see elegance and beauty in every female athlete," Joyner-Kersee writes in her autobiography. "I don't think being an athlete is unfeminine. I think of it as a kind of grace." Gold medal skier Picabo Street says that she "got big and strong quickly" in junior high school, and "it was tough on me." Now she goes out of her way to do media: "It's important for girls to see bigger women with strong opinions, who are also sensitive and vulnerable. I want to tell them, 'You can be a strong athlete and still be feminine.' "

Here is a paradigm shift that helps our daughters expand their choices and enhances their ability to reject what eating-disorder expert Kim Chernin decries as "the tyranny of slenderness." But it's a shift that is only partially accomplished, and there's a lot we can do as parents to help reinforce this change. "We have to socialize girls differently," says Joan Jacobs Brumberg. "We have to teach them about the potential of what a body can do, not what it looks like. Young boys generally benefit from growing up thinking this way."

Playing sports can also help prevent a whole panoply of risk-taking behaviors that have become a contagion among high school girls. High school female athletes are less likely to use tobacco; in fact, they have one of the lowest rates of smoking among all sectors of the high school populace. There is a significantly lower rate of attempted suicide among teenage female athletes than among the population as a whole.

A major 1998 study of athletic participation and sex behavior definitively established the link between sports involvement and lowered rates of teenage pregnancy. Researchers found that girls who were athletes were less than half as likely to get pregnant as female nonathletes. The study, sponsored by the Women's Sports Foundation and a consortium of corporations, also determined that female athletes were more likely to refrain completely from sex throughout high school, and were more likely to use contraceptives if they did have sex. On average, the athletes studied had their first sexual experience later than nonathletes, had intercourse less often, and had fewer sexual partners. The chicken-or-the-egg puzzle remains—do sports attract people who are more responsible, or encourage responsible behavior? The answer for most parents, at least in the case of teen pregnancy, is simple: Whatever works.

High school athletic participation continues to pay off later in a girl's college and professional career. According to the NCAA, female student athletes graduate college at a higher rate than do female students, 69 percent to 58 percent. For African Americans, the differential is greater, 58 percent to 41 percent. Participating in athletics as a high school student can open doors for college scholarships. Beyond that, there is strong evidence that a grounding in nontraditional activities such as sports can serve our daughters well in their work lives. In one study of women business leaders in Fortune 500 companies, 80 percent said they were childhood "tomboys" and were involved in athletics during their youth—a clear signal that playing sports can act as a springboard to greater opportunities later in life. When your daughter has been challenged on the basketball court or soccer field, she will be better equipped to handle the challenges—the need for perseverance in the face of defeat, the hard work required for success—that come her way as an adult. Champion distance swimmer Diana Nyad writes in her autobiography that "marathon swimming is the most difficult physical, intellectual, and emotional battleground I have encountered, and each time I reach the other shore, I feel worthy of any other challenge life has to offer."

Less measurable, more intangible, are benefits such as learning to win—or lose—gracefully, sportsmanship, ethical conduct on the field, the idea that practice cannot always perfect performance, but is of value in and of itself. "Sports, from which I learned all I know about ethics," wrote Albert Camus about his childhood. A constant theme sounded by girls talking about their participation in sports is how much it helped them to feel part of a team. Adult women speak of the lifelong friendships they made pursuing sports in school. At every stage of life, female athletes receive invaluable support from being one of a group dedicated to a common goal. During adolescence, this sense of inclusion helps serve as a buffer against more dangerous influences and peer pressures.

We need to view sports not as a panacea, but as one crucial element in the effort to help our daughters through the difficult transition to adulthood. "Many strong girls," writes Mary Pipher in *Reviving Ophelia,* "have found protected space in which they could grow. There are various ways to find that space. For example, athletics can be protective. Girls in sports are often emotionally healthy. They see their bodies as functional, not decorative. They have developed discipline in the pursuit of excellence. They have learned to win and lose, to cooperate, to handle stress and pressure. They are in a peer group that defines itself by athletic ability rather than popularity, drug or alcohol use, wealth or appearance."

If Ophelia had been on the swim team, in other words, she might not have needed reviving.

So girls are ready for sports, and sports are good for girls. But are sports ready for girls?

Even in this era of athletic golden girls and the Olympiad of the Woman, too many girls who are eager to participate in athletics are turned off by their experiences. Our daughters drop out of sports at much higher rates than our sons, and it tends to happen right on the cusp of adolescence, when girls most need the measurable benefits athletics can provide. While a third of high school freshman girls play sports, that percentage drops to 17 percent in their senior year.

Why does this happen? One reason is that our daughters have inherited a legacy of bias against the female athlete. Old notions die hard, and prejudice endures beyond all reason and expectation. Outmoded attitudes still keep girls from sports today, cut short their dreams, narrow their vision of what they can accomplish. Just when there appears to be a vital way out of the Ophelia syndrome, we are confronted with blocks and barriers to that path, vestiges from a time when women were pushed out of athletics because engaging in sports was deemed "unfeminine."

In the last decade of the last century a Rochester physician named Elias Holloway published an influential series of articles warning women against all forms of physical activity, particularly athletic activity. Initiating what was to be a constant theme over the next hundred years, Holloway voiced a protective if somewhat obsessive concern for the breasts and reproductive organs of the human female. These physical attributes, he announced, were too delicate to be subjected to the rigors of sport. Women were counseled to avoid "strenuosity" in all forms.

It is a view of female anatomy that has proved surprisingly durable. As late as the early 1970s, Dr. Creighton Hale, then president of Little League Baseball, testifying in civil actions attempting to open up his organization to girls, said the "vitals" of the preadolescent female might be threatened by playing the game. A judge in the case heard a medical witness declare there was a danger of breast cancer developing in female players who were slammed on the chest by a hardball.

A potent variation of this view argues that there is something not physically but socially wrong with being a female athlete. Don Sutton, the great major league pitcher, said that he would introduce his sons, but not his daughters, to baseball. "I'm a great believer in little girls being feminine," Sutton said. "And you can't be feminine sliding into third." Bruce Crandall, Kate Greathead's coach, who's been coaching for thirty years, says he still encounters the "conflict" of parents and students alike believing "that the combination of running and sweating is not feminine."

Another line of argument ignores the injury (moral, social, and physical) that sports might do to girls in favor of complaint about the injury that girls might do to sports. To some people, the superior male athlete is involved in the serious pursuit of excellence, while the female athlete is either a freak or a hobbyist. This attitude cropped up with regularity recently when male sportswriters were asked to cover the ABL and the WNBA. One well-respected male sports commentator sniffed that the play was "not quite up to the level of high school junior varsity on a good night." Another groused that he had to give up weekend barbecues and fishing because women had the outlandish idea of playing hoops in summer. To top things off, even the NBA lost its status as a males-only preserve when Violet Palmer and Dee Kantner became the league's first female referees.

George Gilder, who went on to become the architect of many of the Reagan administration's family policies, extrapolated this women-harm-sports argument to near metaphysical realms: "Sports are possibly the single most important male rite in modern society. [The presence of women] reduces the game from a religious male rite to a mere physical exercise." Male athletic performance is "an ideal of beauty and truth," while that of females represents a "disgusting perversion" of that truth.

The double standard was clearly visible in the controversy surrounding Nykesha Sales and the "gift" of her record-breaking score. The University of Connecticut forward ruptured her Achilles tendon when she was one point short of her team's all-time scoring record. Her coach, Gene Auriemma, arranged for her to limp onto the court during a subsequent game with Villanova and make an unopposed two-point field goal. Somehow this translated into a women's issue. Big East commissioner Michael Tranghese suggested that "men compete, get along, and move on with few emotions," while women "break down, get emotional"—and thus Sales required having the rules bent as a form of therapy. The idea was that fragile women need special treatment to make it in the big, bad world of sports. Critics conveniently ignored the many instances in the male sports world of assisted record-breaking—Mickey Mantle broke a home run mark off a gift pitch, openly acknowledging it as he rounded the bases—as well as the weepy emotionality of many male athletes. The controversy indicates that many people are invested in seeing the female athlete as somehow different, less worthy, a pale imitation of the standard-setting male.

Another argument is based on women's purportedly "inferior" level of play, which carries a lot of weight with people obsessed with statistics (which of course represents a large chunk of American fandom). For them it's not a question of subjective opinion, it's simply a matter of objective facts. A woman can throw a softball 240 feet, a man can throw it 360 feet. The women's world record in hurdles is consistently broken by male high school champions. Men run faster, hit harder, jump higher, throw farther than women. Just check the record books. It's all down there in black and white.

The shared premise of all the arguments against women in sports is this: female athleticism is not as valuable as male athleticism. This idea is still effective, as it has been for decades, in putting up barriers that stop or hinder girls who want to play sports. For all the glorification of Mia Hamm and Sheryl Swoopes, for all the hundreds of thousands of girls flooding into soccer programs and softball leagues, onto ice hockey rinks and basketball courts, we still have one foot stuck in the past. As a society, we persist in the belief that the athletic achievement of our sons is somehow more worthy, more natural, more exciting than that of our daughters. But it is a premise that is being challenged and increasingly discredited.

In the early 1970s, Billie Jean King was among the best tennis players in the world, dominating women's tennis from the time she first won the Wimbledon singles in 1966. The women's movement was roiling the intellectual life of the nation, but the world of sports was insulated by what seemed to be an innate conservatism on the part of many athletes, both male and female. King was the exception. When she won the Italian tennis championship in 1970, she received $600 in prize money while the men's champion got $3,500. There were inequities across the board—the Pacific Southwest Championships, for example, posted a $12,500 prize for the men's winner and $1,500 for the women. King called for a boycott and, when the United States Lawn Tennis Association (USLTA) refused to budge, helped found a separate women's circuit. Only a few years later it was among the most lucrative sports circuits in the world, its prize money already three-fifths of the men's and rising.

King had accomplished a neat end run around the line of reasoning which held that sports played by women were demonstrably inferior to men's sports. She and the other organizers of the Virginia Slims circuit simply ignored the objective fact that a men's tennis serve is x miles per hour faster, on the average, than a woman's serve. King approached the game differently, in a purely subjective manner. She asked simple questions: Was women's tennis good entertainment? Did spectators enjoy watching women play tennis? It was, and they did, and one of the world's most successful sports circuits was born. The USLTA caved in, equalizing the women's and men's purses at the 1973 U.S. Open for the first time.

King was not through. In that same year, the ultimate confla-
tion of sports and feminism occurred in the Houston Astrodome
in front of thirty thousand tennis fans and some forty million
television viewers. Aging tennis professional Bobby Riggs, who
called himself the "clown prince of tennis," had beaten the Aus-
tralian Margaret Court the previous Mother's Day. He was now
loudly proclaiming the superiority of the male tennis player. On
September 20, 1973, Riggs met King in a match that was in no
small part a circus. She was carried to courtside on a palanquin
by a coterie of "bare-chested muscle men." Riggs made a grand
entrance in a rickshaw drawn by scantily clad girls known as
"Bobby's Bosom Buddies." According to accounts quoted in Allen Guttmann's *Women's Sports:* "Midgets dressed as dancing
bears frolicked near the dugouts, the university of Houston
marching band thumped out 'Jesus Christ Superstar,' a dozen
cheerleaders in red hot pants swirled pompoms, two dozen
women tennis pros in 'BJK' [for Billie Jean King] T-shirts lined
up along a red carpet." But the lasting impact of the match had
nothing to do with the spectacle. When King trounced Riggs
(6–4, 6–3, 6–3) it was a defining moment, not only in the world
of sports but in the modern-day women's movement. Sports had
become a feminist issue.

Today, no one would seriously suggest matching Pete Sam-
pras against Martina Hingis, because fans know this apples-and-
oranges debate has nothing to do with the excitement of playing,
or watching, a superlative game. The idea that no one will watch
a women's match because the tennis is "less dramatic" has been
thoroughly discredited. In fact, the women's tennis circuit has
progressed to the point where *USA Today* can state that "the
woman's game is deeper, more diverse, and often features
matchups that are more intense and entertaining than those
played on the men's tour." Over the space of a quarter-century,

the female athlete has journeyed from the fringes of the sports world ever closer to its center.

Part of what is driving this recognition is the fact that our daughters simply will not be denied sports as an integral part of their lives. In a curious way, the child has been the mother of the woman. The naturalness and enthusiasm of the girl athlete makes the woman athlete appear not so much an anomaly as an icon. Even if they are not aware of it, Kate Greathead and girls like her are helping to accomplish a revolution. Thousands of educators, coaches, parents, and other adults are also working to allow our daughters to receive the full benefit that participation in athletics provides.

Kate Greathead has achieved that sine qua non of equality, the ability to take it for granted. She reports that girls and boys who play sports in her school get treated "the same" and that being a female athlete at Hastings is "not that big a deal." She hears her name on the public address system on Monday morning if she has run well or won a race on the previous weekend, but otherwise her participation in sports is not often called out or commented upon. For the boys, too, she says, "it's pretty irrelevant" whether or not they are athletes. "For both [boys and girls], it's a good thing. It doesn't make you automatically popular, but it makes people respect you more, or—'respect' is a weird word— they think higher of you, they're impressed."

To qualify for States, Kate had to place in the top five in her section of Class B schools ("Class B" refers to a method of grouping schools in categories for purposes of competition, so that smaller schools are not mismatched against larger ones). She had an idea she might qualify, since she had been running against basically the same girls in all her meets, and she knew she was faster than all but one or two of them. But she didn't know for sure until she placed third at a meet in Wappingers Falls, New York, the Saturday before the state championships, in early October 1997. Then the butterflies began. The day before States, Coach Crandall and she drove out to Long Island, an hour's drive each way, to walk the 5-kilometer cross-country course.

The Saturday of the race saw a heavy downpour. Kate and Crandall arrived two hours before her starting time. Her family was coming to cheer her on but had not yet arrived. She waited in the car with her coach, the rain streaming across the fogged windshield. She could see the vague shapes of the other runners heading to their races or coming back covered in mud. She would be among the last to run. They listened to the radio, Kate getting more and more nervous, until twenty-five minutes before the race, when she decided she had to go to the bathroom. She went out "to this really tiny building" that housed the rest rooms and the concessions, finding a half-hour line when she got there. The whole experience seemed designed for maximum anxiety. When she got out onto the course, sloppy as it was, her jitters disappeared. She was running in mud "up to here, falling and sliding all over the place." As she finished she saw that the lousy conditions had taken two minutes off her time.

Kate wound up placing 56th in a field of 140 at States, and she considered herself "sort of happy" with the results. "I have three more years," she says. "I was pleased that I got to go at all." One of her goals is to run a full marathon someday. Realistically, she knows the Olympics "aren't in my future." She has seen too many other girls who are farther along, athletically, than she is, which she recognizes is a function in part of her getting a relatively late start in serious athletic activity. But she admits she can't help "watching the runners in the Olympics and dreaming about it." She also wants to run in college.

There are complex variables of personality, parenting, and

environment at play here too, of course, but clearly sports are something that have helped focus Kate's life, steadied it, provided sanctuary. She is a fifteen-year-old girl who moved two times in two years and whose parents got divorced during the same time period. In another girl, these same circumstances could function as triggers for depression, anxiety, the various self-destructive behaviors to which teenagers sometimes resort. But the experience of Kate Greathead suggests the degree to which sports can buffer our daughters from the ravages of adolescence.

"Considering how frightening everything is," wrote Gertrude Stein, "it is good to realize that not much is really dangerous." Kate Greathead would probably agree. Asked to list the things she is afraid of, she draws a blank. She knows "there are bad things in the world" but says, "I'm never really worried for my own safety." During her parents' divorce, she says, playing sports "was a place where I got away from everything." In health class at school, she learns about eating disorders, but quotes the simple rule of thumb of her coach: "Eat good, sleep good, run good." She describes herself as a basically happy person. She feels "strong," she says, competent at running and getting better at it. She is a good example of a girl who with the help of her sport is successfully negotiating the conflicts and difficulties of adolescence.

How can you raise your daughter so that she not only survives but flourishes during the crucial years when she is growing to adulthood? How can we, as a society, bridge the gap between a nation of Ophelias and one of centered, self-assured girls such as Kate Greathead? At every step of childhood, from cradle to college, we can encourage the kind of physical activity that will strengthen our daughters.

2

Throwing Like a Girl

Sports and Your Preschool Daughter

Trina Chynoweth's garage door is pocked with grapefruit-sized dents. The eighteen-year-old Chynoweth is a star pitcher on her Appleton, Wisconsin, high school softball team, and the dents represent battered testimony to hours spent perfecting her fastball.

Chynoweth has just graduated high school. Her grades were good but not extraordinary. She has had offers of athletic scholarships at several colleges, but she is unsure if she will take them. With typical pitcher's logic, she thinks she might spend some time in the academic "minors" before getting called up to the major league. "I want to take a year and go to the community college," she says.

From early on, athletics was a constant in Chynoweth's upbringing. Her father was "one of the power hitters of his day," as Trina describes him with obvious pride. She recalls reading over the well-worn clippings of her dad's local softball career, first in high school and later in the tavern leagues. The stories of his prowess helped inspire her. "My mom is the greatest in the world," says Trina, "but my dad is my good luck charm." She feels better pitching when she spots her dad in the stands. "Because he's the one who's pushed me to be who I am now. And I thank him for that. It's made a difference." Trina has four older brothers, who are deeply involved in sports themselves. A few of those dents in the family's garage door belong to them. "I had no choice but to be a little roughhouser," Trina says. There were always games of "pile-on" in the snow in her backyard ("smear the queer," Chynoweth says it was called) and oftentimes she was the target of her brothers. Later in her childhood there were hockey, basketball, and baseball games with neighborhood kids.

But softball is the Chynoweth family passion. The coming summer, Trina is to travel with an eighteen-and-under all-state team that is headed to Kansas for the Softball World Series. She is the most accomplished athlete in her sports-obsessed family. Her brothers boast about her. "I had my picture in the paper and my brother looked at it and was bragging to all his friends, 'Yeah, we taught her everything she knows, and now she's beating all of us.'"

Trina Chynoweth's lanky frame is perfect for whipping a fastball past a batter. She is what some people refer to as a "natural athlete"—ignoring the hour upon hour of practice she put in to make herself that way. If anything, Chynoweth is proof that athletes are made, not born. Her natural abilities helped, of course, but the crucial thing in her life was the support of her family. "Playing sports was really pushed when I was growing up," says Trina. "My parents feel it keeps you out of trouble."

It's difficult to believe that there could be much trouble lurking in the small-town streets of Appleton, Wisconsin. On summer evenings there are well-attended band concerts in the park, where some families remain in their cars and honk their horns as a sign of applause. It's jarring to pick up a local paper and see reports of rural methamphetamine factories, police worries about gang violence, teen murders. Trina Chynoweth's parents sent her into sports as a way of protecting her, armoring her. They were using athletics as an inoculation of sorts, guarding their daughter against present-day social ills. They started to do this surprisingly early. Her parents and brothers introduced her as a toddler to the baseball as a toy. "I was always going around with a baseball in my hands, even as a baby," Trina remembers.

While a lot of time and money and thought has gone into youth sports programs in the last several years, not much attention has been paid to children under the age of five. Of course, many parents think this is proper. Loath to resemble the overbearing stage parent, they reject any move to rush their toddlers into sports. Developmental psychologists are nearly unanimous in saying that preschool is too early an age to participate in all but the gentlest of organized sports activities. Certainly it is too young for competition.

But it is not too young to think about how we shape our children's awareness of sports. Trina Chynoweth's parents first took her to a softball game when she was still an infant. The stretch of time from birth to kindergarten is a period when we can examine our attitudes, rethink our prejudices, root out age-old stereotypes which may be turning our daughters away from physical activity in general and organized sports in particular. Female athletes regularly cite early formative experiences that inspired them, motivated them, and gave them confidence about their athletic abilities. These are keepsake memories of moments which helped shape their idea of themselves as athletes. Olympic figure skater Tara Lipinski tells of standing on a Tupperware container when she was two years old, pretending to mount the platform to accept a gold medal, a clutch of dried flowers in her tiny hands. U.S. skier Debbie Armstrong, a gold medalist in the giant slalom, made her first run down the slopes at the tender age of three. Barbara Ann Cochran, who ended a twenty-year gold medal drought for the American ski teams when she won in Sapporo in 1972, grew up on a small family-owned ski area in Vermont. LPGA great Amy Alcott got interested in her sport because a golf instructional program came on after her Saturday morning cartoon shows. Figure skater Tenley Albright's father would flood her backyard every winter to give his children a rink.

Olympic gold medalist Nadia Comaneci writes in her autobiography about how her earliest experiences contributed to her later performance as a world-class gymnast. As a preschooler, she loved to climb the fruit trees in her grandparents' garden in the countryside outside her native town of Onesti, Romania.

> I remember one day when, after I had spent an entire afternoon perched at the top of a plum tree, my exasperated grandmother, having tried to coax me down with some home-baked cookies, called up to me, "Nadia, why on earth do you spend all your time climbing trees!" "Because they're here to be climbed," I answered. . . . It had never occurred to me before that I needed a reason for climbing. I simply did it because I enjoyed it. I remember those days now as a useful introduction to the problems of the asymmetric bars; after all, a swing around a bough is no different from one on the bars.

Appleton, Wisconsin, is a world away from Onesti, Romania, but Trina Chynoweth tells a story much like Nadia Comaneci's. "My parents knew by the time I was three years old that I was getting to be an athlete, because I picked up a softball and started windmilling it into the fence," Trina says. "I actually started with pinecones, just windmilling them into the fence." She was probably imitating the sweeping underarm pitching style she had seen at softball games. In sports as in everything else, who we are as children shapes us as adults. In order to arrive at a confident, accomplished seventeen-year-old like Trina Chynoweth, we have to look at how she started.

There are good reasons why a three-year-old girl might grow up to be an all-star pitcher. One is that her parents don't mind when their daughter roughhouses or gets her clothes dirty—they see it as an inevitable component of play. They steer clear of the dainty, "sugar and spice" model of girlhood and reject any negative stigma attached to the word "tomboy." Often, these parents help their daughters get a jump on developing skills like catching, throwing, and kicking—the building blocks of playing sports. Or parents might nurture a whole sports-friendly environment, an extended family of siblings, relations, and friends who play, talk, or coach sports. Trina Chynoweth's older brothers were at least as influential in her involvement in athletics as her parents.

It may be an uncle or an aunt who makes a special effort to introduce a child to a favorite physical activity. It might even be a neighbor. Penny Rosario, an Olympic softball player for Puerto Rico in the 1996 Summer Games, remembers a neighbor who got her out on the ballfield when she was a child. "I just idolized her," Rosario says. "I would knock on her door and ask her to come out and play with me. That's how close we were. And she'd say, 'Go play with the grass.' But I still waited for her to come out. She was great; she played third base. She's this little old Italian lady, a real wonderful woman, and she would take me to the ballfield and give me all the little tidbits on how to play."

Ultimately, all the people in a child's life—parents, siblings, relatives, caregivers, neighbors—can show through their actions and their words that it's great to be involved in sports and that no one should be excluded. Or, through an equally powerful set of messages, they can communicate negative ideas about sports participation. Further, if parents are not active themselves, they are less likely to encourage their children, especially female children, because they themselves might hold deeply ambivalent feelings about athletics. Children who grow up loving sports see the people they admire most, their parents, loving sports. Lisa and Rick Wheeler are marathoners and cross-country ski racers who are in their late forties, the parents of two adolescent daughters. As babies, Lindsey and Paige Wheeler saw their parents compete in ski meets, marathons, and athletic contests of all kinds. Both girls are now committed to playing soccer and other sports. They often ski and run alongside their parents.

Of course, we already use this pro-sports influence—but we direct it almost exclusively toward our sons. Researchers have yet to do much investigation on specific ways we treat boys and girls differently with respect to sports. There is no published scientific study, for example, on how much time we spend playing catch with our daughters, compared to the time we put in with our sons. But there has been a whole host of scientific studies which, when taken together, point to reasons why young girls might be less likely than young boys to see themselves as athletes.

Studies show that, from the time they are in the nursery, young girls in our society are nudged along a path that leads them away from participation in athletics. "Isn't she delicate?" we say of a girl, while of a boy: "What a strong grip he has!" Sociologists have scrutinized such "cradle talk," the words parents employ to describe their newborns, to see if there are differences in the way we view our sons and daughters. Mothers and fathers "describe daughters as smaller, softer, cuter, and more delicate than sons, regardless of the child's actual physical attributes," states an overview of this research. "Sons were described as stronger, more coordinated, and more alert than daughters." The cradle-talk study was first done in the mid-seventies. It was replicated fifteen years later, after whole-scale changes in sex roles, and the rise of the working mother. The results were virtually the same.

Of course, we reveal ourselves not only through our words, but through our actions. Here, too, researchers have noticed subtle differences in approach that might serve the future careers of male athletes better than female athletes. "Fathers have more physical contact with infant sons than with infant daughters," concludes one 1993 study. "They engage in more rough-and-tumble play with their sons than with their daughters; in contrast, they are more likely to cuddle their infant daughters than sons." We give our toddler boys boosts in physical confidence in many different ways. Researchers investigated parents' reactions when called upon to assist their children. The mothers and fathers were seated in the center of a room, surrounded by a barricade of soft cushions. On the other side of the barrier was a toddler, who obviously was going to make an effort to get to his or her parents. The researchers found that the parents' reactions differed when their children voiced distress. The parents were more likely to urge the boys vocally to surmount the barricade. The girls they lifted up and over. In other words, we are more likely to "rescue" our daughters when they get into difficulties. We may thus be depriving them of the confidence that comes from surmounting obstacles themselves. Other research reinforces this conclusion. One researcher studied parents' responses when their young children cry. He found that, on average, mothers and fathers go to comfort girls eleven seconds faster than they do boys. A logical conclusion: girls may learn that crying gets results, while boys learn to be self-sufficient, to comfort themselves.

Toys marketed for girls continue to be heavily skewed toward passive or traditional female roles. A recent survey by the Renfrew Center, an eating disorders clinic, found a preponderance of toys and games about makeup, clothes, and shopping. "Combined with cultural messages about beauty that we receive from magazines and television," says Renfrew body image specialist Adrienne Ressler, the toys "can promote thinking that sets the stage for additions or patterns of disordered eating." A few toy designers have developed games that buck this trend. The Purple Moon series of CD-ROM computer games has just kicked off a line of girls' sports titles with *The Starfire Soccer Challenge,* described as "a friendship adventure with cleats." *The New York Times* notes that "a perceived bias towards boys [in computer software design] has vanished . . . and the much-discussed gender gap in computer use has all but closed." But some of the new game software is remarkably similar to the low-tech Easy-Bake Ovens and beauty parlor sets that clogged toy stores aisles in previous decades. The top two selling game software titles in 1997 were *Barbie Fashion Designer* and *Barbie Magic Hair Styler.* But even Barbie is changing: Mattel now sells an Olympic Barbie and a Scuba Barbie. Parents need to ask what sort of messages they are bringing into the house when they buy a toy for their daughters.

In essence, we give our sons a different "job" growing up than we do our daughters. Some difference is natural and necessary. No one wants boys and girls to be exactly the same. But when boys fulfill our expectations and go outside to run and climb while girls stay inside playing fairy princess, the trait of athleticism gets assigned to boys only. The result may not be apparent immediately. Preschoolers are a pretty rough-and-tumble lot. Almost all children (those who are able to) run, jump, or climb at least a little. But the machinery of identity has been set in motion. Studies have shown that by first grade, the association between "sports" and "boys" is already firmly in place in young minds. Later, we may be baffled when our adolescent daughter suddenly drops out of sports. We shouldn't be surprised, however. What we're seeing is the fruit of seeds planted long ago, as early as babyhood.

Even before kindergarten, your daughter may have had to make that arduous crossing of the great boy-girl divide, simply to reach a place where she could go outside and get dirty. She probably experienced some confusion over the mixed signals our society sends out. She wants to be a girl and she wants to play hard at the same time—a false choice in which there are no clear answers. In adolescence, when she decides to retire her ice skates to the closet or quit the basketball team, it could be her way of finally coming to terms with the age-old message "Don't get your dress dirty"—which sounds simplistic and ridiculous but actually carries a whole lot of cultural weight and baggage. It's much easier for her to stop participating than it would be for a boy, because athleticism is not recognized as an integral component of her identity as a girl. It's foreign. It's an import. The "default" position for girls is still daintiness.

In a large chain department store near Trina Chynoweth's home in Wisconsin, it is clearly Packer Country, U.S.A., a realm transformed, Emerald City–style, into the green-and-gold colors of the NFL team. A whole section of the ground floor is given over to Packer regalia, which is displayed in almost absurd abundance. There are T-shirts, hats and jackets, ties, socks, mugs, pennants, pens, blankets, coolers, and assorted knickknacks. There are also Packer crib toys and baby clothes. Green-and-gold rompers in sweatshirt fabric are sized for toddlers, babies, and newborns. There is nothing to stop the diehard fan from dressing her girl-child in such sports-oriented clothing. But the section is clearly designed with boys in mind.

Across the store, in the children's clothing department, are signs helpfully labeling one aisle of clothes "Infant Boys" or "Infant Girls," or "Toddler Boys" or "Toddler Girls." The clothes displayed for boys are in primary colors. A shopper would be hard pressed to find a pair of size 2 corduroy overalls for a toddler boy in any shade but red, blue, or green. The clothes for little girls are almost invariably confections of powder-puff pink and white. Sometimes they are made of sweatshirt cotton, in a concession to the reality that female toddlers can be as tough on their clothes as their brothers. But overall the children's section of this store, like stores across the country, conforms to the idea that girls should wear clothes that appear more "delicate" than those worn by boys.

Despite the enormous changes in roles for men and women over the last decades, we're more "pink-and-blue" than ever. The separation in baby clothes is as strict and uncompromising as the Continental Divide. It is a cultural choice, not a universal law. As late as the 1890s, the color code was reversed, with pink preferred for boys and blue for girls, as it is in present-day Japan. There is nothing inherently masculine or feminine in baby blue, pink chiffon, or kelly green, for that matter. But sports apparel, while not exactly coded blue, is still relegated in our society primarily to the boys' aisle. When parents dress a boy in a Packer romper, they are in effect saying, "You belong to the dream of someday becoming a big, brawny athlete." From the clothing stores to the network airwaves, our society helps our sons forge a link between "boy-ness" and "sports."

If we want to dress our daughters in sports clothing, on the other hand, our society forces upon us a figurative journey, "across the aisle" into boys' territory. The same is true when we want to allow our daughters freedom to roughhouse, or to climb to the highest branches of a tree, like Nadia Comaneci. We find ourselves placed in an awkward position, having to break invisible barriers and bend unwritten rules, just to imagine for our daughters the athletic future that is so effortlessly granted to our sons. The way we normally treat young girls and athletics in this society represents something of a self-fulfilling prophecy. We assume our daughters can't or don't want to play sports, and so we don't help them gain the basic skills necessary for success. When they do play sports, therefore, they don't have fun, because they are ill prepared to play. When they inevitably drop out, we are back where we started, confirmed in our preconception that girls can't play.

The prekindergarten years, before the age of five, can be a time—and for boys it usually *is* a time—when children gain an understanding of the fundamental skills which are crucial for any level of success in organized athletic programs. A grasp of the basics can mean the difference between an enjoyable or an embarrassing introduction to sports. Generally, we prepare our boys for sports by teaching them how to throw, catch, kick, and other motor-building skills. This early start is one reason boys tend to find sports more enjoyable than girls, why they tend to stick with athletics over a longer stretch of their lives. The way children begin their experience of sports, in other words, often determines whether or not they continue to participate throughout their lives.

For a country that professes to love sports, we tolerate outrageously high dropout rates in athletics. Seventy percent of children reject organized sports before the age of thirteen, and the rate for girls is six times that of boys. There are many reasons for this, among them the harsh regimentation of some team play, the stress and pressure children may be exposed to, the overemphasis on winning. For the young child, all these reasons devolve into a single one. Researchers have surveyed kids who quit athletics about why they do so. The overwhelming response is that the kids are not having fun. It isn't fun to be sent into a game and not know what you are doing. Both boys and girls react negatively to their first exposure to athletics when they lack basic skills necessary for them to enjoy the sport.

"What bothers me is that we take kids and enroll them in tee-ball or soccer programs, but we never prepare them," notes Fred Ensch, director and founder of the Palm Beach, Florida– based National Alliance for Youth Sports. "It's like taking a child and putting him in school and giving him calculus in first grade. No wonder there's always been such a tremendous drop-out rate from sports."

Instead of being challenging, the experience becomes daunting and overwhelming. Girls especially lack the fundamental sports skills that many boys acquire by the time they enter elementary school. The situation may be aggravated by an orientation that has been demonstrated among young girls—an eagerness to please, a sensitivity to the judgment of others. Studies have shown that girls are more self-conscious, less willing to "blunder on" without skills than boys are. Boys and girls have different reactions to achievement or lack of it. When girls come into sports and they are not prepared, they are more likely than boys to feel they've failed and thus give up.

So how do we prepare our daughters? In fact, learning to throw, catch, and kick is not at all an effortless process, nor is it natural or predetermined by genetics. It's a consequence of experience and learning. In general, boys get that experience, and girls don't. It follows that we must find ways to give our daughters more experience with throwing, catching, and kicking when they are young.

Basic athletic skills are the result of endless hours of childhood practice. Most of the time, this "practice" appears to adults as mere play. A child might spend an hour seeing how far he can throw stones into a lake, for example, or trying to clear a tree branch with a kicked ball. Boys seem so intent on this work because society has sent a message to them that these skills are part of what it means to be a boy. A boy tossing a ball against a garage door is simply playing, yes, but he's also learning throwing skills, and on a deeper level he is also busily constructing his identity. That's why little boys can sometimes seem relentless in their pursuit of sports skills, while little girls may be lackadaisical about pursuing theirs.

So clear is the disparity in our culture that we even have an expression, "throwing like a girl," which has come to mean throwing badly, awkwardly, ineffectively. James Fallows, writing in the *Atlantic Monthly*, points up an intriguing contrast that occurred on opening day of the 1994 baseball season. Bill and Hillary Clinton both threw out a game ball at separate opening day ceremonies—she in Chicago, he in Cleveland. What was interesting, Fallows points out, were the throwing styles of husband and wife. There it was for all the world to see, a picture-perfect example of the difference in the way most men and many women throw a ball—so perfect, as a matter of fact, that both pictures landed side by side in the pages of both the *New York Times* and the *Washington Post*.

"The President, throwing lefty, had turned his shoulders sideways to the plate in preparation for delivery," Fallows writes. "He was bringing the ball forward from behind his head in a clean-looking throwing action." Hillary Clinton threw "standing directly facing the plate. A right-hander, she had the elbow of her throwing arm pointed out in front of her. Her forearm was tilted back, toward her shoulder. The ball rested on her up-turned palm." Hillary Clinton threw her opening day pitch "like a girl," and she threw it that way despite the fact that, according to her press secretary, she had spent "the weekend before open-ing day, tossing a ball in the Rose Garden with her husband, for practice." The imperfect results of that practice indicate how difficult it is to learn how to throw late in life. Like speaking a foreign language or riding a bicycle, it is a skill best learned while young.

"There are different stages that individuals go through when they are learning how to throw," says Crystal Branta of Michigan State University, who has studied the physiological pro-cess involved in overhand throwing. "Some of the earliest stages involve, for example, kids sitting in a high chair and throwing food down on the floor—that 'chop' motion where the hand is up by the ear and they just throw it right down on the floor." Most girls get caught in an intermediate step of the learning process. "We call it an ipsilateral pattern," Branta says. "That means the same side is used. If a person is a right-handed thrower, then she would step out on her right foot."

The ipsilateral throw, "throwing like a girl," is a perfectly natural stage of the process. Every boy in the country has done it at one point. "It's part of the development," says Marty Ewing, one of Branta's colleagues at Michigan State, who has studied the sociological side of the question. "But boys get to that point and the father says, 'Oh, my God, he's throwing like a girl!' So they go to work with them." When most girls start to throw ipsilater-ally, it's a different story. "The fathers don't get upset and say, 'Oh my gosh, we've got to work on this,' " says Ewing. "It's more like, 'Well, she's a girl, and it doesn't matter.' "

What most boys learn—and many girls don't—are the basics

of the "contralateral," or opposite-side, throw, so called because the thrower steps forward on the foot opposite to his or her throwing hand. When throwing right-handed, in other words, the thrower will step forward with the left side, swinging the lower body, upper body, bicep, forearm, and finally the wrist in a crack-the-whip "snapping" motion that increases the power of the throw.

A strong overhand throwing style is crucial to many different sports. It forms the basis of the baseball throw, the tennis serve, the volleyball spike and serve, the forward pass in football, the javelin toss, and, with some modifications, the shotput in track and field. Trina Chynoweth does not "throw like a girl." Neither do Dot Richardson and the other members of the U.S. national team that won the softball gold medal during the 1996 Summer Games. It's a measure of how much we see sports as strictly boys' territory that the inability to perform this basic action is— wrongly, it turns out—associated with girls. Many otherwise well-educated adults continue to believe that females and males differ in some essential way that makes throwing a ball difficult for women, easy for men. "It's in the shoulder joint," they might say vaguely, or "it's something about the muscles." But there is no biological reason for young girls not to throw just as far, just as fast, just as hard as young boys. The question is not whether our daughters throw like girls, since they surely remain girls whenever they throw a ball. Rather, which girls do they resemble when they throw? Someone like Dot Richardson or Trina Chynoweth? Or someone who has been allowed to remain untutored in the process?

Crystal Branta oversees a study of children's motor development at Michigan State that is now in its thirty-first year. An associate professor of physical education specializing in growth, maturation, and motor development in children, she also runs the Early Childhood Motor Development Study, begun fourteen years ago, which looks at kids from age two through six, assessing their development and motor patterns. In addition, she happens to be the mother of three sports-obsessed sons who play, among other sports, basketball, baseball, tennis, racquetball, soccer, and football. This had led her into volunteer coaching, where she's able to apply some of her clinical knowledge on the playing field. What Branta's clinical experience has taught her is that until adolescence, the developmental "race" between girls and boys is pretty much a dead heat. "Prior to puberty, boys and girls are more alike in their abilities," she says. If anything, the developmental process favors girls for the first dozen or so years of their lives. "There's typically about a two-year difference," Branta says. "The average girl is going to have peak growth at around age twelve, the average boy at around fourteen."

But different expectations lead to different skill levels. That phenomenon can start in the cradle, Branta notes. "In the hospital nursery, the boys will have baseball mitts and other sports equipment put in their bassinets, and girls will have stuffed animals." The key to getting the skill levels of girls on par with those of boys is early instruction, Branta says. Her colleague Marty Ewing agrees. She comes at the question from a slightly different angle than Branta, emphasizing sociological and psychological influences that might shape how parents treat their daughters' athletic abilities. Skill instruction is high on her list, too, as a simple, effective measure parents and coaches can take with preschool and grade school children. "At the younger ages, I would like to see coaches understand that they are developing skill," Ewing says. "I would like to see fathers of young girls get as excited about helping them learn sports skills as they are about their young boys."

Cindy Peterson gets up in front of a group of parents and young children in the gym at Atlanta's Northside Methodist Church and comes right out with it.

"These days," she says, "our girls are learning to throw like boys. There's no reason for a girl not to learn the correct technique. If a boy can learn it, I know a girl can learn it. We're going to get rid of this myth. In six or eight weeks, the girls are gonna leave here knowing the correct technique."

Cindy Peterson runs the sports offerings at Northside. She holds a health and physical education degree and sees her work as a way of getting hands-on knowledge on the way to her Ph.D. The boom in youth sports programs can be measured by the fact that Northside serves more than 500 kids in the three-to-ten age group alone—and that's one of the smaller church athletic programs in the city. The Northside congregation is large, almost three thousand members, and very active in community outreach, but the number of kids in the sports program is staggering even so. There are 600 kids in the church basketball program, 360 in the five-to-eight age group. Fifty or even twenty years ago, it would have been unheard of for a church to have such an extensive athletics schedule.

Peterson grew up "a backyard kid" in an impoverished area of Virginia, and she marvels at the opportunities the church offers to the children of its affluent congregation. She runs basketball, soccer, and tennis programs, as well as a "movement lab" for preschoolers that has its own full-time staffer. Also for prekindergartners, Northside offers Start Smart classes, part of a nationwide program pioneered by the National Alliance for Youth Sports. Start Smart features a basic skills curriculum aimed at three-to-six-year-olds. Parents and their children meet once a week to work on rudimentary skills such as overhand throwing, catching, batting, and kicking. "I like the concept of the parent doing it with the child,'' Peterson says. "So much of what we do in athletics and recreation consists of the parent dropping the child off somewhere. They go run the errands and have no interaction with the child.''

During a Start Smart workshop, the parent-child teams rotate through several stations, each devoted to a basic sports skill and each staffed by a coach to help the mothers and fathers teach their kids. The program uses Koosh products almost exclusively. The idea is to substitute the easily graspable Koosh balls for grown-up sports projectiles like hardballs, which can be threatening to young children.

"The irony is that was why the Koosh ball was created in the first place,'' points out Fred Ensch. Scott Stillinger, a Silicon Valley engineer, was having the same problem many parents have when they get out in the yard to play catch with young children— his kids were afraid of getting hurt by the ball. He started off with a traditional baseball, but it was too intimidating. He found that foam balls had a tendency to bounce out of a child's hands, and even a beanbag was too difficult to handle.

Stillinger set out to build the sports equivalent of a better mousetrap—a ball that would make it easy for young children to learn throwing and catching skills. He toyed around with various designs before coming up with a soft, eminently graspable mass of radiating rubber filaments, "a cross between a porcupine and a bowl of Jell-O.'' The sound Stillinger heard when the shaggy ball was caught—"koosh!''—gave the product its name. The Koosh ball is easy to catch, easy to throw, and almost impossible to hurt someone with. It became one of the most popular toys of all time, in part because parents and children alike recognized its usefulness in helping beginners learn how to throw and catch.

Start Smart is a model sports program for preschoolers. It emphasizes skill instruction and adult involvement and makes no distinction between the abilities of girls and boys. One aspect of the youth sports craze that troubles many experts, Cindy Peterson notes, is the increase in competitive programs for prekindergarten children. She says many parents are troubled by it, too. "Parents come up to me all the time," Peterson says, "and tell me how thankful they are that their kids are getting some motor development skills before they're forced into an organized sports setting."

Peterson believes that many sports programs aimed at very young children partake of the hurried-child syndrome. "Too many four- and five-year-olds are put into tee-ball before they're ready. It does not help self-esteem if a child goes into the outfield and cannot catch a ball. Or cannot throw a ball. Or cannot strike something. It's really frustrating for me," Peterson says. "I hate it for the parents, because it's this competition thing. 'Oh, your child's doing this so I guess mine should be doing it.' Charlie next door's doing it so Timmy should too."

Peterson offers programs that are low-key, not very competitive. "We want you to learn, we want you to have fun," Peterson says. "But don't come here if you're serious about practice five days a week and you're going to go to the national championship. There's enough of that here in Atlanta, where if a player is really serious and wants to go a long way in their sport, there's plenty of programs out there. But here at the church, I'm after the kid who is maybe not going to make her school team. Or who is too shy to really get into a local tournament, but her friends are playing sports and she wants to kind of try the waters. I'm the place for that child. That's what my philosophy is.

"It's to improve her self-esteem, because she'll find out she can be successful here. She'll find out she can do sports, she can do something she might have thought she'd never be able to do. And I think that will carry over in her school life, in opportunities to play in her school. Because she had her first experience here, so she won't be scared to try out for a team in her school."

That philosophy is in direct challenge to the win-at-all-costs one which dominates so many children's sports programs and can even reach down to the preschool level if parents allow it. Winning is so often a grown-up objective, not one that is necessarily high on the list with kids. "Make sure your daughter's goal is her goal, not your goal," says tennis great Tracy Austin, a quote which can be read two ways: "goal" meaning "objective," and goal meaning "a point scored." If her aims are her own, then her achievements, too, are her own. "You shouldn't have Darwinism in youth sports," agrees U.S. soccer gold medalist Julie Foudy. The aim is not to winnow out the weakest, but to make everyone stronger. That can only happen if everyone shares some degree of success.

At Northside, Peterson also offers a Teeny Tennis program, a basic skills course for preschoolers that was developed by Marceil Whitney. Whitney lives in Washington State and has three children, the youngest of whom is now twelve years old. Whitney is a home-based entrepreneur who offers the Teeny Tennis course package to recreation departments, schools, and tennis clubs. She started the program twenty years ago, when she was a high school tennis coach and an avid tennis player. She wanted to get her kids interested in the sport but couldn't find any programs to teach tennis skills to young children.

"I started out because I wanted to teach my kids something that I loved. I saw tee-ball, soccer, basketball, but nothing for tennis," Whitney recalls. "So I started to experiment." While there are now numerous tennis introductory programs, Teeny Tennis has survived even without much hard sell by Whitney.

"My husband would probably like me to treat it more like a business," she says with a laugh. "With my family I made the choice to keep it low-key." Whitney advertises the program through professional associations and a few tennis organizations to which she belongs. She does occasional workshops.

Like Start Smart, Whitney's program works with non-threatening equipment. She leads children as young as three through a series of small incremental steps—a four- or five-ball progression. They start out hitting balloons and beach balls ("at that age, variety and color helps keep their attention"), progress to a nine-inch playball that's a little smaller and much lighter than a kickball, then to a foam Nerf ball the size of a softball, then to a tennis ball–sized Nerf ball, and finally to a real tennis ball.

"The comment I get from parents is that their children learn not only tennis skills, they learn social skills and self-esteem," Whitney says. "I've had some kids who were introverts, real shy, and after a few weeks the parents start making comments about the confidence level of the child. They see that through this experience they're becoming more outgoing."

The basis of her program is to give every child a chance at success. "Very rarely, over the years I've worked with kids, did I have a child who did not succeed, in some way or another. Not all of them are going to become tennis players. But they come out with a feeling of accomplishment. You know, making contact with the ball is a very big accomplishment for little ones."

Accomplishment is a vital ingredient of fun. If you raise the bar too high at the beginning, children won't succeed, and if they don't succeed, they won't have fun. If they don't have fun, they won't play, and we lose an opportunity forever. "You will keep a child's interest if you continue to keep it fun," Whitney says. "To do that you have to make kids feel as if they are succeeding. Their first impression is going to last a lifetime. If they don't enjoy it they're going to set that racket back down."

Anna Marie Rezor and her husband Jorge were beaming at a friend's dinner party one recent winter night. They had good reason to: they were expecting their first child. Anna Marie is a strong, intelligent woman who usually wears an expression of benign indulgence at her husband's antics. On this night, over the good-natured protestations of eight-months-pregnant Anna Marie, Jorge made several of the guests in turn place their hands on her rounded abdomen.

"Feel him kick?" Jorge crowed. "You see? You see? Another Pelé!"

From before our children are born, we invest them with our dreams. Like Jorge envisioning his son *in utero* as a soccer great, we build life dramas for them, casting them in starring roles. A longtime friend is convinced that her three-month-old infant shares in the legendary bravado of her husband's family. "He's got Bill's same sense of adventure," she loves to say. What kind of small "adventures" a three-month-old baby might have or in what ways an infant can embody such a concept as "bravado" are questions left blissfully unexplored. As all new parents do, this new mother endows her son with wonderful attributes that reflect her own values.

Our children might not be able to fill the roles we dream for them exactly—after all, how many Pelés can there be in the world? how much bravado?—but they are eager to respond to our expectations. They are delicate, needle-sharp seismographs, sensitive to the magnitude and direction of our dreams. This might be what the poet Delmore Schwartz referred to when he wrote, "in dreams begin responsibilities." Because young children are so responsive to our desires, we must be careful what we wish for, careful not to limit their futures by limiting our dreams for them.

Even before she entered kindergarten, Trina Chynoweth was well on her way to being an athlete. Her family encouraged their daughters to love sports in the same way they encouraged their sons, and they were rewarded for it. Our responsibility is to create as large an arena for dreams as possible, for girls and boys alike.

Jorge and Anna Marie Rezor had a girl. It's too early to tell if she will be another Mia Hamm.

3

A Game of Her Own

Grade School and Team Sports

The soccer competition of the 1996 Olympic Summer Games was held not in Atlanta but fifty miles east in Athens, Georgia, at Sanford Stadium, the home of the University of Georgia Bulldogs football team. There was a small problem with the field. It had a pronounced bulge, like the top of a loaf of bread. In fact, it rose almost a foot from the sidelines to its center, a relic of an old drainage system. This was fine for football but wouldn't do for soccer.

Olympic planners brought in bulldozers to shave off the crown and flatten out the field for soccer play. To a lot of people around Athens, and to many Bulldog alums all over the country, this amounted to sacrilege. Sanford was hallowed ground, and Georgia was, after all, the heart of the South, where football is sacred and old ways die hard. Those dozers represented the forces of progress flattening the house of tradition. But what happened after the turf was relaid and the field widened helped to prove—quite literally, in this instance—the value of a level field. The American women's soccer team that triumphed in Sanford Stadium that August brought home more than the gold medal. It drove home the fact that in a nation where team play had always been reserved for men, women had finally broken through the "grass ceiling." Team sports would no longer be the sole domain of male athletes.

On a cool, bright Saturday afternoon in mid-October, the town recreation complex in Somers, New York, an hour north of New York City, features all the trappings of a traditional autumn celebration. Under the wooden hexagonal roof of the picnic shelter, children decorate pumpkins and get their own faces painted. The local fire auxiliary serves up cider, sausages, and hamburgers. The local Girl Scout troop sells hot "friendship soup" and cookies. Somebody read Martha Stewart: tasteful arrangements of Indian corn, apple bushels, and gourds decorate the scene.

But this is SoccerFest '97, a sports-minded harvest festival. Six hundred children age five to seventeen, on over forty teams in all, compete throughout the day, each player in an average of three games. The six-acre site is overrun with jerseys and shin guards. The lawn surrounding the shelter is a crazy quilt of newly chalked touchlines, goal lines, and penalty areas. More teams play on the park's upper fields. The town of Somers is a sprawling, wooded exurb of eighteen thousand, and it seems as if a good percentage of the population is in attendance. Hundreds of cars clog the parking lot and overflow onto the lawn.

There is a tribal flavor to the day. The scene seems so natural, so ordinary, that an observer could easily overlook a major difference between this and a sports Saturday of a generation ago. The girls at SoccerFest '97 are as active as the boys. They aren't on the sidelines. Girls compete on the same teams with boys, and all-girls teams play in matches of their own. Mothers act as coaches, referees, organizers. Fathers cheer on their daughters with equal gusto as their sons. Younger siblings come along to watch their older sisters play. This is an integrated family event— in contrast to the football game where the father relives his glory days and the mother is a handmaiden to her son's success. There are no marching bands, no cheerleaders, but the enthusiasm for the competitions is genuine and infectious.

The growth of soccer in this country over the last two decades has been staggering. Even more amazing are the numbers of girls, especially grade school girls, that are now playing it. It's a revolution that we see all around us, on fields behind suburban high schools, in small-town school yards surrounded by corn fields, even on closed-off streets in the inner city. Grade school is a time when we give our girls the most freedom to play, explore, and experiment. Increasingly, they have responded to this freedom by choosing to play sports. And among those grade school girls who are playing sports, the game they are choosing more and more is soccer.

There is a paradox here. While our preschool parenting approach is often stuck in the pink-and-blue sensibility of the past, this current generation of girls, once they hit grade school, has somehow managed to break through those stereotypes. The healthiest, most exciting environment for girls in sports exists today in grade school, through the end of middle school—in other words, during our daughters' preadolescent years. Every time a girl sends a ball into a goal, she is sending a message. I can do this, she is saying, I want to do it, and I derive great pleasure and benefit from doing it. Playing soccer has achieved a singular status in our daughters' lives. It has become a rite of passage.

Twenty-five years ago, team sports before high school were played primarily by boys. Junior high field hockey and synchronized swimming were notable exceptions. Female Olympic stars tended to be not team athletes but those involved in personal-best sports such as figure skating, gymnastics, and track and field—Dorothy Hamill, for example, or Mary Lou Retton. These young women were great athletes and superb role models. But the dearth of Olympic women's teams reinforced the message that girls didn't play group sports. This situation was reflected at the grade school level by parents who urged their daughters toward dance class, while even the most uncoordinated boys played Little League baseball or Pop Warner football. Girls were spectators, if that. The situation of young athletic girls in the sixties was poignantly evoked by Stanford basketball coach Tara VanDerveer. "We waited on the periphery of sports like ghosts, invisible to the boys except when we filled a need, invisible sometimes even to the teachers and other adults in our lives who guided us toward home ec and tennis."

Today, an eleven-year-old girl is likely to keep a pair of soccer cleats in her closet right next to her ballet slippers. The true arrival in our society is not the soccer mom but the soccer daughter. The range of options in sports for girls brings added responsibilities for parents—all the choice in the world can be wasted if the tremendous influence we have over our daughters is somehow misdirected. Mothers and fathers can take steps to expose their grade school daughters to sports, to encourage them to participate, to do simple things such as providing an ample selection of sporting equipment. Fathers are often the motivating parents getting girls involved in sports, since they are more likely to be conversant in the world of athletics and are eager for their

daughters to share their enthusiasm. As the post-Title IX generation reaches childbearing age, women will be even more involved
in passing on sports skills to their children.

Soccer is an ideal game for kids. It is cheap to play, requires
little equipment, and has only a small number of easily under-
standable rules. For many grade schoolers, the game is simply
more fun than the other major team sports. The hoop can be too
high in basketball. Baseball can be frustrating because it forces
kids to wait too much for their turn at bat or a chance to field a
ball. In soccer, whenever children are in the game, they are running. For a grade schooler, you couldn't find a better prescrip-
tion for pleasure, and surveys of young athletes have shown that
fun, as basic as it sounds, is the prime reason kids stick with a
sport.

Soccer puts on a good game face for parents, also. The rules
sharply limit physical contact, resulting in few injuries. The benefits seem immediately tangible. While the game's strategy can be
endlessly refined, the basic rules are so simple that even very
young children are often up and playing in their first practice
session. The game "gives good visual." Parents see their young
children exercising outdoors, right before their camcorder, in a
healthy environment.

But there is another reason why soccer is booming—its popularity with girls. The soccer daughter is more prevalent on the
American landscape than, say, the softball daughter, because soccer has been especially welcoming to girls. It presents them with
the closest thing to a level field that they'll find today in athletics.
When girls began playing the game in earnest in the late seventies and early eighties, soccer hadn't yet been "claimed" for boys
the way, say, football or baseball had been. Everybody, boys and
girls as well as parents, learned the sport more or less at the same
time. With everyone a novice, girls couldn't be pushed off the

field as readily as they are in other sports. It is also a sport which honors not brute strength and speed but agility and endurance, both categories in which girls naturally excel.

"SOCCER HAS GRASS-ROOTS APPEAL" reads the bumper sticker, and there is something of a kitchen-sink flavor to the numerous recreation department leagues, school tournaments, church teams, and neighborhood games that have sprouted in response to the sport's newfound popularity. It all happened without professional league tie-ins, virtually without promotion. Girls and women make up fully 50 percent of U.S. soccer players. In Division I college play (the highest category administered by the NCAA), women's soccer programs actually outnumber men's, 238 to 209. More than 6 million women and girls played soccer across the United States in 1987, 7.25 million in 1996.

Mia Hamm is the golden girl of the U.S. national team that triumphed at Atlanta's Sanford Stadium during the summer of 1996, a volatile, explosive player, a striker who in 1997 led the national team with 15 goals in ten matches. Some people call her the best female soccer player in America, some say the best in the world, and some drop the "female" qualifier altogether. Hamm embodies qualities most parents would wish for their daughters as they mature. A strong, confident individual, she got that way in large part by playing sports. *People* magazine named Hamm one of the fifty most beautiful people in the world, maybe the first time the magazine so honored a woman with thigh muscles like banded steel.

Athletes such as Mia Hamm help girls think about their bodies in new, less restrictive ways. Parents worry about the negative influence of the starvation-thin ideal set up by fashion magazines and celebrity waif models. When girls admire Mia Hamm and other women like her, it provides them with a more robust image of female beauty. In place of a passive female figure, girls can emulate someone who, in the words of Anson Dorrance, can "accelerate like she was shot out of a cannon." Dorrance is the North Carolina coach who recruited Hamm off a high school field in Texas and the man largely responsible for maintaining a dynasty in University of North Carolina Tar Heels women's soccer.

Mia Hamm is a child of Title IX. She was born in 1972, the law's inaugural year. Her chance to excel in soccer was the direct result of the opening of sports to women that was brought about by Title IX. In the same sense, the thousands of grade school girls across America who tear up the soccer fields every Saturday morning are also daughters of the law. But Mia Hamm has gone farther than almost any other American woman in the sport, and girls are enthusiastic about following in her footsteps. This is an important, exciting dream, and the female athlete represents a striking new addition to their pantheon of role models. Through their choice of champions, our daughters are telling us that they want to be strong, capable women.

Seventeen-year-old Kate Morrel is a member of the first generation of American daughters to be raised with women sports champions for heroes. Morrel's family has already woven tales of Kate's early athletic prowess into family legend. "They were weighing me on that scale at the hospital that they lay the baby in," she says, "and I guess I kicked something down from the shelf above. That was my first goal." When Morrel's mother was young, she had been a runner, a tennis player, and a dancer. Kate enjoyed the dance classes her mother enrolled her in as a preschooler, but her love of team sports won out at an early age. Spectator sports were big in the Morrel household: "My dad was a huge sports fan and my mom is probably the biggest woman football fan in the country," she says. Growing up in the town of Carmel, Indiana, just outside of Indianapolis, Kate dreamed of being a professional quarterback ("I'm going to be the first woman in the NFL," she recalls thinking at age six). She switched from football to soccer because, she says with a laugh, "I liked the shirt." When she was four she saw a neighbor in a soccer uniform and asked her mom to sign her up.

As soon as she started playing soccer herself, Morrel says, "I kind of got idols." Mia Hamm was chief among them. When the women's national team played an exhibition game in Indianapolis in 1988, Morrel was there to get autographs, including those of Hamm and Michelle Akers, who before Hamm was the media favorite in U.S. women's soccer. Even now, almost a decade later, an autographed Akers poster remains on the wall in Kate Morrel's bedroom. As a child in elementary school, she saw herself as a tomboy, attaching no stigma to the term. She unself-consciously wore her Adidas, gym shorts, and T-shirts to school, her hair in a ponytail. She was known as the best athlete, girl or boy, at the small private academy she attended for academically gifted students. In grade school, Kate didn't confine herself to soccer. She started playing basketball in second grade, and by the time she entered middle school she was starting on both the girls' and boys' teams. She especially enjoyed playing with the boys, she says, because of the challenge and "because I felt really cool when I did well and the boys on the other team were [saying things] like, 'Oooh, she's good.' "

But soccer remains her first sport. "You're always moving," she explains. "That's the thing I like about soccer, to play a ninety-minute game at full speed. At center midfield, which is what I play, you're right in the middle of everything, you're playing offense, you're playing defense." She likes the feeling of good physical conditioning the game gives her, relating it to an important side benefit: being able to eat what she likes, when she likes. More important, she loves soccer because she excels at it.

She intends to play in college and as a high school junior has already been recruited by Harvard, the U.S. Naval Academy, and Duke, among other schools. Her only problem is that she insists on attending a college "where I'm their best player, basically," because she wants maximum playing time.

Kate Morrel wrote a poem for an eleventh-grade English class about the joy she takes in playing soccer. The poem forms the centerpiece of a collage in her grandmother's house, featuring photo highlights of Kate's participation in sports from the time she was very young. "It is now game day, and my nerves shake with energy," she begins. The poem ends, "The intense competition, the fight for ultimate glory. . . . And I strive someday to earn the title of Olympic champion."

The psychological benefits of hard physical play have proved important to Morrel during rocky times. When Kate's father unexpectedly died of a heart attack the summer after her sophomore year in high school, playing gave her "a release" she needed. Her father had always been a major supporter during her games, she remembers. "He was always on me, screaming at me to hustle." There were conflicts about this during her father's life, including one time he yelled at her from the sidelines to get in the game and she yelled right back at him—and got in trouble for it afterward. But now, after his death, she writes "Dad" in permanent marker on the tape of her shin guards before every game she plays, taking strength from the memory of her father's pride in her athletic accomplishments. Her team members, who are "like a family," also give her strength. At the time of the funeral, they were constantly around her, helping out, bringing food, just being there. It was an extended support network of the sort that sports have traditionally offered boys and men.

Of course, even in the sunny picture soccer presents, there

are shadows. Vestiges persist of the skew toward boys' sports, small things which nevertheless are meaningful in the context of how girls succeed or fail at their athletic endeavors. In Kate Morrel's school, a group called the Soccer Hoppers mounts various activities in support of the boys' soccer team. All day on game days, Soccer Hoppers stop the players in the halls and present them with cookies and candy for good luck. "They don't have anything like that for the girls," Kate says. "I think we should. I think we should get boys to do it." She even spoke to the members of the boys' team about it, and they were agreeable.

Unlike her counterparts of a previous generation, Kate Morrel may even take for granted the inspiration of vigorous, successful female players such as Mia Hamm and Michelle Akers. What has been equally important to Morrel is working with female athletes up close, in a sports camp or clinic situation. Kate draws inspiration from a Notre Dame college player named Jen Grubb, who coached her in a summer soccer camp. "I see in her how I could be," says Kate. "I heard Michelle Akers speak one time, and she said, 'When we were growing up there were no athletes for us to look up to that were women.' I think it's important for girls to see that women are doing well in sports, too—not just men."

Sooner or later, the heroes need to come down off the posters and enter girls' lives for real. The most obvious role models for the very young child are always parents or close family members. Through attending games with them or running the track alongside them, girls adopt the values of mom and dad. But as girls grow up through grade school and into adolescence, they begin to cast a wider net. They look outside their immediate family circle to find other people to emulate and imitate. They want someone like themselves, but not of themselves. Their first choice might be a fantasy figure, an impossible ideal. But as they grow older they may want someone who can help make those fantasies become real, a coach or a mentor.

Sportsbridge ("Empowering Girls through Sports") is a San Francisco mentoring program that matches area athletes with young girls in sports. "Recognize her strength," is the nonprofit program's trademarked motto. "Encourage her dreams." Although Sportsbridge currently focuses on adolescent girls, the goal is to make the program available from grade school onward. "We know you have to start at age eight or nine," says Sportsbridge founder Ann Kletz. "At that age, all of their notions about themselves are already happening. The boys start developing their sports skills when they're four or five. The girls don't." She likes to cite the statistic that says if children are not playing sports by the age of ten, there's only a 10 percent chance they'll be playing when they are twenty-five.

The organization has also piloted an overnight sports camp, during which Kletz acts not as an administrator but as a soccer coach. A standout soccer player herself, she makes it a point to always practice with participants. "As a coach, I offer myself as a role model," Kletz says. "During my career I'd had only one or two female coaches. I felt it was incredibly important that the girls see me playing soccer, or see other women who were better than them, college players. I was able to show them videos of the national team. It's hard for them to visualize that level of play, because it's just not out in the media."

Sportsbridge was founded by "a real product of Title IX," as Kletz describes herself. She was born in 1969 and played soccer "exclusively" from grade school through to college. In the seventies, she was in the vanguard of the girls' sports boom, becoming one of the first females to play organized soccer in the Bay Area of California. When she tried out, Kletz recalls, she was one of two girls in the entire league. The other girl soon dropped out.

Kletz still remembers "vividly" some of the incidents that followed. Before every game officials would line each team up shoulder to shoulder, facing the other team, for an equipment check. It is traditionally a time for the teams to take each other's measure. Inevitably, during these lineups, the other team would spot Kletz. The whispering would start. "This one particular game they were whispering really loudly, and you could hear what they were saying: 'Look, look, there's a girl on their team—they're going to be so easy.' I have never, ever forgotten that. I remember my reaction being, 'Oh, just you wait.' It just fueled my fire. I attribute those early experiences to a lot of the determination that I've carried with me through my life."

As a teenager, Kletz was growing up just as the Olympic Development Process, the way in which girls are currently chosen for Olympic teams, was evolving. The system involves first trying out for what is called the "select" team, then the district team, then the state team, then the national. "I was playing soccer all year round, which you can do in California, either on my high school team or on one of these select teams." She made the under-nineteen national team in 1988, but at that point organized women's soccer had not progressed very far. "It was a paper team because we didn't have anybody to play," Kletz says. She was just a step before her time. "Had it been four years later, it would have been a real team."

After almost two decades of playing soccer, Ann Kletz had nowhere to go. She had hit the "grass ceiling"—the lack of professional outlets for female athletes. Despite the WNBA and the start-ups of various women's professional leagues, the grass ceiling remains a reality. In years past, it was absolute. With the exception of barnstorming baseball teams, and despite almost perennial attempts to put one together for basketball, American women had no league of their own in any sport. Until the very recent past, the most any American female athlete could look forward to was a physical education or coaching position at a high school or college, or an expatriate career in the European leagues. It's a vicious cycle. The grass ceiling leads to a lack of female role models in sports. For young female athletes to be motivated, they have to be able to dream. No matter how remote his chances, every boy can at least imagine a future for himself in the National Football League, say, or in major league baseball or professional soccer. He can dream of becoming a Brett Favre or a Dwight Gooden.

After her stint with the opponent-less national soccer team, Kletz accepted her fate and went quietly into that good twilight which represents the end of so many women's sports careers. The nonprofit bug bit her, and she helped organize an effort called the Urban Service Project to help get kids involved in community service. After almost three years with the project, "wearing every hat you can imagine," Kletz decided she was ready for something new. She knew she wanted to stay in the nonprofit realm. She just didn't know exactly how to direct her energies. "I was pretty confident at that point in my life as a woman, and I wondered how I became that way," Kletz recalls of her time of soul-searching. The answer came easily. "It was definitely sports. That's where I learned so many lessons that translated into my life—how to deal with success and failure, how to realize that if you work hard at something, it will pay off—all these lessons."

Kletz decided she wanted to work with girls, and she would use sports as her vehicle. On leave from the Urban Service Project, she spent six months working the phone "ferociously," as she puts it, calling at times thirty people a day. She was "trying to see if anything existed in the Bay Area by way of a girls' program that used sports as a primary tool." She found there was nothing.

She started digging deeper, gradually realizing that there was next to nothing for girls, period. She looked at the YWCAs, and not a single one in the Bay Area had sports programming. She looked at the Boys and Girls Clubs, and even though they were coed in name, they were still serving only the boys. She'd go to the basketball games and there would be three girls in the whole league. She broadened her search to the whole country, trying in vain to find a model organization.

This was in 1994—an indication of how freshly minted the girls' sports boom really is and how far the male monopoly on athletics extended until very recently. But Kletz did not give up. "I couldn't find a model," she recalls, "so I just started visualizing what I would have wanted when I was a young girl." What had she wanted back then? What Kate Morrel wanted, what so many young female athletes want: role models who become real flesh-and-blood mentors.

When she was growing up in Berkeley, Kletz recalls, one of her favorite activities was to attend the games of the California State Women's Soccer Team, a barnstorming amateur team that was the closest thing, for Kletz and other female soccer players, to a league of their own. "I'd dream that one of them would want to work with me," she remembers. "They would come play with me and tell me what I had to do to get into college and play at college. They were my heroes. I would stand there, and my dad would come with me, and once in a while I'd maybe muster up the courage to say a word or two." Kletz's father convinced one of the team members to play with his daughter a couple of times. "But then she was too busy so it didn't work out," Kletz says.

Through Sportsbridge's mentoring program, Ann Kletz is "giving back" to young female athletes something she herself lacked. Sports was such a huge influence shaping her life that she wants to pass it on to a younger generation—all the while trying to eliminate the obstacles, hassles, and disappointments that she herself faced. She recognizes that historically, the biggest challenge of setting up a mentor program has been finding qualified, committed mentors, and in this regard she feels lucky. "There's a whole mass of women out there that have played their whole life or started playing later in life that are real sports fanatics. They have all gone through this cathartic experience of realizing what sports can do for them, and they want to give back. They want to make sure that the girls growing up have the same opportunities."

The reality of Sportsbridge and programs like it amounts to a social movement, not officially organized and largely unrecognized, made up mainly of women who came of age after Title IX opened the door to female athletes. These women are trying to influence athletics from within. Their passion for coaching or mentoring allows them to do two things at the same time—to stay in the game and to do something good for the generation coming up behind them.

It is a grassroots phenomenon with small, "home-made" organizations spread throughout the country. Alongside Sportsbridge in the Bay Area, for example, a twenty-seven-year-old former college player named Jenni Liner spearheads the lesser-known Women's Soccer Resource Center in Marin County. Liner matches female coaches with girls' teams. In Chicago, there is A Sporting Chance Foundation, a nonprofit group dedicated to empowering girls through athletics, founded by Kathy Chuckas, another "soccer baby." Nationally, the young women who run the new Girl Scout program GirlSports and sports-oriented initiatives at Girls Inc. are also from the first generation of female athletes to spring up after Title IX. At the head of other grassroots organizations are women with similar credentials. These are forceful advocates who were shaped by the soccer revolution's can-do atmosphere—self-described children of Title IX who never experienced a world bereft of sports opportunities, but who realize we have a long way to go.

The soccer boom has primarily benefited children of the suburbs. But there are individuals committed to bringing the game to the inner city. Carolyn McKenzie is a bubbly, charismatic woman who was raised in rural Georgia by a sharecropper mother. Although she was a promising runner as a child, her school lacked sports programs for girls. Now in her mid-forties, she had never seen a soccer game when in 1989 she accepted the start-up leadership position for an urban sports program called Soccer in the Streets (slogan "We boldly go where no other soccer program has gone before"). Aimed at children in public housing, Section Eight, and other low-income communities, Soccer in the Streets is now in fifty-five cities, teaching young kids rudimentary soccer skills. McKenzie has helped introduce soccer to over sixty thousand inner-city youth, girls and boys both. "The needs of the girls in the inner city are so different, because the girls in the suburbs have at least one parent, at least one role model, someone to say these are the classes you have to take, these are the sports you need to be registered in. The girls in the inner city don't have that kind of infrastructure that provides them with role models. They don't have a map. They don't have a book. They have to get out there on their own and figure out what they want to do with their lives. I give them sports as a way to provide a map for life. It just so happens that sports is a fun way to shape your life."

McKenzie describes herself the "ultimate soccer mom" because she develops a personal bond with as many kids in her program as she can. She has an instantly intimate style with people, and uses it to help garner support from such major corporations as Reebok, Umbro, McDonald's, Chick-Fil-A, and Delta Air

Lines, among many others. Corporate underwriting has not hindered her bracingly individual approach to her mission. She is about to launch two separate but related programs, for "urban soccer girls" and "urban soccer moms," with heavy emphasis on parenting skills and mother-daughter bonding. For the U.S.-hosted 1999 Women's World Cup, McKenzie has proposed a measure which gives some idea of the flavor of her promotional style. "The mothers and daughters will be given free tickets to go to the game together, provided that they do one thing: hold hands. That's all they have to do. They've got to promise me that they'll hold hands, not the whole time, but while they're walking into the stadium and while they're walking out. And during the game, when they get excited, they have to hug each other."

In the world of youth soccer, at least, girls today play on a relatively level field. They can look up to charismatic stars, as well as receive guidance from first-generation athletes and other dedicated adults who are consciously seeking to encourage others to enjoy the sport. Such role models have helped produce a second generation of confident young women like Kate Morrel.

It is a rainy Saturday afternoon, and Lucy Morgenstern tosses a foam football over and over against her basement wall. Rangy and tall for a ten-year-old, she wears a billowing, tie-dyed T-shirt with an oversized black peace symbol on the front, well-worn jeans, and athletic shoes. The caroming ball narrowly misses several pieces of expensive sound equipment in the basement (Lucy's dad is a musician), but the girl always seems to snag it just before it does serious damage. When the family moved from Riverdale in the Bronx to Hastings, Lucy immediately signed up for the village recreation center's softball program for girls. She had played tee-ball in North Riverdale and was developing a passion for baseball. But she was disappointed with the game of softball, which she saw as a pale imitation of the real thing. "It's just stupid," she says. "They just copy baseball with a bigger ball."

Lucy Morgenstern would have quit playing ball the next year were it not for a one-man baseball promotion machine named Chris Evans. Evans has played baseball for forty of his forty-five years, although never professionally. To him it is a "true Zen experience," a game of timeless purity. "It's the definitive American sport," Evans says. "I think it defines us as a people." Last year, when his son was in fourth grade, Evans realized that kids in the village had only limited chances to play baseball, so he started a junior level of Little League. Due to the success of that venture, he is now chairman—he styles himself "commissioner"—of Hastings Little League.

As a national organization, Little League has a decidedly uneven record of accommodating girls who want to play. From the beginning, however, Evans made it a point to welcome everyone. Lucy Morgenstern, he says, is "a great player, someone who really loves the game." He extols the play of the girls in the league, giving chapter and verse of one girl's great feat of fielding at home plate as if it happened yesterday. Evans is at times accused of being "too p.c.," a charge that was leveled against him when he named the teams in the junior Little League after those in the old Negro leagues. "It's a great bit of history," Evans says. "Why not honor it? What are we going to do, 'dis' Jackie Robinson?"

The baseball league Evans founded has only a handful of girls who play; more get involved with Hastings rec center's softball. There was, in fact, some friction between Evans and the rec department, which wanted the female prospects for its softball team, as well as the women softball players in town, who thought it would be better if the girls started playing softball right from the start. "They were discouraging me from encouraging them," Evans says. The players told him, he says, that playing baseball is not good preparation for playing softball later. "I haven't quite bought into that," Evans says. "If you have the reflexes to play baseball, softball is a lot easier."

With Lucy as the only girl on the roster, her team, the Barons, went up against the unbeaten Giants for the league championship during a miserable June heat wave. "It was like 110 degrees," Lucy recalls. "We were all dying out there." The game took place on a diamond at the local elementary school, which happens to be the high school girls' softball field. Lucy remembers being a "tiny, tiny bit nervous that we would lose," but mainly she was thinking how much she wanted to be pitcher and frustrated that her coach probably wouldn't let her. (At this age, no positions are assigned and players customarily rotate all around.) It was a good game for the Barons and for Lucy. Her team won, 8–5, and she was responsible for half of those eight runs, knocking a double into center field for one of her two hits. "You could not have found a more exciting series of games if you were watching the World Series," says Lucy's mother, Anita. "The parents were going nuts." When the game was over, the kids ran to the nearby public pool and jumped in en masse, some of them in their uniforms.

Lucy's devotion to the game of baseball has lately extended to a rooting interest in the New York Yankees and a passion for the fine points of baseball strategy. But she was ready to quit the game altogether at one point. She had been playing on a Riverdale team, with inspiring coaches and exciting games, and she was beginning to get enthusiastic about baseball as something that might figure into her adult life. "Then she found out that there were no pro women's teams," Anita Morgenstern recalls, "and she was very disturbed by that. She said to me, 'Well, I'm not going to be a baseball player. What's the point?' "

There are two schools of thought about women and the "stick-and-ball games" that have been, to a greater or lesser degree, this country's passion for almost 150 years. One school, represented by Lucy Morgenstern's rejection of softball, holds that only the game played with a ball "not less than 9 nor more than 9¹/₄ inches in circumference" (to quote the rule book of Major League Baseball) is deserving of the name of baseball. "Hardball: The Real Thing" is how author Barbara Gregorich puts it in her excellent history of women in the game. The other school contends that preserving hardball as a predominantly male sport and softball as predominantly female slights no one, leaves no one out in the cold, and results in excellent athletic offerings for everyone. "Have you ever watched women play their fastpitch [softball] games?" asks Chris Evans, himself a supporter of girls playing hardball. "They've got their own field of dreams." Evans coached the rec department's girls' softball team in response to parents' requests.

Seven million girls age seven to seventeen play softball every year, in school leagues, club leagues, summer leagues, bar leagues, and amateur leagues. The inaugural season of the Women's Professional Fastpitch League in 1996 saw crowds averaging two thousand coming out to watch women players in a seven-city league. The creation of a professional league for women can only spur the interest of young girls in the game. But the popularity of softball for girls serves to mask a fundamental truth. Unlike soccer, say, which has boys and girls, men and women playing essentially the same game, baseball in America has evolved a two-track approach. Classic hardball is reserved primarily for men and boys. A modified version of the game is widely considered more appropriate for women and girls.

Softball was created in the early 1900s as a way to play baseball indoors or where space was limited. Although it was always played by both men and women, from the 1930s onward the game—called variously "kittenball," "mush ball," or "powderpuff ball" but eventually labeled "softball"—was increasingly identified with women. Softball was thought a suitable activity for females because it did not, in the words of a pair of male commentators, "bunch muscles, give girls a weightlifter's figure, develop varsity-club leg, the usual penalty of fiendish exercise." Here, of course, is one more echo of the turn-of-the-century view that male sports were too strenuous for women. Women's barnstorming teams and semipro leagues abounded throughout softball's heyday in the 1930s and 1940s. It was always something of a blue-collar pastime, and, as sport historian Susan K. Cahn notes, strength in women was valued more by the working class than by the middle class, and "delicacy [was] more of a liability than a virtue." In amateur leagues today, the working-class flavor of softball endures, and it is a sport both men and women play. But the tradition of softball as a "women's game" still lives on in school leagues, and in the Little League organization as well.

The segregation is by no means absolute. Boys play a lot of softball, and there are always a few girls like Lucy Morgenstern who love hardball and will accept no substitutes. There are female hardball players, mostly on boys' teams, at the grade school, high school, college, and even semipro levels. In recent years a professional women's hardball team, the barnstorming Colorado Silver Bullets, played against college and minor league competition. After the 1997 season, the Coors Brewing Company, which had been underwriting the team (to the tune of $4 million), dropped its sponsorship, and the future of the Silver Bullets is uncertain.

Softball as a designated sport for females has yielded a vibrant subculture of leagues, trainers, clinics, championships, and playing seasons. Once again, as it did for soccer, the 1996 Summer Games at Atlanta provided a defining moment for softball, with the American team taking the gold medal. Dot Richardson's fielding and hitting heroics provided instant inspiration to legions of young girls hungry for female role models in their favorite game.

But without taking anything away from the girls all across the country who love the sport of softball, the two-track, "separate but equal" approach of distinct games for males and females seems to ignore women's long history of playing the hardball version of the game. Baseball thrived at Vassar, Smith, and Wellesley in the last half of the 1800s, and from 1890 to 1920 "bloomer teams" of professional female baseball players proved that women could play hardball and play it well enough to attract paying crowds. Always, though, the prospect of females playing hardball triggered intense, almost hysterical reactions. The whole idea was objectionable not only physically, it seemed, but also symbolically. Particularly in the hallmark century from 1860 to 1960—before the rise of football as the nation's premier spectator sport—baseball was sacred male turf, and woe to the girl who trespassed.

A coed game that took place at the University of Pennsylvania in 1904, for example, had the male students enthusiastically cheering the female players (including one who hit a double), until the school authorities caught wind of the contest. They immediately halted the game, instituted a rule that no female could play on campus, and instructed police to break up all such games in the future. All this in response to a pickup game of ball. Throughout the early years of the century, despite disapprobation, pioneer female athletes such as Maud Nelson, Alta Weiss, and Lizzie Murphy had long careers in hardball, using the same rules as men. It was not until the 1930s that female participation in the sport was effectively channeled into the game of softball. Then it was as if women had never played the "male" version of the sport. Early female players were forgotten. Baseball became another chapter of the secret history of women that is often ignored or suppressed by society as a whole.

The movie *A League of Their Own* celebrated one passage in that history, the time in the 1940s when the All-American Girls Baseball League thrived in midsized cities in the American Midwest. Organized because male baseball players were fighting in World War II, the AAGBL continued until 1954, long after the war was over. The league started playing what we would today recognize as softball. The pitcher threw underhand, and the ball was a fat 12 inches in diameter. By 1948, though, and to the end of the league in 1954, an overhand, major league style was adopted, and the ball eventually shrunk to $9^1/_4$ inches—virtually the same hardball used today.

The story of the AAGBL typifies the ambivalent feelings many people in this country harbored about women playing hardball. That ambivalence came to a head in the early 1970s, when the national Little League organization spent almost $2 million fighting to prevent girls from participating. Girls had been clamoring to play Little League baseball since its inception in 1939. The national organization, based in Williamsport, Pennsylvania, resisted, repeatedly threatening to revoke the franchise of any local league that allowed female players. That was where things stood in 1973, when civil rights lawsuits were mounted simultaneously in many states, including Michigan, Connecticut, and New Jersey. When viewed from today's perspective, the battle to integrate Little League baseball seems baffling and a little quaint. We're moved to ask, along with New Jersey Superior Court judge George Gelman, who ruled in favor of eleven-year-old Frances Pescatore's right to play the game, "What's the big deal?"

But in those not-too-distant days it was a big deal for a grade school girl to want to play with her schoolmates on a hardball team. The New Jersey Little League teams voted to suspend activities rather than allow girl players. Boys, girls, whole families marched on Trenton, the state capital, bearing a petition with fifty thousand signatures against the move to integrate the teams. Judith Weis, an attorney and representative of the National Organization for Women who argued the New Jersey case, was surprised by the vehemence of the reaction. "This particular issue is as fraught with emotional backlash as any I've ever seen," Weis said at the time. "We're seeing the same hostility and fanaticism on behalf of segregated baseball as from the right-to-lifers."

The no-girls policy was simply a matter of preserving decorum, averred Little League president Dr. Creighton Hale. "It just wouldn't be proper for coaches to pat girls on the rear end the way they naturally do boys," Hale was quoted as saying. "And suppose a girl gets hurt on the leg? Why, that's just not going to go over—a grown man rubbing a little girl's leg." Today such arguments reveal more about the fevered imaginations of those who invoked them than any objective reality. On June 12, 1974, the national organization of Little League Baseball officially abandoned its boys-only policy.

Significantly, though, the organization had another response to all the girls clamoring to play ball. In the same year it opened its ranks to females, it also started a new division, called Little League Softball, "to provide young girls with the same opportunity to participate in organized ball as their male counterparts in Little League Baseball." Despite the either/or sentiment invoked in those words (which were taken from the official

Little League Baseball Web site in 1997), today any interested school age girl can choose many different versions of the game, including hardball in Little League. Tee-ball, in which the ball is not pitched but is hit off a stationary tee placed in front of home plate, is now a fairly common way to start children off (as young as age four) in the game.

As of the mid-1980s, Little League Softball, too, has been open to boys and girls both, the result of yet another court ruling. But the softball league remains overwhelmingly female. Over 400,000 girls play Little League Softball, as opposed to what Little League spokesperson Lance Van Auken estimates as "eight boys worldwide." According to Van Auken, Little League created its softball division after the court battles of the seventies because "even then, softball was considered the sport that girls play." Van Auken says that no high school or college he knows of fields a women's hardball team, and therefore it would be "an exercise in futility" for Little League to create a girls' hardball division. "I don't think any league out there would have had enough girls to field even one team," Van Auken says. His explanation: "There is no place at the upper levels left for them to go as baseball players."

The softball/baseball duality is a self-perpetuating system. Few girls play hardball when they are young because there are few chances to play when they are older, and there are few chances because there are few experienced girls to play. "If baseball had been open to women for the last 150 years," writes baseball historian Barbara Gregorich, "we would have already seen female major leaguers. The game is closed not because women can't play, but because the men in power don't want women around."

That may change if people such as Chris Evans succeed in

83

"leaving it to the kids" to decide what game they want to play. "Lucy Morgenstern could go on and be a star softball player," he says. "Here's my thing, though: who am I to say that Lucy isn't the first female major leaguer? What do I know? And why should I deny her?"

4

Reclaiming the Court

Girls' Basketball Comes of Age

Dave Curtis drove his nine-year-old daughter Kimberly and four of her friends to a basketball game at Furman University in Greenville, South Carolina. Curtis's twelve-year-old son Brian sat in the front seat with him, and the two of them listened to what Dave later described as a "giggle party" going on in the backseat.

Brian turned to his father and rolled his eyes. "Dad, when is this going to end?"

"Not until we get there," Curtis said. The grade schoolers were indeed a "giggle gaggle" all the way to Furman, but once they got there, they settled in to watch an exhibition game by the school's Lady Paladins basketball team. They may have been more attentive since they had met some of the players at a multisport clinic put on for girls age six through fourteen by the Greenville YWCA.

Curtis is an enthusiastic man, and his conversation runs to superlatives. As far as he was concerned, the chance for his daughter to see college-level female athletes in action was just one more aspect of the "superfantastic" YWCA girls' basketball program. Kimberly loves participating. "The girls get to do stuff that the boys do," she says. "When the girls wanted to play, they couldn't before, and now we're getting a chance."

Kimberly and her friends had recently attended what Curtis describes as a "fabulous" basketball clinic that featured Lynette Woodard, the first female Harlem Globetrotter, "a broker on the New York Stock Exchange, just a very successful young woman, a role model and a half for these girls." The girls got to talk with Woodard one on one, get her autograph, and see themselves on local television news afterward.

Curtis had put Brian through grade school in Los Angeles. But when Kimberly was just old enough to go to school, the family moved back to the rural hamlet of Slater, Curtis's hometown, outside of Greenville. "I was becoming a single parent," he recounts, and was also a little unsure about how to raise a girl. "I knew that I wanted to get my daughter involved in all kinds of things." It was a difficult proposition. Rural areas in general have fewer recreational opportunities for children than do cities, and there are added transportation and scheduling problems. Curtis had participated in Cub Scouts with Brian in Los Angeles and wound up being heavily involved. But he felt he probably wouldn't be welcomed into the local Girl Scout program, so he searched for something else to do with Kimberly.

Greenville-Spartanburg, a collection of once bucolic hamlets strung along Interstate 85, is a modern southern success story. The landscape gets green in March and hot by the end of April.

It's easy to break a sweat without playing sports at all. In the summer, there's nothing much for kids to do apart from hanging out to cool off at the local Hardee's, where the a.c. provides some relief from the heat. Manufacturing concerns have recently relocated in the area, and the huge BMW factory alongside the interstate churns out everything from sleek roadsters to luxury sedans. But it's difficult for the newfound prosperity to reach the deep pockets of rural poverty scattered all over the area.

Curtis found out about the YWCA basketball program through a flyer handed out at a PTA meeting. After the clinic with Lynette Woodard, the Y organized another clinic in the gym at Furman University, this one running through the fundamentals of soccer, softball, volleyball, and tennis as well as basketball. That's where Kimberly had a chance to meet and learn from a few of the Furman college players. The clinics are part of an ambitious campaign by Myra Jones, program director for the Greenville YWCA. A resourceful, energetic woman in her mid-forties, Jones had enjoyed sports all her life and wanted girls in and around Greenville to have a chance to experience the benefits athletics can provide.

Jones looked at the offerings of the local school system, which offered no organized athletics at all until high school (middle school girls are eligible for the high school junior varsity teams), and then only for the elite athletes. She wanted something that would serve the middle range of girls who weren't talented enough to play varsity ball, the girls who perhaps had not had any skill instruction at all and thus were unlikely to enjoy sports or stick with playing sports. She started to cast around for something that might work in the big, heterogeneous area that the Greenville Y served. There were low-income city kids, mostly African American, and equally impoverished rural children, white and black both. At a YWCA convention she attended in

California, she encountered the basketball program run by the Santa Monica Y, which began in 1988. It had become a raging success, with more than two hundred girls participating.

The Santa Monica program got started, recalls national YWCA program director Alpha Alexander, when a group of parents became frustrated over their experiences with the local coed basketball leagues. "The fathers went to the YWCA and said, 'We're tired of seeing our daughters sitting on the bench. Can you offer something that's just for girls?' " Since then, Santa Monica had become the flagship girls' sports program of the national YWCA. Myra Jones observed it at the convention and came away impressed. She asked its director what it would take to start such a program in Greenville.

"He said, 'eighty thousand dollars,' and I said to myself, 'Wow,' " Jones recalls. "I knew I couldn't do anything like that initially. I took their idea and started to do something different, which was a low-cost program."

That was in 1994. The next year Nike joined the national YWCA in sponsoring basketball programs like Santa Monica's around the country. Myra Jones had her program up and running, so it was perfectly positioned to benefit. The sponsors kicked in $3,000 of seed money and $1,000 worth of equipment. Even with that level of support, Jones had to depend a lot on volunteers and had to give scholarships to many of the girls who could not afford the $20 program fee. One of the people she recruited was Dave Curtis, who first coached basketball and wound up coaching volleyball and softball, too, when the program expanded. This despite the fact that Curtis did not know a lot about the rules of any of these sports to begin with. "I was the kind of kid who did the chess club when I was growing up," says Curtis. "I learned a lot." Myra Jones is a difficult woman to turn down.

The Greenville basketball program now serves eighty girls, and Jones was successful in her efforts to keep its tone low-key and inclusive. There are two sites, one in downtown Greenville and a rural one that meets in the Slater-Marietta elementary school gym. "We cater to the masses," Jones says. "Instead of having twelve girls that are going to play high school ball, we have forty girls that play every week." They work on basic skills, with each session split between practice and a loose, informal game. They don't keep score, and the coaches referee. Sometimes the coach will stop the action to give impromptu instruction. "We try to give them not only a chance to play ball, but to have fun and do it in a noncompetitive environment," Jones says. "A lot of these girls will lose interest if it starts getting real competitive, because they know that they can't compete. Their skill level isn't high enough. They're not going to be those elite few. They'll see that they can't keep up with the other girls, they can't shoot as well, or they can't dribble as well, so they'll drop out."

The sports programs spearheaded by Myra Jones demonstrate how athletics can transform not just the lives of girls but the vitality of a whole region. So underserved were the rural residents of northern Greenville County that when Jones showed up in the gym of Slater-Marietta elementary school it seemed like a miracle. "I know God answers prayers," says Patsy Hunt, whose daughters Tatiana, age twelve, and Tristan, age seven, joined the Y program. "I knew for sure he had answered mine when Myra came up here. It seemed like she came out of nowhere! I was so thankful. My girls were getting restless. They had nothing to do."

Hunt is most thankful for the changes that learning to play basketball and baseball has wrought in the life of her elder daughter, Tatiana. "She was transformed over a year's time," Hunt says. "Myra showed Tatiana her natural abilities. She's big for her age, and Myra showed her what to do with that size. She showed her where the advantage was. And boy, she has really learned from it. She has more self-esteem. I had no one to do that for me when I was young." In fact, watching her daughters go through the Y programs has forced Hunt to reappraise her own life. She used to be athletic. "To look at me now you wouldn't believe that," Hunt says with a self-deprecating laugh. At thirty-five she is heavyset, but she recalls a time in sixth grade when she and her best friend came in second and first, respectively, in the 100-yard dash. "I wish I had stuck with it," she says.

One of the things the Y program did for her daughter, Hunt believes, is furnish her with role models, not only in Myra Jones, but in the female athletes Jones brought in to talk to the girls. "I could tell that [Tatiana] began to think, 'If those ladies can do it, I know I can,' " her mother says. "Some of the women talked about the backgrounds they came from, and I think Tashie started to relate to them." Hunt naturally measures herself against some of the athletes she and her daughters meet through the Y program. They too went to see Lynette Woodard. "That lady was close to my age," Hunt says, "and here she is, getting ready to get started in the pros." But she liked what the exposure to women professionals did for her daughter.

"After seeing Woodard and seeing that league, my daughter started to say things like 'Mom, I could do this one day.' You would not believe how good she's gotten about her diet, about her appearance. She was complaining about how she felt when she was running. I told her, 'The worst thing you can do is sit in front of the TV all day.' So she started getting out and riding her bike." Tatiana was shy at first, unsure of herself. But after working in the program she became enamored of basketball and baseball both ("She is a slugger!" says her mother). Jones's emphasis on a noncompetitive atmosphere and basic skills training turned out to be just the right tonic.

"Tatiana has really blossomed, and not only athletically," Patsy Hunt says. "It has changed her completely. It sounds like a cliché, but she has morphed from one phase to the other. I saw her grow up in a year. I saw her mature. I know definitely that her getting involved with the sports program had a lot to do with her self-assurance."

In Myra Jones's judgment, the question of coed versus single-sex play is simple. "Single gender is the key," she says, primarily because of the difference in skill levels between girls and boys of the same age. If the girls can't play competitively, or if they are just sitting on the bench, then their experience with athletics won't be a positive one. The average girl on a boys' team, Jones says, is not only wasting her time, she's forming opinions about how much she likes—or dislikes—sports.

"My biggest concern was that the girls have fun," Jones says. "Yeah, they learn some things, but I haven't been that concerned about the finer points of technique. We want to give all the girls an opportunity, and if someone is good, if she is going to be one of those elite few, we have no problem sending her on to another program where she can refine her skills."

"Separate is never equal," states Deborah Slaner Larkin. Larkin is a past executive director of the Women's Sports Foundation, a member of the President's Council on Physical Fitness and Sports, and an initiator of the council's report on girls in sports—a mover and shaker, in other words, in women's athletics and an outspoken advocate for the benefits girls can gain from participating in sports. In her mind, coed competition is a way to demand the best from, and for, our daughters.

Larkin puts her time where her mouth is, coaching her own daughter on her grade school soccer team. (A lifelong athlete, she says her daughter's first words were "mommy sweat.")

Larkin has seen girls who have played other girls exclusively start to go up against girls with experience in coed leagues. The result is a mismatch. The girls who have played with boys are much more advanced, more aggressive, willing to take the initiative. The girls who have played only against girls find themselves at a disadvantage.

It is a thorny question, whether girls are better off competing against only girls or on coed teams. The answer gets clearer, of course, after adolescence, when the growing upper-body strength and added muscle mass of boys makes for uneven competition in most games. Even then, there are exceptions, and the difference really matters only at the elite, varsity level of play. For many parents, the question isn't an issue simply because there are not enough offerings to make a viable choice. Only in popular, successful soccer programs such as the one in Somers, New York, are parents able to have the luxury of many different options. In Somers, coed teams are the rule until third grade, after which girls and parents have a choice, through seventh grade, between all-girls and coed teams. But the only reason this is possible is that there is so big a pool of players from which to draw.

Often the choice is between coed play and no play at all. If the boys' team is the only game in town, then a girl who wants to play has nowhere else to go. Roberta Butcher, one of the first girls to wrestle at the high school level back in 1974, faced a problem girls are still confronted with a quarter-century later. "If there was a girls' team, I would go out for it," she told reporters. "But since there isn't, I have to stick with the boys." Some girls, like Lucy Morgenstern, insist on playing with boys, because they want to play the game the boys are playing and consider anything else second best. When she was young, Tara VanDerveer made sure she bought the finest basketball then available so she could use it to lure boys into playing with her. WNBA star Sheryl

Swoopes recalls having to prove herself over and over again on the playground courts and rec center gymnasium of her Texas hometown. Once she did establish her game, however, her male peers accepted her without question. And for some girls, beating the boys is what it's all about. "Basketball chose me," says national team standout Teresa Edwards, "because as a child it was the one sport in which I could outperform the boys."

Different sports present the question of coed competition in different ways. Track and field, gymnastics, and other personal-best sports have long-established categories of competition for males and females. Again, the impetus has always been fundamental biological differences that rendered a sprint competition, say, between top male and female runners an unfair and basically meaningless exercise. There is abundant evidence that the gap between the sexes in personal-best sports is diminishing. The difference between the female and male world records for 800-meter freestyle swimming, for example, fell from 21 percent in 1910 to 5 percent in 1980.

With two professional leagues and with high school and college play burgeoning in popularity, women's basketball is firmly established in this country. But there will always be a few elite female players—in every town, on every playground—who want to mix it up with the boys.

Que-Lam Huynh learned to play basketball in local pickup games of what she calls "streetball."

She lives with her mother in Phoenix, Arizona, out near the suburb of Glendale, in the midst of the kind of undifferentiated residential sprawl that forces people to identify their neighborhood in relation to the nearest mall. Her street is lined with small, low-slung bungalows with parched, postage-stamp lawns. Across the way is a vacant lot studded with three radio towers.

Que-Lam (pronounced "way-lahm") doesn't look like the stereo-typical basketball player. At five-two she's small for the game, but she has an intense, scrappy style, all elbows and squeezing in low. She has delicate features and gently permed, shoulder-length hair, and her loose-fit jeans and T-shirt seem to swallow her up. Around her neck she wears a jade Buddha with a diamond crown, a gift from her mother after a trip back home to Vietnam.

The two of them arrived in this country in 1990, when Huynh was in fifth grade, settling in Phoenix. Other immigrants told her horror stories of unwary newcomers getting impaled on cactus. "They were just trying to scare me," Que-Lam says. She's older now, thoroughly acclimated. Her T-shirt is emblazoned with a series of gag photos featuring Dick Clark wearing the hair-styles of rock stars. She drives a used Toyota pickup with a re-placed left front fender. Displayed on the wall of the family living room, beside the television and VCR she uses to scrutinize her game reels, are three Asian zithers, an instrument she played with some proficiency from age six until shortly after she arrived in America.

Back then, she had barely even heard of basketball. When she was young in Saigon she remembers playing badminton with her mother and her aunts, going out onto the street at four in the morning, when it was still cool, "before the cars and bicycles started coming out." She would also practice aikido moves with her mother, My Nguyen, who as a child was one of the few girls in her neighborhood to practice martial arts. Her parents, Que-Lam's grandparents, complained about their daughter's involve-ment in "self-defense." My Nguyen recalls, "I told my mother, 'instead of hanging out with bad people, I go to school, I do my work—what do you want?' "

My Nguyen shares with her daughter a quietly determined, iron-fist/velvet-glove personality. She is polite and positive, despite her past hardships, which she recounts matter-of-factly in accented English. In less than a decade she has managed to achieve some measure of the American Dream: she owns her home and has a full-time job where, as her daughter says, "she has, like, a space suit on," working with microelectronic wafers. Her long hours make it difficult for her to attend Que-Lam's games. "I always did the right thing," she says, "but the situation is such that I am struggling here." Despite any financial stress they might feel, she tells her daughter not to work during high school. She would rather Que-Lam concentrate on her studies than work at a low-paying job which, her mother believes, would never allow her to make enough money to pay for college anyway. She should go for a scholarship instead and spend her time on extracurricular activities and community service (Que-Lam volunteers at a local hospital and at a food bank). My Nguyen believes that sports helped her daughter through the difficult transitions of the immigrant experience. "Education is the most important thing in her life," says Que-Lam's mother firmly, and she sees athletics as an integral part of that education. "I feel she is more confident when she is involved with sport."

In grade school in Vietnam, Que-Lam played soccer, but when she got to Phoenix and transferred into a predominantly white middle school, she couldn't find a game. It was before the soccer craze hit. One reason basketball attracted her then is that, unlike soccer, it was easy for her to practice by herself. All she needed was a rim and a ball. Soon she began to get up early to shoot hoops. She stopped playing the zither. She became, in her words, "a basketball freak," hurrying her lunch, playing after school. She was "the scrawniest one out there," she says, and the only girl playing streetball. "I couldn't afford to play on a team," she recalls. "I didn't know there were teams around. It was easier to play with the boys. The boys were better at basketball anyway, so I figured if I wanted to get better at basketball, I better play with somebody good."

All that street training paid off. She made the varsity team as a sophomore at Washington High School ("Home of the Rams"), playing point guard. She exudes the easy confidence of a student leader as she talks about her school, describing activities she's involved in, which range from student council to a "cultural diversity club" called Ram's World. Even for the booming immigrant mecca of Phoenix, Washington is a multiethnic stew, with Chicanos, Asians, blacks, whites. When there are gang fights, Que-Lam says, the Asian faction sometimes derides her for not automatically taking their side, but she'd rather act as a conciliator or a mediator. As counselor at a Ram's World retreat the summer before her senior year, she saw how sports can act as a bridge between groups. She spent time with a group of Native American teenagers who hadn't said a word to anyone else outside their group until they happened to choose Que-Lam for a basketball team. "It's easier to talk to people when you're in sports," she says. "You have something in common right away."

She has taken her game back to Vietnam twice so far, on month-long visits to her relatives. On the first visit, during the summer she was fourteen, she found she had to explain what basketball was to her grandmother, who had never heard of it. "I said, 'There's a round metal rim and you throw the ball in there, and you can dribble and pass the ball.' I tried to show her and she just laughed at me." Searching out games led her to a crumbling athletic club in downtown Saigon. The floor of the outdoor court was warped and the rims were bent crazily from the baseboard, but every day Que-Lam got there when the place opened at 5 A.M. The players ranged from fifty-year-olds to teenagers, both boys and girls. They played a competitive game, but to Que-Lam's streetball-trained eyes, it was "polite": heavy on fundamentals, a lot of bank shots and layups, no air, clean, no-trash talk, and hardly any fouls. She was able to impress the other players with a spin move and fancy dribbling.

" 'Oh, she's an American!' they'd say," Que-Lam recalls, "because nobody around there does that stuff."

The game of basketball provided Que-Lam with an informal civics lesson. She talks about going to Phoenix Mercury games in the summer of 1997 with her friend Szudia, "an African American with an African name," and the "feeling in the pit of [her] stomach" that happened every time she stood for the national anthem. "Sometimes I would sit there and be watching the game and all of a sudden tears would want to come out."

Que-Lam has the heart for the game, but not the height. At five-two, she is just under what she feels to be the cutoff point for college basketball. A little wistfully, she names a college player who is five-three. No worthwhile college, she feels, will offer her a sports scholarship. Her 4.0 academic record has gotten her full-ride offers at "all the Arizona schools," but she's holding out for a private San Diego school, and her eventual aim will be a medical degree. Inspired by the example of the Steingards, a Phoenix-area family of physicians specializing in orthopedic sports medicine, she wants to someday work in the field.

"There are still people out there that think that girls shouldn't be playing basketball, or shouldn't be playing sports, period, and there are some at my school," Que-Lam says. "But I think 99 percent of the people are open to it." She feels the boys appreciate the girls who are athletes, and she tends to date athletes, though not necessarily the ones on the boys' basketball team. She still shoots hoops with the boys once in a while, and although she likes having girls for teammates, she relates better to the way boys play the game. They are physical, she says, they practice more, they play more, and their skill level and dedication is a lot higher. "I think I might be the most serious girl about basketball at my school."

Que-Lam has transformed her room into a shrine to basketball in general and Michael Jordan in particular. Papering three walls are poster images of Jordan. There is a Michael Jordan bedspread and, uncharacteristic for a drug-free student, a neon beer sign ("Chicago Bulls Lite"). Within dunking distance of her bed is a Nerf basketball net. Her nightlight is a small glowing basketball. On the room's western wall, facing away from the door, hangs the sole item of decor not related to basketball. It is the yellow-and-blue flag of the Republic of Vietnam, now gone from the world's flagpoles. Que-Lam's aunt, who lives in Australia, sewed it after Que-Lam admired the flag at an acquaintance's house, and her mother couldn't find one in a store.

For Que-Lam, basketball helps quiet the storms of adolescence. Beneath her polite exterior she harbors a fiery temper, and during a game she sometimes has a tendency to kick and punch the air, or to "disrespect" the referee, but in order to stay in the game, she has to control herself. She thinks it has carried over to her off-court life. "If I get mad at one of my friends," she says, "I don't just go off. I don't explode. I think about what I'm getting mad at. I think, Is it worth it? I let myself sit down and think, just like I would let myself calm down on a court so I don't get a technical."

The game provides an outlet, she says, for when she's "angry, needs to think, needs to resolve something" within herself. "I go and play basketball and it clears my head. When I'm frustrated I go and play basketball. When I'm happy I play basketball. It fills an empty spot in my life." Yes, she likes to win, something, admittedly, her team doesn't do too often. But for Que-Lam the main thing isn't victory. "I just like being with my teammates. If we're working together well, you feel like you're walking on water."

Girls' basketball has gotten a big boost in Arizona recently with the debut of the Phoenix Mercury, one of the premier teams in the WNBA, coached by former USC and U.S. national team standout Cheryl Miller. The fans at the America West Arena are known as the most vocal on the WNBA circuit. The Mercury and Nike sponsor the Plan-It League, a citywide program designed to use basketball to foster leadership and self-esteem among grade school girls.

Both Que-Lam Huynh and her friend Szudia are coaches for a Plan-It League team. The program uses a mix of teenage coach/mentors and high-profile athlete advisers to inspire its young participants. Each Plan-It League team has a Phoenix Mercury player assigned to it—Que-Lam's team had standout power forward Jennifer Gillom, who came to a practice and helped motivate the kids. Afterward, Que-Lam says, the girls were starstruck, in awe of the star who had just helped carry the Mercury to the WNBA quarterfinal.

Another Mercury player who worked that season with the Plan-It League is Nancy Lieberman-Cline, at thirty-seven the oldest player in the WNBA and a Hall of Fame legend. Lieberman-Cline is one of the pre–Title IX pioneers in women's sports, a premier player of her generation, the grande dame (although she might loathe the description) of women's basketball in America. As of the 1998 season, she is coach for the WNBA expansion team, the Detroit Shock.

A few months after graduating high school, Nancy Lieberman helped the U.S. women's team win a silver medal in the 1976 Olympics. She went on to become a college force at Old Dominion, and was the first female to play on a professional men's team (the Springfield Fame of the U.S. Basketball League). Beyond the court, she has campaigned tirelessly throughout her career to promote basketball for women and girls.

When she was growing up in Far Rockaway, New York, her mother did everything she could to discourage her daughter from sports, even puncturing her basketball with a screwdriver. "It's okay, Mom," the confident Nancy would say, "I'm going to make history."

She played as often as she could, and until her sophomore year in high school she played exclusively with boys. Stories about the teenage Nancy Lieberman are the stuff of legend: how she took the subway to the city in search of the best, the toughest basketball games around. She knew that Julius Erving, Connie Hawkins, and Kareem Abdul Jabbar (then Lew Alcindor) had played ferocious games of street hoops. "I always wanted to be the best," Lieberman-Cline recalls. "I figured that to be the best, you had to play against the best. I don't know why, at twelve, thirteen, fourteen years old, this is how I conducted myself—I never studied psychology or any of that stuff—but I knew all the best players were playing in Harlem, so I would just take the train, by myself, at night, and get off and walk to the park."

She remembers being only "a little scared" on those treks. She used to stuff extra T-shirts in the arms of her jackets to make herself appear to have large muscles. "I'd kind of glare at people on the train, like if they thought I was crazier than them, they wouldn't mess with me." Once she got to the courts, she would throw out that age-old playground query, half-question, half-challenge, Who's got next? "Nobody would say anything to me," she recalls. She'd repeat her question, and when she was still met with silence, she'd throw down the gauntlet. "Since none of you guys want to play," she'd say, "I've got next, and I'll be sitting over there if you guys want to play. You just see me." The Harlem players finally wound up respecting her brashness, taking her under their wing. Lieberman-Cline says the fundamental thing she learned in those playground games was how to play a creative, instinctive, high-risk game, "not to be scared to try something, whether it was around my back or through my legs." A quarter-century later, the WNBA pluralized Nancy Lieberman's playground claim when they adopted "We've Got Next" as their official motto.

Lieberman-Cline is one of those successful female athletes who believe in the principle of giving back. It's what she's doing at her Plan-It League appearances and also in clinics she has sponsored for sixteen years in her home base of Dallas. For her, helping inspire the younger generation is not an onerous duty. "It's a dream come true," she says. "It's not worth having what you have, or the experience, if you can't share it. Because it's all about passing it down. I mean, there would be no Michael Jordan without Julius Erving. There would be no Julius Erving without Elgin Baylor. Everybody has to set the place for the next generation."

In the Plan-It League, elite athletes like Lieberman-Cline work with eight-, nine-, and ten-year-old players. More than four hundred girls from throughout Phoenix participate, and twenty-eight area high schools send referees or, as in the case of Que-Lam Huynh, coaches. The WNBA players are free to choose their level of commitment. Some of them conduct a single workshop with their designated teams, others do more. Tara Williams had her team over for a pool party and sleepover, during which they stayed up late and watched horror films.

Lieberman-Cline believes "if you can't see it, it's very difficult to dream it." How would anyone know that a female could run for vice president of the United States, she asks, were it not for Geraldine Ferraro? When she played with the Mercury, she looked out upon thousands of young girls who filled the stadiums every night. She saw it in their eyes, she says. "They're dreaming. They're thinking, I want to be number ten. I'm going to wear a Mercury uniform one day. It's fueling their dreams and their hopes and all their aspirations."

Basketball's informal hierarchy might furnish a model for all sports: a level of recreational sport open to all girls, a varsity level of rigorous girl-against-girl play, plus an open acceptance that there are girls out there ready to play against boys in their leagues. The sport has a distance to go to realize that ideal. But the way to solve the question of coed versus single-sex play is finally not to resolve it at all. The world would be a poorer place if girls like Que-Lam Huynh and the young Nancy Lieberman were not allowed to play up to their potential, to learn from the best opponents and teammates, just as the world would be poorer if all girls were dragooned into playing on coed teams. What we owe our daughters is maximum access and opportunity, regardless of the sport and regardless of who they have to play against to realize their dreams.

5

Soul Strengthening

Sports During the "Ophelia Years"

Crowded into an office cubicle at a community center are nine high school students, all teammates, all from the Washington Heights neighborhood of Upper Manhattan. As these young women talk about themselves, it becomes obvious the ways in which sports shore up their lives and help them weather the storms of adolescence.

Yanel Cordera, dressed in a red-white-and-blue Tommy Hilfiger sweatshirt, baggy jeans, and running shoes, says that getting into athletics enables her to avoid "being pressured into having sex." Since the high school senior began playing sports with regularity—she plays volleyball, softball, and basketball—she finds herself being more critical about the relationships she chooses. The guy she goes out with now, she says, is the kind of guy who supports her for who she is. "He'll bring my shorts to my game," she says, prompting appreciative laughter among her teammates. "Once you play a sport, something you have control of, you tend to see things a little bit differently, so that's how you end up choosing your relationships a little bit differently," she says. "You won't just pick any boy from the block. You begin to set up standards."

Control is a word the high school girls come back to again and again. As a concept, it speaks to a concern, an obsession almost, that teenagers have with freedom, independence, trust, and choices. Girls with low self-esteem tend to feel they can't control anything in their lives—life just "happens" to them. Confident nine-year-olds too often transform into self-destructive fourteen-year-old Ophelias with "no inner direction," as Mary Pipher describes them. Behaviors such as disordered eating patterns, cigarette smoking, early pregnancy, sexual promiscuity, or abuse of drugs and alcohol often represent attempts, however misguided, to assert some measure of control over their lives. Physically active girls are not immune to such scourges, but they engage in them far less often than their nonactive peers.

Athletics offers teenagers a chance to assume independence without losing control. In sports they can make choices, take risks, be assertive, and be independent within a safe setting. It's a positive form of independence, whereas many of the other strategies are flawed, false, or prone to backfire. "You feel when you start playing that you have this sort of control," says Aida Ramos, one of Cordera's teammates. "You feel, well, hey, if I'm playing good, if I'm practicing, then I can control the rest of my life. I'm the one that's going to have a say in what's going to happen in my life and what's not."

Washington Heights is built along a spinelike ridge of Upper Manhattan, where the island narrows to a little over a mile in width. A large segment of the neighborhood population is Dominican, and Yanel and her teammates are mostly children of immigrant Americans. A recent Columbia University–City College study found that the Dominican community in New York City is at the very bottom of the income scale and losing ground. Even though statistically there is less crime in New York than in many large cities, the perception is that the streets of Washington Heights are unsafe, severely curtailing after-dark activities in parks, playgrounds, and gymnasiums. The youth population of the neighborhood numbers around 56,000. The typical school operates at 110 to 140 percent capacity. P.S. 128, in the heart of the Dominican community, was designed for 900 students but currently enrolls 1,600. Another school operates on double session, which means many students aren't dismissed until after four o'clock—again, severely curtailing extracurricular athletic activities.

Yanel Cordera and her teammates both define and defy the concept of teenagers at risk. Many of them come in close contact with friends who have babies, with drug users and sellers, with street violence. Yet for all this the girls come across as surprisingly intact. Playing sports is an anchor—perhaps *the* anchor—in their lives. These young women are bright, energetic, funny, and strong.

Cordera, especially, is inclined to laugh off her troubles, though with a dark-edged sort of humor. Confident and outgoing, she has strong features and long, wavy black hair. With a smile, she speaks of the reception her girls' softball team received when they played in High Bridge Park, along the Harlem River. "Crackhead Alley," one of her teammates calls it. "Don't get me wrong," Yanel says, with a knowing sidelong look at the others in the group, "there's something funny about a crackhead cheering you, but . . ." The girls laugh, and Yanel shakes her head. *But I wish we didn't have problems like these* is the unspoken thought.

By the time the Washington Heights girls' teams were organized in the early 1990s, by a long-standing group of local community activists called the 280 Dreamers, their league had to compete with long-established programs for field space, a case of last come, last served. It's a problem all over the country. Girl athletes in suburban Los Angeles recently filed a class action suit against the city, claiming that for years their softball league has had to scrounge for piecemeal temporary permits to play on substandard fields, while boys' Little League teams played year after year on well-maintained, secure fields, with perks such as concession stands and electronic scoreboards. One official commented favorably on the suit. "We want to make sure that historical accident doesn't mean the boys have a lock on the best facilities in perpetuity." In Washington Heights, the girls were forced to play their games at 9:30 on Sunday morning, when the drug users were just letting go of their Saturday night turf, because the boys' teams had sewn up all the more desirable fields and game times long ago. It was an especially difficult schedule for family members with church commitments.

The girls also deal with parental indifference at home. Aida Ramos says that as often as not, the reaction from her mother about her sports participation is "Another game?" or "Another practice?"—as if her activities are nothing but an inconvenience. On a Saturday morning, her mother would rather that she help with the grocery shopping than play softball. The girls say that their parents don't generally get a chance to attend the games. Cordera says that her biggest fan is her baby brother—and that's out of necessity: she has to bring him along to the field, since she babysits for him. Whenever the girls pick up a ball and bat, they are heading upstream against the current of tradition. Although there is a rabid baseball culture in the Dominican Republic, and recent National League Cy Young Award winner Pedro Martinez has been raised to the level of folk hero in the Dominican community, girls are generally not encouraged in athletics. Whenever she or her sister got their hands on a ball growing up, Aida recalls, their mother would take it away and throw it in the trash.

For Yanel Cordera, sports participation is a way out of a sometimes suffocating predicament, a response to a world that increasingly closes down her options. She describes how she feels on the way to a game. "Once you get out of your house, life is just a little different," says Yanel. "When you're home all the time, you tend to be exactly like your mother, exactly like your brother, exactly like everybody else. You don't get to do much of what you want. I like to be exposed to things and get out on my own and have the feeling that I know how to do something, that I know how to do this." She searches for the right word. "It's just more *realistic* when you get out of the house."

For everyone, boys and girls alike, the high school years are an emotional crucible. Social demands increase just when the process of self-definition becomes painfully all-consuming. Some girls at this age, such as Yanel Cordera and her teammates, might have additional challenges of poverty, lack of social resources, or degraded home environments to overcome. Participation in athletics is perhaps the only viable broad-spectrum answer to a whole range of problems confronting our daughters. Those problems may challenge the well-off and disadvantaged in radically different ways, just as they might challenge a shy girl, say, differently from a girl who is more outgoing. The good thing about sports is that they represent a flexible, adaptable resource for girls in many different situations.

It is only about fifty miles as the crow flies from the barrio of Washington Heights to the wooded enclave of Suffern, New York, but the social distance is far greater. Suffern High School might as well be light-years away from the overcrowded, underfunded city schools where Yanel Cordera and her friends scratch out their softball careers. Suffern High has furnished its fair share of high school champion teams over the years. While it's not a nationally ranked, high school sports powerhouse, it takes its athletics—including, to some degree, its girls' sports—very seriously.

Lisa Philips is a junior at Suffern High. On a chill October evening she is running late for her usual Monday night batting practice with her hitting coach, Penny Rosario, a former Olympic softballer who offers private training sessions. Lisa shows up still in her volleyball uniform from a high school game that afternoon. It is already dark. Rosario and Philips are using the batting cage that dominates the backyard of Suffern High School's softball coach, Ray Buteaux. Buteaux is a model train enthusiast, and wide-gauge model railroad tracks wind through the yard, past the beds of impatiens, looping all the way around the batting cage. Visible through the plate-glass windows of the Buteaux family room are the coach and his wife watching Monday night football. He's relaxing, but his standout player—"the best first baseman I've ever had," as he describes Lisa—is ready to hit away.

Rosario flips a switch and the high-powered halogens above the cage burn blue-white through the fall mist. She takes a seat on a bench just outside the netting, where she can scrutinize each of Lisa's swings and offer comments and correctives. Behind a net shield inside the cage, Rich Philips, Lisa's father, loads the pitching machine. He simulates the windmilling fastpitch motion each time as a visual cue for his daughter. This is the first of two drills they will do tonight, with coach, father, and daughter making up a single collaborative unit, each element contributing to the overall effort. The short-term goal is to bring Lisa's swing as near to perfection as possible. The long-term goal is to get her into the Olympics. But the ultimate purpose, for both Rosario and Rich Philips, may be to shape Lisa's character through the struggle and challenge of perfecting her game.

"If I can teach a girl to hit an 0–2 fastball," Rosario asks, "what will it do for her self-esteem in school?"

Penny and Lisa have developed something integral to most elite training regimens, a mentor relationship whereby an older athlete passes on skills and strategies to a younger one. Rosario has been to the Olympics, playing for the Puerto Rican team in 1996. "Penny's been where I want to go," Philips says. "She started right here in Clarktown South. I've always had the dream of playing for a Division I college and going to the Olympics, but to see someone from Rockland County actually go there gives me hope." She didn't get into organized sports until she was in seventh grade, but growing up a few miles from Philips's hometown, Rosario had an active childhood. "I was always hanging out with the boys, I was always playing. You couldn't get me off the field. I would come a bloody, muddy mess," she says. She played baseball, stickball, basketball, and football: "Wherever there was a ball, I played." She played with boys because "back then, you couldn't get together a pickup football game with ten girls."

What Rosario learned from her own mentor, an older neighbor named Nancy, was something along the line of life lessons. A formative moment for Rosario came the day Nancy was playing third base and "there was a rocket right back at her that hit her right in the eye." Rosario panicked and ran out onto the field. "Her eye blew up so big, and I looked at her and I was crying, I was so upset," Rosario recalls. Nancy turned to the eleven-year-old Penny, saying, "You've got to be brave," and went back into the game. "I've never forgotten that lesson," Rosario says.

One reason Rosario has invested so much of herself in teaching others is that she has seen her share of less than helpful coaching. Her high school coach taught her the negative lesson of "how to throw a tantrum, how to get upset" over a loss. Rosario's fiery temper would express itself when she threw her bat and helmet after striking out, a habit it took her a long time to break. "You can still see the imprint of that coach," she says. She is now trying to leave a more positive imprint on Philips.

"That's the one, right there," Rosario says, as Lisa cuts at a fastball and sends it into the net. Rosario is working on getting Lisa to relax her swing. She speaks to her in a conversational tone, hardly ever raising her voice, heavily emphasizing the positive. She has teaching points she calls "key cues," breaking down the elements of the swing into separate motions. Each practice concentrates on only a few key cues. Lisa has what ballplayers call "quick hands"—she tends to pull the ball, getting her bat around quickly to hit into left field. The key cues Philips is working on tonight are "wait"—waiting for the ball so that she doesn't swing too quickly—and "opposite hand"—concentrating on her left-hand motion. Those are the two key cues Rosario believes will help Philips relax with her swing.

Rich Philips picks up a dimple ball, one of the softer, lighter practice balls they use in the cage. He displays it to his daughter in a three-quarter-speed pitching motion and then feeds it into the machine. Lisa smacks it foul. "From your ear to the ball," Rosario says, then, after Philips fouls another, "Wait a touch longer—right back at your dad." The next swing is a solid connect, and the ball booms off the bat to smash the net near Rich Philips, who instinctively ducks. "Nice!" Rosario says to Lisa. "Do you feel the difference in the extension there?" Rich is still smiling and shaking his head at the near miss. "Don't worry, Dad," Rosario calls to Lisa's father, "I know CPR." Over and over again, for nearly a hundred balls, they continue, Lisa batting, Penny counseling, Rich feeding the machine and trying to stay out of the way of line drives. "Nice shot, Lis'!" Rosario says. "Way to rip the ball." By the end of the drill, Philips is ripping everything that comes past her.

Afterward, as the three of them gather up the balls littering the ground inside the cage, Lisa talks to Rosario about her play of the day before, which, she mentions proudly, got her name in the local paper. She also reminds Rosario of the all-star game in Edison, New Jersey, that is coming up. "Are you nervous?" asks Rosario. Lisa hesitates. "Wellll . . ." College scouts will be at the game, and Philips wants to make sure she performs well. Rosario offers her advice, based on her own hard-won experience. "They're looking at the whole package," she says. "They're looking at the ones who throw their helmets, the ones who do the cheering—and they're looking at your raw talent, not necessarily whether you even get a hit that day. So just check your attitude. Be sure that if you strike out, you walk back, put down your helmet, go sit down. The first person that throws their helmet, the coach will never look at them again."

"Yeah, all right," says Lisa.

"So just go and have fun, okay?" says Penny. "You'll be great. You're not nervous, right?" Lisa nods.

"The thing that's in her favor, she's hot now," Rich Philips says to Penny as he puts the last of the dimple balls into a crate. "She's not in a slump now."

Rosario drags the purple plastic milk crate full of balls over to Philips to begin the second drill, speed work. Rosario sits close to Lisa and throws up ball after ball for her to hit, rapid-fire, a dozen or more per minute. There is no conversation, just the whistle of the red aluminum bat and the solid "thwack" as Philips tags every ball. She's not thinking about her all-star game now. When asked later what is on her mind during a speed drill, she says, "I just concentrate on trying to hit that ball right through the middle and break it in two. I want to smash it and kill it. And I want to get better."

There is a limited pool of national athletic talent, numbering perhaps ten thousand girls nationwide, from which the Division I colleges recruit their star athletes and from which the various U.S. national Olympic team organizations develop their gold medal hopefuls. Lisa Philips is attempting to become a member of this elite club. The sports experience for this class of girls has become ever more rarefied in the last decade, a world of weekend clinics and summer camps, trainers and professional coaches. It's expensive, exhausting, demanding of time from child and parent. "From June to December, we have no life," Rich Philips says. Above all, it is a world of specialization. Lisa Philips has just dropped out of varsity basketball. "When you stop having fun," she says, "you shouldn't play anymore. You're letting down your teammates, you don't care as much, you're not trying your best." The reason she was on varsity in the first place was simply that she is tall and the other center could not be relied upon to show up for practice. From now until she graduates, she is concentrating on her main sport, softball. For her, it is a year-round endeavor. In addition to her high school varsity season, she plays in a special fall league, attends winter batting clinics and training sessions, and participates in "summerball," an elite traveling squad. Philips continues to play volleyball in the fall, because colleges like multisport prospects and also just because she enjoys the game, but softball is her passion.

The club system has been criticized by some athletes and parents of athletes, who feel club-sport participants can get a very small return on the high investment of money and time, especially if they are spending games on the bench when they could be honing their skills. But Lisa Philips and her parents feel the sacrifices—the fees paid, the vacations given over to tournaments, the scheduling hassles, the missed dates and parties—are a worthwhile trade-off.

There is a gulf between girls like Yanel and girls like Lisa, and it is not just cultural. Lisa has entered an intensive sports training track that is simply not available to all girls in this country and is difficult for the underserved girls of Washington Heights to access. But for all their differences, Cordera and Philips experience a similar pattern of slights, shortage of resources, outright hostility, and blatant backlash that seems automatically to come with being a female athlete. Philips has an extensive support network to balance out any negatives in her environment with strong positives. Looking at Philips, an outside observer would almost conclude that there are no barriers associated with girls in sports. Lisa herself downplays the negatives to the point of denial. Perhaps the best way to illustrate obstacles still remaining for girls in sports even at an elite level is to compare Philips not with Yanel Cordera, but with an A-list male athlete from Suffern.

From high school onwards, a male baseball player will have newer uniforms, better facilities, four times the college scholarship money, and better access to all aspects of the game, from field time to doctors, trainers, and physical therapy. If he's good enough (that is, if he's at a comparable level in his sport with Lisa Philips in hers), the male star will have a college career followed by a chance at professional play in an extensive farm system of minor league and semipro teams. And he'll have a chance to grab at the gold ring of "the Show," the major leagues.

Lisa Philips, for all her bright future and in spite of the fact that she would never complain about the disparity, faces a far different sports career than her male counterpart. Her father, Rich Philips, notes that the Suffern girls' team just got around to getting new uniforms two years ago ("Before that," Philips says, "they were playing in ones that were years old"). The girls' team is not assigned practice time on the main Suffern High School ballfield, the well-manicured field with dugouts—that's reserved for varsity boys.

As a junior, Philips is already being scouted by college teams, even though by rule college representatives are not allowed to speak with her. She has her eyes firmly focused on her immediate future. Her wish list includes a scholarship to a prominent softball college and then the Olympics. But beyond dreaming of a possible Olympic triumph, the future gets hazy for a female athlete in this country, and this is another way in which a high school girl's sports participation diverges from that of her male peers. Perhaps the professional softball league that just started up will have a place for Lisa Philips. She thinks that coaching girls would be "fun" at some point in the future. Perhaps athletics won't figure in to her adult livelihood at all. Her role model, Penny Rosario, augments her coaching activities with a career in physical therapy.

The reason Lisa Philips faces a dead end while her male counterpart has a clear shot at a sports future is supposedly based on objective measures of their skill. It isn't personal, many commentators in the sports media seem to believe, it's just part of the cold calculus of sports. Lisa Philips can hit a softball two hundred feet, and a top-notch baseball slugger can belt a hardball more than twice as far. The disparity in distance, the reasoning goes, accounts for the disparity in opportunity. The argument fades in the face of Lisa's passion and determination. For her, the political element of girls in sports doesn't even qualify as background static. She doesn't think of herself as anyone's symbol. She's too busy competing. "When I see a really good team out on the field warming up, I still get intimidated very easily. Then to go out there and prove to them, and make *them* intimidated by *me*—it's such a great feeling," she says.

She wants the other team to look across at her warming up and be cowed. "I want them to say, 'Look at number twenty-eight. Who is she? She's the big hitter, watch out for her when you go up, look at her arm, she can throw." She scopes out the other team without letting them know she's doing it. "I want them to be scared of me. I want them not to want to hit to first base." This is a glimpse into the face of girl power, of the kind of confidence our daughters all should enjoy.

Philips customarily gets straight A's and says she is miserable when she falls short of that record. She has a focus and determination rare in a sixteen-year-old. "In sixth or seventh grade," her father says, "she told me she knew what she wanted to do: play softball and go to college with it. She had her head together from an early age." Lisa's parents are divorced, and while her mother supports her play and attends her games, it is her father who lends it a passion. Rich Philips has been a mainstay of his daughter's career. He attends her games, acts as a coach and number one fan, pays the $1,500 or $2,000 a year for Penny Rosario's help and all the clinics and camps his daughter attends.

The sports father may in time become as much a cultural archetype as the stage mother, representing an evolution in the way fathers and daughters can connect with each other. Former executive director of the Women's Sports Foundation Deborah Slaner Larkin says that in her experience, "the fathers are always more involved." There are reasons for this. Fathers may have more sports experience. The father is traditionally the parent responsible for the athletic training of a family's offspring. Mothers may be more heavily committed to other aspects of their children's lives and not have time for sports. This may have unintended consequences. Sports for girls are being "policed by fathers," says current Women's Sports Foundation executive director Donna Lopiano. The current crop of sports fathers are the first generation "who have . . . grown up believing that your daughters will have equal opportunity." The growth in girls' sports, Lopiano says, has been spearheaded by dads who are "really teed off" to find that their daughters don't have the same athletic opportunities as their sons after all.

Their daughters' entry into the sports equation represents something new for most fathers. It can result in their having a new awareness of their daughters' capabilities and may eventually translate to an overall increase in men's respect for women. When a father witnesses his daughter smash a softball (or slap a hockey puck, drain a jumper, or strike a soccer ball), he is no longer as likely to think of women as delicate or passive. A sports father might develop something that is still rare in this culture: an appreciation of girls and women as competitive and physically strong.

Sports fathers and athletic daughters both are present in force at a batting clinic Lisa Philips attends after the finish of her fall softball season. The three-session, Friday-night-through-Sunday-afternoon clinic is offered by Ralph Weakly, head of the softball program at the University of Tennessee (a college traditionally strong in women's sports) and the head coach of the Olympic women's national softball team. Weakly's presence brings out a bumper crop of girls from all over Rockland County and northern New Jersey. The clinic is conducted in a partitioned Suffern High School gym, one side devoted to pitching instruction, one side to hitting. Each side of the gym has a single step of the bleachers pulled out for spectators. Seated in line or standing hands in pockets, soberly assessing their daughters' progress or speaking quietly among themselves, are a half-dozen fathers.

They have each paid $100 for their daughters to attend the clinic. For three hours, the girls rotate two at a time among the twelve batting stations set up on the hitting side of the gym. The stations include a fully rigged batting cage with a Jugs pitching machine, tees in different configurations, several swingaways (softballs tethered to elastic cords), and a small pitching machine called a "spitter." Each station focuses on a single element of the swing: hitting a softball off a double tee, for example, teaches the batter to swing down on the ball, while hitting a basketball off a tee improves strength and follow-through.

In every Olympic sport there are clinics such as this, grooming grounds for future gold medalists. More than the WNBA, the Women's Professional Fastpitch League, or the women's professional soccer, hockey, and volleyball leagues that are forming, the Olympic level of play represents the pinnacle of women's sports, the goal to which the most serious female athletes aspire. Women's professional play is just too new, too uncertain to represent a tangible dream for most high school girls (as opposed to the grade school girls, many of whom are convinced they are heading straight to the WNBA, if not major-league baseball or the NFL).

Weakly conducts clinics all over the country. He speaks with professional authority to his students, insistent in his conviction that there is something attainable called a perfect swing. "When you leave here Sunday," he announces on Friday night, "you're going to be a better batter, and you're going to be a better batter because we're not gonna accept anything less." He tells them that good players hit 250 balls a day. He talks about coaching Olympic star Lisa Fernandez, whom he deems the best softball player in the world right now. This will be the second year in a row that Lisa Philips has been to Weakly's clinic (later in the year, she also will attend a weekend clinic conducted by Penny Rosario, as well as other training sessions). There is an unspoken acknowledgment that such clinics are a two-way street. The girls are here to soak up as much as they can from one of the world's best softball coaches, but they are also here to audition, to impress him, to make him remember them four years down the line when it comes time to pick the members of the year 2000 national Olympic softball team. He is here to teach them, but he is also here in an informal scouting capacity, both for his Lady Vols and for the national team. Traveling all over the country as he does, seeing elite players in every state, Ralph Weakly is a roving Rolodex of softball in America, holding in his mind the constantly shifting and developing hundreds-strong lineup of Olympic hopefuls.

"He remembered my name," Lisa confides, as if she can barely believe it. The coach singles her out several times during the first night of the clinic, describing her as one of only two or three girls attending who "had 'it.' " (The other girls, in contrast, "almost had it," or "were still going for it.") Rich Philips recalls that at last year's clinic Weakly told him outright, "Keep her with it—if she keeps on going this way she'll go to the Olympics." Lisa beams whenever the coach mentions her. She is, he says, a hard worker, but she is also a natural. "You can't coach size, you can't coach speed," Weakly says, meaning that you can't as a coach create these qualities, even if they're the very things you want in a player. Lisa Philips, who at age sixteen is a strapping five-ten-and-a-half, qualifies.

"I think my height, because I was always bigger, helped me a lot," Philips says about growing up playing ball. "I like being the best. I had sort of a reputation, and I saw it. When I was up at bat, my name was just known. And becaue I got that recognition—I loved it—I wanted to get better, to improve it, and keep it. So I think if I was bad at the sport, truthfully, I don't think I would have kept up with it. But I liked the competitiveness of it, I liked being up there and hitting a two-hundred-foot ball and everyone like, 'Oh my God, who is that?' I loved that feeling.''

Lisa Philips is reaching for a sports experience that extends beyond high school, setting her sights on a college scholarship and, conceivably, the Olympics. But how does a girl who is not necessarily a star get through high school? There are many girls for whom involvement in athletics is not part of some long-range life-planning strategy, but a coping mechanism for the here and now. Sports can help them focus and improve their academic performance, allowing them to deal more easily with heavily freighted adolescent issues such as weight and personal appearance.

Erica Lewis, seventeen years old, is a senior at Walnut Hills High School in Cincinnati. When she was in grade school, all her friends were on soccer teams. "When I was younger, I was a big, heavyset girl," Erica recalls. Her weight didn't hold her back. Far from it. She became a fullback, one of the defense positions in soccer, a player who hangs back to protect the goal. Lewis was known for her great booming kicks to clear the ball, sending it all the way into the opponent's territory. "That was the best part of playing soccer," she says, "that everybody just loved when I kicked the ball. Everybody would say 'Ahhhh!' and then that clapping would begin." The only time her coach put Erica on offense—at left wing, a position that requires almost constant motion—she struggled. Once she got back to her familiar position, Erica says, "I stayed there and I knew what to do."

Lewis did not remain in soccer beyond middle school. When she switched schools in seventh grade, she began to feel that her new classmates—especially those who had access to summer soccer camps and who played on the spring tour—had a literal leg up on her. But the sport represented a crucial rite of passage in her life, as it is in the lives of many girls who participate in the national soccer boom. It showed her the pleasure and pride she could get out of moving her body—even a body that did not necessarily conform to cultural models. She comes from a sports-minded family—her older brother played soccer in grade school, her stepsister, stepfather, and mother were all athletes—and that helped keep her in the game. Even her grandmother, who never specifically encouraged her own daughter to play sports ("that's not how she raised her children"), came to Lewis's early soccer games.

When teenage girls give up a sport, there is a danger that they will drop out of athletics altogether. But Erica Lewis is, in high school, more an athlete than ever. She plays softball, volleyball, and basketball. She keeps playing, she says, primarily because of her mother's influence, even though at first she wasn't physically in shape. "When I first started playing [basketball], I had a lot of weight on me. I lost forty pounds between seventh grade and now. But I don't think losing the weight is what brought my confidence up. Getting better in the skills of my sport is what brings my confidence up."

Erica Lewis could easily have fallen victim to the many dangers that face our daughters every day. She knows many Ophelias—they are her friends and classmates. She still meets up with soccer teammates from her old neighborhood. "A lot of the girls I know have children," she says, "and they have children because they stopped playing sports." She sees people from her high school now who dropped out of school and "they're still working at Taco Bell." She herself considered dropping out of athletics at several points during her adolescence. "I have my times when I feel like just throwing my hands up." What kept her going was her mother, who as she was growing up taught her to approach each decision by consciously laying out the pros and cons. "She makes me make the decisions, but after you weigh the pros and cons you're pretty sure to pick the right route."

Erica is not a product of a privileged background. Girls like her walk the edge of a precipice, but sports give them balance. "Playing sports kept me out of trouble," she says. "I don't drink or smoke, but my friends who don't do sports, they do. If they haven't had liquor or a beer, they smoke cigarettes or something else. I was always too preoccupied with sports to do stuff like that, or to run around with boys. So I didn't end up pregnant." One reason Erica is such a surprisingly forthright cheerleader for sports participation is that she coaches a group of twenty eight-to-ten-year-olds in Cincinnati's new YWCA basketball league for girls. She sounds the same themes with her young players: "My mind-set is, this is all about just helping children. If I can change a child's mind, that's great. Instead of having her just sit in the house and watch TV all day, if I can have her, instead of that, come play a sport, or come read a book, I feel like I did something."

Every morning at Walnut Hills, the principal comes on the PA system to note the achievements of the school's athletes from the day before. Hearing her name puts a "big smile" on her face, Erica says. "I will glow a little bit." She has to make that crumb of praise last, since the lack of support for girls' sports at her school is one of the disappointments in her life. For a boys' basketball game, the crowds fill up the Walnut Hills gym, while for a girls' game, "you might just get a stand, just one little bleacher." The only people Lewis and her teammates can count on are their relatives and friends, while for a varsity football game, say, or a boys' basketball game, fans come from all over the area, some who don't know any of the players involved, "just because it's a guys' game."

"It kind of makes you feel down sometimes," says Erica, "when you're about to play a sport and the gym is empty or the field is empty. You don't have anybody there watching you. Especially if you do something good. Your catch in the outfield, or your three-point shot—you don't have nobody there to see it. It takes away from performance. Guys, if they know the people are watching, they try to impress them, try harder. But for us, no one's ever there." The girls' basketball team did manage to "catch a crowd" when they played against the junior high school boys, a matchup that makes Lewis wince a little ("I know it sounds bad"). "We loved playing them, because they tried to beat us and we tried to beat them—because we were trying to prove that we could beat some guys, and they're going to get humiliated if they're beat by some girls." The game turned out to be fairly even. The boys' team was stronger underneath, but the girls' guards were faster and deadlier than their counterparts. The girls squeaked out a win.

Erica Lewis's older stepsister recently graduated from the University of Cincinnati on a basketball scholarship. Erica wondered how her sister had time to study, with the endless practice sessions and game days. She thinks she may have the grades to earn an academic scholarship like her brother, now an executive at Procter & Gamble. For now, sports is helping, not hindering, her academic performance. "As a teenager in high school, I of course think about skipping school," she says. "Well, if you don't go to school, you can't play in that game. Or you cannot practice, and not practicing will lead to not playing in that game. So sports gets me up in the morning: 'Well, I want to play today.' That happened a lot. I'd be laying in bed, and I would say to myself,

'We play our rivals today' or 'We play my friend's school today.' So then I say, 'Let me go to school!' ''

The experience of Erica Lewis demonstrates the promise that sports involvement holds out to reshape the way adolescent girls think about their bodies. As girls endure the complicated cultural pressures of adolescence, the ideals of size and shape can become tyrannical nightmares. The world of big-time sports can participate in this tyranny, with its pinup-style cheerleading squads and kick dancers. What does it say to girls when by far the most visible presence of women in *Sports Illustrated* is models in swimsuits?

Lewis remembers being a "big girl" when she was a child. In a culture where even grade school girls go on diets, this could have been a liability. Through sports, she had an opportunity to see her size as an advantage. Her body represented something she could feel good about. It was no longer decorative but had instead entered the realm of the useful. The confidence Lewis gains in her sports involvement spills over into all aspects of her life, most notably her academics. What if she didn't have a game, a practice, to lure her into school on a lazy morning?

Lisa Philips also manages to sidestep the adolescent's obsession with conformity, remaining strong and confident through her accomplishments as a ballplayer despite her uncommon height. No doubt about it, she's a big girl, with a solid, broad-shouldered frame. Traditionally, this would be a burden for a sixteen-year-old, but for Philips it's a gift. An athlete's body image goes far beyond the passive, objectified, commodified mannequin touted by Madison Avenue, glorified by the media, and accepted by her more impressionable peers. "I *like* it when I weigh more," volleyball superstar Gabrielle Reece told *Mademoiselle*. "I feel stronger, more dominant. I feel meaner. I love it when I hit the ball and there is no resistance." When a girl is justifiably proud of her volleyball spike, her batting average, her booming kick, she is considering her body as a functioning physical tool, not an object on display. She connects to physicality in a way that promises to enhance her confidence, mental health, and life as a whole, integrated person.

The girls from the decade-old Eureka program, which combines sports with tutoring in science and math, gather at summer's end for an awards ceremony at Brooklyn College's Gershwin Auditorium. The women's rest room is crowded with teenagers dressed in formal wear. A group of them huddle in front of the mirror, applying makeup. This is a day these girls have been working toward, and their pride in their achievement is palpable.

Not all of the girls in front of the mirror have the long, rangy body typically associated with the female athlete. There are huskier girls here too, heavyset girls, some of whom have conquered fears of the water to excel in swimming, say, or developed a passion for softball—an indication of the wide embrace athletic programs can enjoy.

On the face of it, the idea that athletic participation can help raise the math and science scores of adolescent girls might seem overreaching, even if it has been strongly suggested statistically. The disparity in the performance of girls and boys has presented an intractable problem for educators and child professionals, who are searching for any measure that promises to help narrow the gap.

The success of Eureka is a tribute to the vision of the late Alice Miller, former director of the Brooklyn College Women's Center. In 1986 Miller started a program designed to help high school girls in areas where they tended to be weakest. Casting about for something to address the traditionally lower test scores for girls in science and math, Miller recognized that simply offering science tutorials during the summer might not do the trick. By offering access to a wide range of sports—from softball and basketball to swimming and volleyball—she could get the girls interested enough to keep coming back. At first Miller used sports simply as the hook or carrot to entice girls age twelve to fifteen into her program. The middle school girls also appreciated the chance to spend time on a college campus.

As the program developed over the succeeding years, however, Miller began to appreciate more and more direct parallels between sports training and science and math education. That link is still largely unexplored by social scientists, but there are indications that girls who are involved in athletics do better at math and science. Since these are areas in which there has been a perceived difference in the achievements of high school boys and girls, everyone, it seemed, was looking for a way to address the problem. Eureka was a pioneering program in this respect. It took two years for Miller to put the program in place, and Eureka officially kicked off in the summer of 1987 with thirty-five girls studying physics, chemistry, and biology and at the same time working out at swimming and basketball.

Like a lot of nonprofit endeavors held together by the vision of a single charismatic person, Eureka started small but seemed to feed off its founder's energy. Each year brought incremental levels of expansion, until Eureka was a full-fledged summer enrichment program featuring more sports, including karate, track and field, aerobics, and speedwalking. Area colleges and universities offered research internships to the Eurekans, as they called themselves. But in 1996, just as Eureka began to receive national attention, Alice Miller died of cancer.

Now a year after her death, sixty girls are gathered for the end-of-summer awards ceremony. They sit in the front rows of the auditorium, talking among themselves with the easy familiarity of friends, while their family members fill the rest of the seats. Onstage is a table full of trophies; almost every girl, it seems, will receive some kind of award. Evelyn Roman, the director who took over for Miller, embarks on a tribute to the founder and then segues into an inspirational slide show. As images of the girls' summer appear on screen (often to shrieks of recognition from the front rows of the theater), Helen Reddy's "I Am Woman" blasts over the PA. Roman narrates with hallmark phrases of the Eurekans, a mantra of self-esteem: "Trust, family—supporting each other in moments of fear," she begins, and then, over an image of six of the girls in hard hats and harnesses, participating in an Outward Bound-style mountaineering program, Roman says, "So girls can feel they are powerful." She continues, "learning from other women . . . exercise of the mind . . . learning to succeed in competition with each other . . ."

Roman ends with the group's catchphrase, their translation of the Greeks' ancient cry of discovery, now echoing the cry of the outfield: "I've got it!" The girls roar it back at her.

Eureka is structured as a three-year protocol beginning in the summer after eighth grade. The girls study mathematics as well as science (with components of architecture, engineering, computer, and environmental sciences). They spend the third year on an internship at an area hospital, university, or other institution. The first year a girl is a "new girl," a phrase Eurekans use as one word, like "freshman." Among the first prizes given is one to Alexis, for Most Improved among the new girls, because, says Roman, she "never quit." Other prizes are awarded in sports—for example, best offensive and best defensive play in basketball. A new award this year is the Alice, named for Alice Miller, given to the girl who most embodies the values of Eureka.

Nicki Ematwali first participated in Eureka at Brooklyn College in 1990, the summer after eighth grade, when she was thirteen years old. Although it is a program aimed at kids in Brooklyn and Ematwali's family resides in Queens, she managed to get accepted. In summers following that, she completed internships in science and space. This summer she went back as an instructor, teaching computer science.

Ematwali had been well prepped for her Eureka experience. At the elementary school level, she attended the Astor program for gifted and talented students at P.S. 183, and then in junior high, at P.S. 180, went to the Scholastic Research Institute, also aimed at advanced science and math students. These programs as well as Eureka were designed to put Nicki exactly where she is now, beginning her college career at Johns Hopkins University. She has also continued in sports, garnering first-place medals in 100- and 200-meter sprints at the spring championship meet with the university's track team.

"One of the biggest messages when I was a new girl at Eureka was always 'I've got it!' " Nicki says. "To me, it meant that even before I started, I knew I could do whatever it was I was trying to do. There was no doubt in my mind. It was important to have that self-esteem before I started, because then I really didn't have worries about accomplishing something."

Eureka was successful enough to attract nationwide interest among the loose alliance of organizations whose goal is to help girls succeed. The program seemed to get to the heart of several seemingly intractable problems associated with our daughters, from their underrepresentation in the hard sciences, to keeping them active and healthy, to helping motivate underserved urban teenagers. Success stories such as Nicki Ematwali's are what Heather Johnston Nicholson likes to hear. Johnston Nicholson is the research director at Girls Incorporated, formerly Girls Clubs of America. Girls Incorporated received a National Science Foundation grant to replicate Eureka in settings all over the country. The Brooklyn College Eurekans, Johnston Nicholson says, "became our mentors" in that effort, and there are now Eureka programs in Lynn, Massachusetts; Birmingham, Alabama; and Oleander, California, with others planned.

"Grown-ups claim they can learn stuff while sitting at a desk," Johnston Nicholson says. "The connections in Eureka seem to me to be the right connections. Girls of all ages have better bodies if they're moving a lot, and their brains work better when their bodies are in good shape. But even more than that, learning while doing is a much better way of learning anything."

A lot of emphasis in Eureka is placed on continuity, on getting the girls involved not just for one year but for three consecutive years—or more. Ematwali has been involved with Eureka for six years in all, first as a student and then as a teacher in computer science. "I wanted the same respect from my girls, as a role model, that I had for my teachers when I was a new girl in the program," Nicki says, citing the fact that Eureka had amazing coaching talent, including one coach who went on to the national Olympic volleyball team and several coaches who played for Division I schools in college. "It was very gratifying to be in a position to give in return something I had gotten from my coaches so long ago, but which I vividly remember. I never thought I would be in a position to give back to the program the way I did."

Nicki knows there are downsides to athletic participation. At Johns Hopkins, where African American females make up a small percentage of the student body, she sees that women athletes are not automatically accorded respect and popularity. "I notice that a lot of athletes don't get asked out to the formals or aren't really popular," she says. "You're wearing gym shorts and sneakers to class." Women's sports on her campus, she notes, are "less favored" than men's sports. Athletics is considered a "nontraditional" choice for women. She also knows of girls who have had eating disorders associated with their sports, including a tennis player who began taking laxatives to lose weight, in order to "get that look," as Nicki says, when she wore her short-skirted tennis uniform.

The important thing about Eureka, Ematwali says, is that it helps counter prevailing attitudes about women in sports, including stereotypes about what constitutes an "athletic" body. "For me, what was real eye-opening, when I was a new girl in Eureka, with sports, was there were a lot of people all shapes and sizes, and they could do everything that I did and more. Everyone has this perception that you have to have a certain physique and body type to do a sport. After my first year at Eureka, I realized that anybody can do it. It's not a question of how you look—you don't have to have a tall, slim, muscular look to do anything. All the girls in Eureka learn how to swim. All the girls in Eureka learn how to play basketball or volleyball or run track or do something else. Their size didn't matter. That was something important that was reiterated in Eureka: it doesn't matter how you look, you can do any sport you want to do."

A foil in her outstretched hand, Erinn Smart awaits the referee's call to fence. At age seventeen, she is one of the top female fencers in the world. Her lamé vest is hooked by a body cable to an electronic scoring mechanism, attached by a retractable reel. The tunic reads "SMART USA" across the back, signifying her past participation on junior and cadet world teams—but also alluding to her future Olympic hopes. Smart, a freshman at Barnard College, is at Harvard's Malkin Athletic Center for the Columbia University fencing team's first intercollegiate meet of the season. There are four "strips," or fencing lanes, in the small third-floor gymnasium, two at the far end for the men's team and two at the near end for the women. The atmosphere is relaxed, the coaches mill casually in the space between the strips, and there are few spectators. The walls are studded with photos of past Harvard teams—all the team members male, many of them seemingly doing their best to convey, by expression or posture, the elite background of the sport.

Erinn Smart is another example of a well-grounded young woman who, like Lisa Philips, has used involvement in a sport as an organizing principle in her life. Though the two girls come from different middle-class backgrounds—Smart from an urban one, Philips from a small-town suburb—they both illustrate how much the landscape has changed for our high school daughters. There are new dangers, yes, posed by the widespread availability of illegal drugs, by an already pressured sexual atmosphere over-heated through the media, by the threat of AIDS. But the lives of these girls indicate that athletics can provide an exciting new strategy to help them negotiate the rocky terrain of adolescence.

Women are only a very late arrival on the fencing scene. Two enlarged black-and-white photos on the Harvard gymnasium wall, of recent women's team captains, only serve to emphasize the unequal male-to-female ratio of the display. The scoreboard has been hastily reconfigured to accommodate the presence of women's teams. "It's a traditional, aristocratic, Eastern European sport," says George Kolombatovich, Erinn's co-coach at Columbia. He says this by way of explaining the resistance to women in fencing, talking about the difficulty he has had in getting the International Fencing Association, the governing body, to accept innovations such as women referees. Even today, women at the college level do not fence sabre—the most physical, violent, and aggressive version of the sport—and are limited to foil and épée (women's sabre will be a demonstration sport at the 1998 cham-

pionships). Fencing still retains evidence of its martial beginnings. Matches are "bouts," and the blades are referred to matter-of-factly as "weapons."

At the Harvard meet, subtle variations are evident in the
ways the men and women approach the sport. The men's meet
begins with sabre, and there is much cheering, shouting, and
some howling as the boys encourage their own. A few times during the bout a sabre charge goes awry, and the fencer thunders
off the strip, slamming his weapon at the floor. The women's end
of the gym is quieter. Erinn's teammate Kelly Camamis has a one-
word explanation for the difference in sound level: "Testoster-
one." The women's play appears more cerebral, almost like
chess. The men fence as if it's either that or fisticuffs. Due largely
to superior coaching, Columbia is a dominant force in college
fencing, and at this match the Lions slowly overwhelm the Crim-
son.

In the single row of seating along the gymnasium's far wall, a
Harvard player nudges another. "That's Erinn Smart," he says.
"Check her out—she's great." Smart is leading, 4–0 (she has
gotten four "touches" on her opponent, while her opponent has
managed none on her), in a five-touch bout. The director, or
referee, an elegantly dressed woman in a navy blue suit and high
heels, holds her hands apart, calls out "Ready," and then closes
her hands together, calmly, almost laconically giving the word to
begin: "Fence." Smart and her opponent shift warily in front of
each other and then suddenly drive forward. Erinn flicks her
blade with faster-than-the-eye quickness. It is all over in the space
of a moment. An electrical circuit is completed by the point of
Smart's blade touching the other's lamé vest. A green light
flashes above the scoring table. The referee raises her hand, signifying a point awarded to Smart. She has won the bout, the first
of four she will win that day, two by shutout.

Thirty or even twenty years ago, Erinn Smart would have made an improbable fencer, a black Brooklyn-born female who began her life far outside the sport's tight Eurocentric orbit, which has Vienna and Budapest as its twin suns. Once again, as happened with soccer, the American contingent was instrumental in opening a primarily European sport to women. Erinn is among the first generation of girls to benefit. She grew up on Flatbush Avenue in Brooklyn, and began her career at the New York Fencers Club, a rather scruffy street-level space on Manhattan's Upper West Side. When she was eleven she began to study fencing in classes offered by the then brand-new Peter Westbrook Foundation, which is devoted to introducing urban kids to the sport.

Through her participation in fencing, Erinn has traveled all over the country, all over the world. She customarily spends a month during the summer studying in Budapest and has traveled to meets all over Europe, most recently in France, where she took a bronze in the Junior World Championships. This is a long way from her home in Prospect Park, where she comes from a strong, stable family that encouraged competition and achievement. Fencing was supposed to be her older brother's sport. Erinn's father saw a newspaper ad for free lessons at the Fencers Club and sent both her and her brother to take advantage of the offer. Her brother dropped out, only to take up the sport again when he saw how well Erinn was doing with it.

At first her parents drove her in to the city to practice, but eventually she and her brother took the subway. At the Fencers Club, she fell under the tutelage of Aladar Kogler, a fencing master from Hungary who was a coach of the U.S. Olympic team. Encouraged by Kogler, Smart started attending regular practice sessions on weekday evenings. "It would take an hour just to get there each day," she recalls. She would study or sleep on the train or do schoolwork in a branch of the public library near the Fencers Club, getting her homework done and then returning to practice. After the four-hour practice session and the hour-long commute, she would arrive back in Brooklyn at ten or eleven o'clock at night. It would be a demanding regimen for anyone, but especially for a teenage girl. "I just loved competing against other people," Smart says on why she stuck with it. "I wasn't able to be lazy about my schoolwork. I couldn't just slack off and say, 'I'll do it another time.' Because there wouldn't be another time."

Erinn Smart got her chance at fencing because of Peter Westbrook, who himself represents a remarkable story of achievement against all odds. In the projects of Newark, New Jersey, where Westbrook grew up, fencing was not "a natural sport," he admits. But as a boy he was bit early on by the Zorro bug, carrying a rapier and wearing a mask on successive Halloweens during his childhood. His mother still had to bribe him with a five-dollar bill to get him to go to his first fencing class. He pretended not to like it at first, to keep the five-spots coming, but soon enough he was deeply involved. He took it all the way to the Olympics in 1984, when he won the bronze. Westbrook is of mixed Japanese-African-American ancestry—on the Japanese side, he claims to descend from a long line of swordsmen—and he was the first non-Caucasian champion in the sport.

"I'm so grateful that I'm not a statistic," Westbrook says. "If it were not for the sport, I would be like most of my friends—about 90 percent of them are dead, and 10 percent are alive, in Newark, New Jersey, still in the housing projects, or incarcerated, or on drugs." When he started his foundation, "everyone told me I was crazy, to get boys and girls to fence—out of the question." But he was stubborn. He began offering the free Saturday morning lessons at the Fencers Club as a way of identifying promising young people like Erinn Smart. His objective is two-fold. He wants to create great Olympians, and he wants to help kids.

"Fencing saved my life," Westbrook says. "Sports is a great life saver."

For Erinn, one of Westbrook's success stories, fencing is a great life enhancer. She says she doubts that she would have gotten to travel to the places she has traveled to or achieved all that she has achieved were it not for fencing. One of the ways it has made her a stronger person, she says, paradoxically, is that it has taught her how to lose. "If I lose in competition, I can't get depressed. I have to stay strong and move on." She still participates in weekday evening practice sessions, which she says are much easier to get to now that she lives in a Columbia dorm, only forty-plus blocks (as opposed to a whole borough) away from the club. She remains under the tutelage of Kogler. The two of them make an arresting picture: a wiry, middle-aged European master facing a strapping young African American. But as soon as they don the masks, it is clear why fencing is a great equal opportunity sport. It's impossible to tell if a fencer is black or white, young or old, male or female.

On a weeknight coaching session at the Fencers Club two days before the Harvard meet, Kogler and Smart practice a fencing figure over and over, refining a nuanced response to a thrust that in a bout will pass in a fraction of a second. Kogler's graying blond hair is chopped straight across at his neckline, he has a hawklike, ragged face that in another century no doubt would have accommodated a sabre scar. But he is the author of ten books, a man whose presence in New York and at Columbia is enough to render them both centers of fencing in America. "Come on, woman!" he encourages Smart in heavily accented English. A fencing gym is not a particularly calm place. Practice bouts happen on either side of Smart and Kogler, the scoring machines emit constant high-pitched blips, and the clash of steel sounds throughout the whole gym. Junior high boys, no doubt attracted by the elaborate outfit and rig of a fencer (expensive, too: a beginner's outfit can run as much as $250 with sword), gather for an intermediate-beginner class in a nearby room. They are joined there by an almost equal number of young girls. One of them, a student of Peter Westbrook's, pauses to watch Smart work with Kogler. "I want to be like Erinn," the young girl says.

On the day of Lisa Philips's all-star tourney in Edison, New Jersey—the one that she hopes will establish her in the eyes of the college scouts—the weather is unseasonably cool. Lisa arrives before dawn. As the spectators gather, her father hunches over a cup of hot coffee in the stands, nervously scanning the crowd for the men who may be deciding his daughter's college future.

The cold seems to be affecting Lisa's day at the plate. She does manage to send a booming foul shot over the fence. She makes up for it on defense, stretching her five-eleven frame for errant throws to first, digging balls out of the dirt. But at the back of her mind is her conviction that only a big bat will make her stand out. She approaches the batter's box mentally cataloging the key cues Penny Rosario has drummed into her during all those evening practice sessions in her coach's backyard. Focus. Wait. Opposite hand. She watches a ball and a strike, then unleashes a waist-high fat one and sends it soaring into center field. It fades at the last minute, dropping into the outstretched mitt of the fielder—but it was a big shot all the same. Would it be enough for the scouts? Will she stand out? Will they know her when it comes time to dole out the full rides?

Up in the stands, her father is looking over the shoulder of a middle-aged guy wearing a warm-up suit and holding a notebook, whom he takes to be one of the college scouts in attendance. He is satisfied when the guy ticks off "Lisa Philips" on his roster after she has a nice pick at first. It turns out he is a college scout, from Temple University in Philadelphia. Even though contact at this age group is strictly proscribed, Rich talks to the guy anyway, at first not letting on that he's the standout player's father. When the guy asks which girl is his daughter, of course Rich is going to tell him.

Her second time at bat, Lisa comes up with the bases loaded, a chance to do her team some good. With two strikes on her, she feels a subtle shift in her concentration. Suddenly it all sinks in— the college coaches walking around with their roster sheets, the idea that she is being measured and judged. Rich has already whispered at her through the fence about the Temple scout, so she is feeling the pressure. When the next pitch cuts the inside edge of the plate, she's frozen up. The umpire's cry of "Streeike!" is like a stab at her heart. She has struck out looking. The inning's over, and so is her chance to show them what she could do. The day's frustration boils up in her. She is about to toss her helmet in disgust when Penny's admonition comes back to her. *They're looking at the ones who throw their helmets. . . .* Lisa carefully lays down her helmet, lays down her bat, and walks methodically back to her place in the dugout. It is a small personal victory. To show she is not moping, she gathers up her glove and hustles back onto the field. She even remembers to smile.

6

A Question of Heart

Saving the Lives of Girls Through Sports

Athletes today talk about "heart" the way drill sergeants used to talk about "guts," meaning courage, drive, spirit, a passion for the game. Lisa Philips says she chose not to play basketball because "I didn't have heart in that sport, but I've got it in softball." Erica Lewis says that "for basketball and softball, my heart is really in it, I really want to win." In sentimental formulations, heart is all that it takes. A kid with enough heart, enough determination, enough moxie, will somehow find a way onto the playing field, no matter what obstacles are laid before her.

It is disturbing, then, to see so many teenage girls who have plenty of heart, but who through lack of opportunities or support will lose out on the benefits athletics can offer. A mind is a terrible thing to waste, and so is a 12-second 100. "Self-esteem" has become a universal catchall phrase for whatever is good in the development of a young person's character, but people who use it sometimes fail to consider the entire package: mind, body, and soul. What does it take for a girl to feel confident, secure, and in control of her world? It seems formulaic to engender self-esteem by having a child repeat "I like myself" ten times every morning. Children learn to feel good about themselves through accomplishment. The crucial element in self-worth is not consistent success, but the experience of progressing, of becoming better, of succeeding where you've failed before.

Some of these lessons are inherent in the athletic experience at its best. Athletes are constantly encouraged to achieve, to overcome obstacles, to practice to the point of proficiency. They may learn about sacrifice, commitment to a greater good, responsibility to others. The stereotypes of the dumb jock and the athletically inept egghead have by now become anachronistic. It seems clearer than ever today that athleticism feeds intellectual and even moral development. "When you use your senses, your body, you tap into a different kind of intellect," says climbing enthusiast Heather Mitchell. Denying girls the feelings of mastery and pride and the opportunities for growth that sports can offer is blow not only against their cardiovascular fitness (for example) but against their long-term human potential. To squander any measure of our daughters' athletic abilities might be to squander their academic, social, and emotional capacities in ways we are only just beginning to understand.

We cannot assume that girls and boys take the same lessons from their athletic experience. There is wide appreciation, for example, for the different ways in which girls and boys approach play. Research by developmental psychologists Jean Piaget and, more recently, Janet Lever has suggested that girls tend to have a flexible, pragmatic understanding of rules—they are more likely to adjust rules in midplay to ensure fairness to all participants. Boys are more likely to consider adherence to rules as a method of fairness in and of itself. In her landmark study *In a Different Voice*, the developmental psychologist Carol Gilligan explores the contrasting ways in which girls and boys react to competitive situations. Girls, who tend to put a premium on social relationships, may experience competition as a threat to those relationships. These are archetypes that may change as girls experience athletic competition in greater numbers than ever before. But to help our daughters get the most out of sports, we have to be able to adjust our approach to fit their needs.

Carole Oglesby, a Temple University kinesiology professor who is a leading authority on the sociology and psychology of women athletes, suggests that the either/or approach to coaching females and males may not work. What coaching strategies work for girls? "I deal with administrators all the time, and they want a short, simple answer," she says. "It's not that simple." On the one hand, the idea that "basketball is basketball" no matter who plays the game is "really wrongheaded." But equally misguided, Oglesby says, are the coaches who keep their female athletes away from all writing and advice that is directed to men. "There's a middle ground," she notes. What you have to pay attention to in coaching girls is "how you deliver feedback, use of personal space, socialization procedures." As an example, Oglesby suggests that girls are not accustomed to getting specific content-based feedback—teachers and other authorities tend to give them more positive, general reinforcement. "That gives them a readiness to hear certain things and a lack of readiness to hear other things," Oglesby says. "The more attuned a professional person is to that, the better."

Having the heart for the game can drive a young athlete to unimagined accomplishments, but in many cases it is simply not enough. We need to be aware of the special needs of female athletes—and know that those needs may be different for girls of color, for girls at risk, for elite athletes, and for those with physical handicaps. Huge research gaps exist in studying these specific groups. What research has been done reveals that social and economic groups may have markedly different experiences both in sports and in growing up. For example, adolescent African American girls exhibit higher self-esteem and better body image than their peers—an intriguing finding that has yet to be followed up with further research. One expert noted that disabled boys are more often encouraged to meet the world, whereas disabled girls are kept from it. Virtually no varsity athletic opportunities exist for the physically disabled, even though 10 percent of the college student population have disabilities. We need to understand that the population of girl athletes is not a monolith, but has many variables and differences within it.

For girls today, there are fewer resources and not as much encouragement of athletic success as for boys. We as adults need to match girls' determination—we need to demonstrate as much heart as they do. We need to provide the coaching that will enable girls to thrive, the role models and mentors to encourage and guide them. We need to eliminate the stigma that labels athletic girls as too masculine. We need to make sure there are facilities and equipment for our daughters to use and ensure there are safe ways for them to get to practice—something that suburban kids may take for granted but that can be a daily concern for inner-city athletes.

All over the country, individuals are helping to change the way adolescent girls feel about their lives, forging a link between a passion for sports and girls' mental and physical health, a link that scientific research is just now beginning to recognize and gauge. Many of these individuals have discovered that connection on their own, through direct experience. They've seen the girls under their charge not only resist damaging influences and self-destructive behavior, but actually blossom through a commitment to a team and to a sport. The problem is that there are not enough of these pioneers. Though many new grassroots sports organizations have been started in the past five years, they could be duplicated many times over and still not nearly meet the need. It's inspiring to look at some of the girls whose lives have been touched by sports.

Tamelia Brown went to a movie with a boy last summer. For the majority of high school girls in this country, that would be unremarkable. But because Tamelia Brown is a member of Oakland's Acorn Oscar Bailey Track Club, not only her running career but her life falls under the unofficial stewardship of coach Darrell Hampton. For Hampton, a casual date is worthy of comment, and of action. There is an informal, unwritten, but nevertheless very real set of rules for the girls on the track team based at the Acorn Apartments housing project. They are members of one of the premier track and field clubs in the country, a perennial contender at the Oakland Athletic League games, the Pacific Association Championships, the U.S.A. Track and Field Junior Olympics, the Hershey Nationals, and the American Athletic Union Junior Olympics. Brown will have to make sacrifices if she expects to remain one of the elite. No fast food during training. No dates. No boyfriends.

"I didn't see why I shouldn't go out with a boy one time in my life!" Tamelia complains. So she did, but it was the last time. Darrell made sure of that, which was no surprise. One year recently, the members of the team did go to their senior prom. They went as a group, without male escorts. "They had a ball," insists Hampton. Given the fact that the teen pregnancy rate in

West Oakland is among the highest in the country, maybe it's not such a sacrifice. Maybe it's an appropriately extreme response to a dire problem.

Tamelia Brown is a pretty, long-legged sixteen-year-old with large brown eyes, the tallest girl on the team. She lives with her mother, stepfather, little brother, and sister about a twenty-minute drive from Acorn. Her willingness to speak her mind borders on what some would call "attitude." Brown knows a lot of girls who have gotten pregnant and had babies while they were still in their teens, some when they were younger than she is now. She says of them: "When y'all was little, they'd say, 'I'm not going to get pregnant!' and now what they got? A baby." Maybe they were pressured into it, she says. For a few, the decision was deliberate. "Some of them come up to me and say, 'Well, I wanted a baby.' I say, 'Well, you're crazy then.' I ask them, 'Where you at now?' You're in the house, watching that baby. Dropped out of school. They say something like, 'I don't know, I just messed myself up, I guess.' I guess!" Getting pregnant, Tamelia Brown says, "takes away your whole dream."

As of early 1998, only a third of the Acorn Apartments housing project, the part bordering Adeline Street, has escaped the bulldozer. The rest of it is chain-linked or demolished completely, a flat lot of paper-littered gray earth stretching a full city block. Acorn was built in 1968, under the aegis of Lyndon Johnson's Great Society, but by the mid-eighties, crack cocaine had sent the whole neighborhood into a downward spiral of neglect, violence, and poverty. About this time the phrase "defensible housing" came into vogue among urban design professionals, referring to public housing built with security concerns in mind. Acorn epitomized the exact opposite. It was a housing cop's nightmare, a warren of blind walkways, abrupt cul-de-sacs, and truncated sightlines.

142

Acorn is to be rebuilt in the latest spasm of urban renewal, with 227 "individual residential housing" units replacing the original 667 apartments. A refurbished community center and an Olympic-sized swimming pool are on the planning table wish list. Darrell Hampton will believe it when he sees it. Interstate 880 slices right past Acorn on its way to the Bay Bridge. Hampton, a former high school wrestling star, first encountered Acorn on a spring day in 1985, when he took a wrong exit off the Nimitz Freeway and found himself making a quick turnaround tour. He recalls thinking that for all its reputation, the place "didn't look so rough." Three weeks later, when he saw a newspaper ad seeking applicants for a recreation aide at the complex, it seemed as if fate had intervened. He got excited about the possibilities. He himself had come from a solidly middle-class background, a world away from the projects. His parents and friends tried to warn him off. "They let me know, 'Hey, this is not a place that you're used to.' They did not think I could cut it."

Hampton had always been involved in sports—at age twelve, he recalls, he used to sign up neighborhood kids to "baseball contracts" and organize them into teams. After high school, he even qualified for the Olympic trials in wrestling but couldn't raise the fare to travel to Indianapolis, where the trials were being held. He had taken a job in an auto shop and was "just living, trying to be responsible" when Acorn changed his life.

The job was offered only because Acorn's management company, Condor Management, was mandated by the state to provide it. The thinking of policymakers was to mount some sort of response to the drug plague racing through the projects at that time, locking residents inside their apartments, turning the whole neighborhood into a virtual free-fire zone. "People would sleep in their bathtubs because of the gunfire every night," Hampton recalls. Sports were an important part of the culture, especially for the boys. There were the "playground legends" of the project's basketball courts, players who had ferocious physical skills but never moved up to organized ball. It made Hampton sick to see the wasted talent among these young men. "The brothers, the reason they can take all these bullets, is because they play basketball all day," Hampton says. "They're in excellent aerobic and cardiovascular condition. Some of these kids have got so many bullets in them they couldn't go through a metal detector, but they can run and jump. They're outstanding, they're just incredible athletes."

At first, Hampton says, "the kids ran every game on me possible." They told him they didn't have any money to eat, that someone had stolen their wallet. They seemed magically to know which days were his payday and hit him up for "carfare" especially on those days. The kids on his teams were amazed that the dodges worked on him. "I fell for all of it!" he says with a laugh. "I didn't know any better. But we got beyond that stage." He began to get a feel for which kids were in trouble, which of them were, as he puts it, "doubles"—children with both parents addicted to crack. Hampton started coaching boys in football and basketball, as well as in the sport he knew best, wrestling.

In 1987, two twelve-year-old girls from Acorn came to him and asked if they could do something, anything. Hampton cast around and heard that the Oakland Police Athletic League was starting a summer track program, so he suggested track. "The two of them said yes, and we went out to the track and practiced and went through a few drills," Hampton recalls. "They were so excited about it that they recruited two more of their friends, and we had a relay team." The Acorn Track Club was born. "We trained that summer and we got better," Hampton says. "And as the girls got better, their self-esteem grew. You could see them becoming more and more proud of themselves. By the last meet of the year, downtown at the junior college, everybody's parents came out, and these girls ran a 4-by-1 relay, and they beat the boys."

Success begat success, and more girls were attracted to the club. Early on, one of the main difficulties was simply getting the girls to meets—even area meets were beyond the club's resources. It all seemed like a bad rerun of Hampton's own wrestling career, terminated for lack of travel money. Then a man named Oscar Bailey, the father of speed-demon twin daughters, contacted Hampton and asked if the club was open to girls like his, who lived outside the project. Bailey stepped in and was instrumental in arranging travel not only to state but to national track meets. When he died suddenly, the club was renamed the Acorn Oscar Bailey Track Club.

By the early 1990s, the club had emerged as a perennial contender at meets all over the country. In 1994, club member Aisha Margain set the AAU 400-meter national record with a time of 56.54 seconds. There were gold medals, championships, high-visibility wins at the Junior Olympics and the Hershey Nationals. When writer Marilyn Levy wrote a young adult book about the club, called *Run for Your Life,* a pair of Hollywood producers optioned it for a movie. The first script turned in—written, ironically, by African American screenwriters—Hampton instantly rejected. It featured a fictional track club where each girl had to shoplift something in order to become a member.

Hampton is at pains to point out that the club has transcended its beginnings, that it now attracts girls from all over the city and from all income groups. "We even had a cardiologist's daughter," he says. But the team plays on its "ghetto girl" reputation. At meets, its members limber up to a choreographed aerobics routine backed by a thumping beat. The purpose, Hampton says, is threefold: conditioning, building teamwork, and "intimidating" the opposition. The other teams, seeing the smoothly coordinated exercises of the Acorn girls, have got to be impressed, and Hampton is very big on the psychology of winning. "A lot of races are first won in the mind," he says.

As Acorn is slowly eaten away by the bulldozers, the track club is being squeezed, too. Hampton used to have five staffers, and now it's just he alone. His office and the club's weight room were moved from the shuttered community center to makeshift quarters in an unheated apartment. Preparation for a meet might include meditation time to screen out outside distractions, but the jumbled nature of this transitional period seems only to add to them. On a blustery winter day, for example, club members are forced to practice inside, running through conditioning drills and baton-passing practice on the top floor of the empty community center. "Hold your breath," Hampton instructs the girls as they walk through the building's lobby, "they're tearing down the walls, and there might be lead dust and asbestos in here." The wall of the vacant second-floor hall sports a remnant of its days as a Head Start lunch room, a sign that reads, "Adults may not share children's food." As the sky clears, Hampton packs eight team members into the back of his small pickup for a quick training cycle at nearby Crab Cove beach, where the girls limber up with six sets of double 100-meter sprints. Throughout, the girls giggle and complain by turns. But they complete the regimen, as they customarily do six and sometimes seven times a week.

The routine doesn't leave time for cultivation of bad habits, the girls say. And, of course, that's the point. "I'm trying to change behavior," Hampton admits, saying that the whole culture of fast money and easy sex was playing havoc with the lives of adolescent girls. His rules are an attempt to extract his players from the prevailing culture and substitute the culture of sports, competition, and achievement. "They can have friends," Hampton says firmly, "but they're too young to be dating." Hampton jokes that at times he may "go overboard," physically patrolling the lives of his players, scaring off predatory males. "No, no, no, not that one," the athletes say to him if they really like a guy. "Let *him* through."

"I used to say—I've stopped saying it since all the sexual harassment stuff became so prevalent—but I would tell them that I was their 'boyfriend' until they were thirty-two, and no one else was allowed to talk to them." Hampton is also determined to keep his kids away from illegal drugs, which he understands as one of his main challenges. A club athlete whose mother had used marijuana will avoid the drug, he promises. "It's not going to happen, because I'm going to keep her on my right hip," he laughs, half-serious. Hampton is almost as harsh on the subject of pot as he is on crack, decrying marijuana's casual prevalence around the neighborhood, citing lung disease as among its many health repercussions.

Tamelia Brown joined the club when she was ten years old. She recalls telling her mother she didn't want to play softball anymore, that she wanted to try something else. "Well, you could run," her mother suggested. (Brown's mother had also run track in school.) She took her daughter to the running track at nearby Laney College. Darrell Hampton happened to be working out there with his Acorn girls. "They looked like they were having fun," Tamelia Brown recalls. "They were laughing. He would tell them to do something and they were like, 'Okay!' and they did it. They were running so strong." Brown had her mother ask if Tamelia could train with them. She's been on the team since then.

Hampton, who is going to school for a graduate degree in kinesiology, praises Brown's "kinesthetic awareness," her ability to pick up a complex series of movements just by watching someone else do it. She recalls him asking her, "Do you want to do a different event?" She told him she wanted to try long jump. "I think you'll be good in the triple jump," Hampton told her, " 'cause you're tall, you're long." Brown hadn't heard of the event before, but she said she was game to try. "He told me what to do and I did it," she says. "Very good," Hampton told her. "Very, very good." Brown was puzzled. "I don't know what I just did." You just triple-jumped, Hampton told her. She is a "natural," he says, "a potential All-American" in the event. The only problem with Tamelia, he says, is that she sometimes has difficulty with the discipline the club requires. "We try to give her structure," Hampton says. "She resists it"—for example, the single time she went out with a boy.

Brown remained with Acorn, but recently, Hampton had to turn her away, prohibiting her from traveling and even training with the team, because her grade-point average fell to 2.2, three-tenths of a point below the club minimum. "I told her, 'Stay home—I don't even want to see you,' " Hampton recalls. Brown returned to the club after getting A's and B's on her next report card, higher grades, actually, than when she had first started slipping. She brought up her grades with old-fashioned hard work, and the reason she did it is so she could come back to the club. For girls who have stayed in his program, Hampton claims a "100 percent high school graduation rate, a 100 percent college acceptance rate." Oscar Bailey's own daughters, for example, graduated and currently attend UC Santa Barbara. Other Acorn girls are now at UC Davis, Sacramento State, Nevada–Las Vegas, Columbia University.

Hampton has been repeatedly raked over the coals at Acorn complex community meetings, criticized for being too achievement-oriented, for trying to leverage children out of the neighborhood environment into what he considers to be better lives elsewhere. A troubling aspect of his tenure is the overall lack of support he has gotten from the residents. Not from the parents of the players, he hastens to say. "They thank me, they love me." But there are adults in the complex who do not approve of what he is trying to do. To them, he says, he is "controversial." This stems in part from a 1990 incident when Hampton was assaulted by police in front of the recreation center. The police version of the story was that Hampton was disorderly, but Hampton says he only cautioned an officer who was driving his patrol car at unsafe speeds in an area where children were playing.

Hampton received a $250,000 settlement from the city of Oakland as a result of the incident (most of which, Hampton says, was plowed straight back into the club budget). He marks down negativity about him and about the club to "jealousy" and the culture of failure that has been spawned among the "oppressed people" who reside in the housing project. Hampton uses the word "oppression" repeatedly to ascribe the source of the conditions around Acorn. To counter such conditions, he says, parents have to be eternally vigilant, starting very early on. By age fifteen, when many parents bring their kids to him, Hampton says "it's already too late"—not too late for athletic achievement, perhaps, but too late to extricate them from the quicksand of poverty, violence, and drug and alcohol abuse that is the fate of many in the neighborhood.

Track for Hampton is only a "medium," a means to an end. Academic acheivement, he says, is first, and athletics are used always with the aim of securing the girls a higher education. "Their parents can't afford to send them to college. So how are we going to get them in?" He tells his athletes there are "people who will pay because you can put your feet in front of each other faster than the next person." Even academics represent a means to an end. The ultimate goal is to get the girls college degrees and stable employment, to get them out of the projects, out of "gangster culture."

A first step is showing girls like Tamelia Brown that they can do things that other people assure them they cannot do. A competitive person, Brown has a long memory for slights. When she was still in elementary school, she tried out for a basketball team. A boy her age—"I ain't never going to forget"—taunted her that girls could not play basketball. "You cannot do what we do," the kid insisted. When she wound up on the team, "he just could not get by that." She recalls her schoolyard taunt back at him: "Ha, ha, I can do what you do." Later on, when she was on the Acorn team, she remembers the "little comments" boys from another team made when they were all trying out for the Hershey Nationals, an annual high school track event in Pennsylvania. "There go Darrell's girls," Brown recalls one boy saying. "They think they're going to come out here and beat us. But guess what? Boys are faster than girls." "You don't know that," Brown said to him. "Some girls might be faster than you, you don't even know that." The guy put her off with a wave of a hand and a "whatever." Brown pauses, then remembers, "I think he got beat by Aisha."

Byron Shewman worried that volleyball "was in danger of becoming a white middle-class sport." Shewman spent four years on the U.S.A. men's national team in the late seventies, and he believed the game should be open to all. He likes to cite William Morgan, who invented volleyball, and his belief that the greatest value of the sport is to bring people together. "I was having so many arguments about affirmative action," says Shewman, "that I decided I had to shut up and do something." This was in the early nineties. College scouts—the source of thousands of dollars in scholarship money—were forgoing the democratic chaos of high school leagues to concentrate their efforts on elite club team tournaments. The club system, which has become increasingly prevalent on the high school sports landscape not only in volleyball but in soccer, basketball, and softball as well, presents the scouts with what are essentially all-star rosters, the best players, preselected as it were, to make the job of picking standouts easier. The problem that Shewman saw with this is that not only are club teams made up of superior players, they also consist almost exclusively of girls from middle- or upper-class families, whose parents can afford the $2,000 to $4,000 annual club membership fees. Athletes from less affluent backgrounds, who might be playing excellent ball in their school leagues, were being shut out of college scholarship money.

In the summer of 1995, Shewman recruited Olympian Kim Oden, captain of the 1992 U.S.A. Women's Olympic team and currently coach at the University of North Carolina. Together they founded the first Starlings Volleyball Club in San Diego, Shewman's home base and perhaps the country's premier volleyball city. They tracked down funding from Nike, the Amateur Athletic Foundation, and the Sporting Goods Manufacturers Association. That first Starlings team enlisted girls in the San Diego area who wouldn't ordinarily get a shot at a club team. By 1997, Starlings Volleyball Clubs USA had teams in New York City, Chicago, and Los Angeles. Gabrielle Reece, perhaps the country's only volleyball celebrity, and 1988 Olympic captain Karch Kiraly also signed on.

At around the same time, a couple of states east, in the Four Corners area of Arizona, a high school volleyball coach named Rich Foley was trying to recruit some big-name help for the girls on his team. Foley is an East Coast transplant, raised in Smithtown, New York, on Long Island, and he is an exuberant promoter. Foley has close-cut salt-and-pepper hair and crinkly blue eyes, and he talks volubly about Native American high school athletics. He recently married a Navajo woman from Ganado who was, in her day, a high school volleyball player. Michelle Foley works on a long-term research project on diabetes, which is epidemic among the Navajo. They live in housing provided by the Ganado school district that would be called modest in other communities but is luxurious by reservation standards. "NO WATER HAULING" reads a sign near the parking lot, and Foley says that many times his outside spigot has been surreptitiously used to fill containers by outlying rural residents who are, in this arid landscape, chronically short of fresh water.

Over the last decade, Foley has become a man with a mission, an ambassador for Navajo girls' volleyball. He wants to help his team members gain more educational opportunities, and the one way he knows how to do it is to use athletics. Foley is all too aware of the skew toward club ball that is developing in the sport. "Club volleyball has really changed the recruiting process," he says. "Why does a college coach need to go watch your eight-foot daughter, when he can go [to a club tournament] and see seven hundred eight-foot daughters? No matter how good we are up here, no matter how much we play the recruiting game in the press, there's only one way we'll get exposure."

In the spring of 1995, Foley was able to get Dave Rubio, the well-respected women's volleyball coach at the University of Arizona, to help conduct the annual Navajo Nation Volleyball Clinic for the Four Corners area. "We treated him like royalty," Foley says. The clinic organizers presented Rubio with a turquoise-handled knife and a "real nice bolo tie" from the venerable Hubbell trading post, Ganado's main claim to fame. Hosting Rubio wasn't only about volleyball, it was about showcasing the heart of the Navajo people, their passion for sports. The Navajo players had so much going against them; they were short, poor, and isolated, afflicted with health problems and low self-esteem. It was all the more amazing, then, that they consistently beat teams from much larger high schools in the Phoenix area. They came to the net giving away inches and managed to triumph anyway, through quickness, technical virtuosity, and force of will. Teams from Ganado or another Four Corners high school, Monument Valley–Kayenta, have won the Class 3A state championship three times in the last five years.

Rubio came away impressed not only with the quality of the athletes but with the whole phenomenon of Navajo volleyball. The audience at reservation high school games was four or five times the size one could expect at large suburban schools in affluent communities. And these people cared about the game. It was breathtaking to hear hundreds of people shouting out the names of these fifteen- and sixteen-year-old girls as if they were NBA all-stars.

Next thing Foley knew, Byron Shewman was calling him, tipped by Rubio about what was going on in Four Corners volleyball. Shewman showed up for the Native American Festival Games in the summer of 1996. "Byron walks in the gym," Foley recalls, "and there's 2,500 people watching the volleyball match, and he's just as excited as heck."

Foley had the advantage of being at first an elementary school and then a middle school physical education teacher in the same small community. He developed what was in essence a volleyball pipeline, teaching the game from about third grade up through high school. "Realistically," Foley says, "I was coaching them for nine or ten years, the same kids." When he first took the Ganado coaching job, people had told him to forget about volleyball on the reservation, that Native Americans simply could not play the game. He was patient, and he discovered that a lot of the girls he coached were fierce competitors. "The parental support is outrageous,'' Foley says. The nearest movie theater is fifty miles away, so a sporting event is prime entertainment, and whole families show up for games. Luauna Nez, captain of Foley's 1997–98 Ganado team, says her ''tribe''—her extended family of parents, siblings, aunts, uncles, and cousins—comes along with her to meets in ''Flag'' (Flagstaff) and even five hours away in Phoenix.

Oden and Shewman recognized an opportunity to expand the Starlings' reach, and eventually they were able to hook Foley up with funding to sponsor a Four Corners club team. ''One of our big focuses is not to be exclusionary, not to just be looking at who lives in the right area,'' Oden has said. ''There aren't many programs in the inner cities or in rural areas, so let's go there.'' You can't get more rural than the region around Ganado, which is still largely given over to pursuits such as corn cultivation, cattle ranching, and sheepherding. The reservation is the largest in the United States, and the tribe is the nation's most populous. For the new Starlings team, Foley recruited girls not only from Ganado but also from Fort Defiance High School near the Navajo Nation capital of Window Rock, and from Ganado's archrival Monument Valley–Kayenta High School in the northern part of the state.

Unlike the other Starlings teams, which were sited in inner-city environments, the Four Corners club had to overcome the huge distances of the western landscape. The weather in the area, which Foley understatedly calls ''exciting,'' can make it difficult for girls to get to games and practices. ''Not like in Phoenix, where the kids go to practice in shorts and T-shirts—our kids have got to go to the gym wearing warm, warm clothes, and they have to travel treacherous roads.'' Foley recalls an occasion when a sudden storm forced him to cancel a Starlings practice. ''We have two kids who have to come from Window Rock over the mountain, ninety miles round trip, and the pass is seven thousand feet [high]." He was able to tell all the local kids of the cancellation, but he could not reach one of the Window Rock girls. In the middle of the storm, there came a knock on his door. "Christie Cooke is there, and I mean there's a foot of snow on the ground." Her mother and father had driven her ("real slow, in a four-wheel") over the mountains.

Maggie and Carlson Cooke represent a rock of stability in an area where many families are broken by poverty, alcohol, lack of opportunity. Grounded, as Carlson says, in "the traditional ways, the traditional wisdom" of the Navajo, the two have raised three daughters, sending Christie's two older sisters, Melissa and Carla, to college. Along the way they have demonstrated a knack for combining the old with the new to good effect. Christie proudly displays a clan chart of her Navajo ancestors. Featuring names like "the charcoal stream of the red running into the water people," the chart, prepared for a Navajo culture class in school, was done on the family's home computer.

"If you don't know your clans, you don't know who you are," Christie says. Christie Cooke is a girl who can discuss the possible advantages of various college scholarship offerings one minute, and the next give detailed procedures for butchering, grilling, and eating a sheep—brains, eyeballs, entrails, and all. The stomach sac, she says, is good for making blood sausage, but Navajo elders say you risk blindness eating the pupil of the eye. She doesn't think tradition is all good. She rejects the persistent custom of arranged marriages—"to some extent, that's actually like selling your daughter, just for sheep and cattle." She also bridles at "the main stereotype men have of women on the reservation—they say you're supposed to be at home taking care of your family." She plans to return to the reservation after college with a teaching degree. Her parents, she confirms, "want me to have a career. They want me to excel in volleyball and my education.''

Ball games for Native American women and girls were known throughout the Southwest before the arrival of the Europeans. In 1868 a New Mexico U.S. army major described a half-mile footrace with a field of some one hundred Apache and Navajo tribespeople, men and women both, won by a seventeen-year-old girl. The matrilineal Navajo society values the input and status of women relatively more than some other cultures do. Christie and her teammates report few discouraging words about their participation in sports. They are accustomed to seeing photos of female volleyball and basketball teams on the front page of the *Navajo Times*.

In her position as a setter, the player who sets up the ball for the spike at the net, Christie was awarded a Most Consistent Player trophy in her junior year. She attends Fort Defiance High School (''Home of the Fighting Scouts''), just outside Window Rock. With all three of their daughters, the Cookes have deliberately encouraged volleyball as a path to higher education and also as a way to shield them from the dangers inherent in growing up in the modern world, dangers that are in many cases widespread, and heightened, on the reservation. Although Christie is still too young to be actively recruited by colleges (they are limited merely to sending a form letter asking for test scores), she has had interest from several colleges and universities, including Georgetown, the University of Arizona, and Syracuse. Her parents say that if Christie does indeed wind up at college in some faraway state, they would relocate there.

On a midwinter day the Cookes walk up to Window Rock National Monument, a natural red sandstone arch that is surrounded by the government buildings of the Navajo Nation. They hike a trail over half a foot of snow, through a shadowed gorge of stunted pine and yucca that also serves as the sled run for the neighborhood children. Carlson jokes with a tourist couple, coming down the trail as he goes up. "You see any sheep up there? I lost my sheep." He is an emotional, self-effacing man with a wry sense of humor about some of the sadder aspects of his past. "I am a refugee," he says, describing his peripatetic childhood, when he was shuttled between government schools, separated from his family, and discouraged from speaking Navajo or embracing the tribal religion. "It took me fifteen or sixteen years to get my freedom." Maggie also had a less than settled upbringing. Her father was a railroad man on the Santa Fe line that runs alongside the old Route 66. "All we did was move, move, move." As a teenager she was sent out for "placement" to a Mormon foster family and wound up attending Brigham Young University.

Even though Carlson was raised in a succession of Catholic environments, and Maggie still considers herself a member of the Church of Latter-Day Saints, the Cooke family's spiritual life clearly revolves around long-established Navajo practices. Before each game, Maggie gives her daughter a packet of bitter-tasting herbs called *t'glisz*, used for its protective power, which Christie sprinkles over her Nikes and rubs on her clothes and in her hair. There are ceremonies and all-night "singings" for protection of a child who is leaving home, for success at a tournament, for the onset of puberty. Melissa Cooke went to college at the University of Kansas at Lawrence, in tornado country, so the medicine man conducted a special ritual against strong winds.

For Christie, being a strong athlete doesn't conflict with the "new traditionalism" of her parents. She doesn't date—her parents haven't forbidden it, but she doesn't think they would like it—and yet she was elected homecoming queen, alongside a "good friend" who was homecoming king, a boy Christie describes as "a skateboarder and a graffiti artist." Every summer Christie spends time on her father's family ranch, two and a half hours away from Ganado. She herds sheep, shucks corn, and sometimes sleeps in a hogan, the traditional pre-European house of the Navajo. Even with all her enthusiasm for the old ways, she recognizes that the Navajo language—of which she has limited understanding and no speaking knowledge—is dying out among her generation. She knows only one girl who has taken up the traditional art of weaving. But she's putting a life together that includes both *t'glisz* and volleyball, and with her parents' support she's thriving.

If Christie Cooke represents the stable end of the spectrum of Navajo family life, the experience of her teammate Lynette ("Nettie") Martinez may be more common. Just after Christmas, she sits back on the couch in Rich Foley's home, hugging to her chest a white, fluffy stuffed bear her boyfriend has just given her as a Christmas present. A year younger than Cooke, Nettie comes across by turns as fragile, wistful, and softly defiant. She often looks to her friends on the Starlings, in particular to Cooke, for advice and support about her family situation. Martinez lives with her grandmother and her uncle. Her mother has a drinking problem and often "goes off and doesn't come back for a long time," and her father stops by only occasionally. "If this kid didn't have volleyball," says Rich Foley, "I don't know where she'd be."

A national survey of fifteen thousand Native American youth found the highest levels in any ethnic-racial group of stress, depression, suicide, obesity, and alcohol, physical and sexual abuse. "Indicators of distress are phenomenally high, particularly among girls," stated Michael Resnick, the director of the University of Minnesota Adolescent Health Research Center, which conducted the survey.

While her fellow Starlings are beginning to toss around names of colleges, Nettie is not so sure about the future. Her "academics," she worries, might not be good enough for college (this despite her 4.0 average). She speaks vaguely of leaving the reservation. "I just want to go somewhere. Maybe to school overseas. Maybe in Paris." While Cooke's parents drive her to practice through blizzards and team captain Luauna Nez sees her "tribe" in the stands at every game, Nettie's family at times constitutes a drag on her aspirations. "In my family, they don't ask me, 'What do you want to be?' " she says. "I just kind of think about that: why don't they ask me what I want to be, what I want to do? If they don't ask me, then they probably won't be able to support me either. They don't encourage me at all."

The ledge Lynette Martinez is standing on is very narrow. She typifies a teenager at risk. Coach Foley is one of the few healthy, positive presences around. He literally bangs on Martinez's door to get her out to games, to tournaments, to practice. Her maternal grandmother, an X-ray technician at the local hospital, "really struggles" to keep the family together. Her uncle, her mother's brother, was afflicted with night blindness as a child and his vision is still deteriorating (when he once attended one of Martinez's games, he could see only "a little white glare going back and forth" and hear the crowd screaming her name). He actively discourages his niece's involvement in athletics. "You play too much volleyball," he says. Unemployed, demanding her constant care and attention, her uncle "has a short temper," Martinez says. "So it's like if I ever talk back to him or something, I get afraid."

He did not want her to attend the U.S. Junior Olympic Nationals in Denver in June 1997, where the Starlings Four Corners club was going to compete for the first time.

"Do you have to go?" he asked her. "Can't they go without you?"

"I don't *have* to go, I want to go!" Nettie told him. When her grandmother supplied spending money for the trip, her uncle became angry. "You're going to have to give that money back—we need that money and you're not going!" She managed to make the trip only when Foley interceded. Her uncle "doesn't like Mr. Foley," says Nettie. "He says [Foley] doesn't know what he's talking about, he doesn't know what it's like" for Native Americans. Her uncle also talks down her mother, his own sister ("If she really wanted you, she would stay here and act like a mother"). He doesn't believe in "daydreaming," she says, he "just thinks about reality and how hard it is." She quotes her uncle so much that it is clear his voice is always ringing in her head, even when she gets out of the house, away from him.

Martinez worried in the weeks before Christmas that her mother would not come home for the holiday, but at the last minute she walked in the door. "I guess she expected everybody to go up and give her a hug," said Martinez, "but I don't know . . . I didn't. She had been gone for a week. And she kept telling me, 'Give me a hug, give me a hug, I missed you, Merry Christmas,' but I was looking at her like, 'Golly, how could you . . . I mean, on Christmas?' " Then Nettie came down with the flu, and her mother "kept giving me tea, and rubbing my legs and stuff, and I felt bad." She told her mother she was sorry for "just . . . making a pain, I guess." Nettie asked her where she had been.

"Nowhere," her mother said. "I was okay."

"That's good," Nettie said. "Just as long as you were warm and had a place to sleep, I guess."

Volleyball, Martinez says, helps her get through tough times with her family. "It makes me stronger," she says. For Cooke, playing with the Starlings is a great experience as well as a possible ticket to a good college her family couldn't otherwise afford, and Foley is a cheerleader, a facilitator, and a booster. But for someone like Martinez, the Starlings are a surrogate family, and an energetic, purposeful ally such as Foley can mean the difference between survival and oblivion.

Lynette Martinez doesn't know if she will be able to continue in volleyball for the remainder of high school, given her lack of family support. It will probably be harder in her junior and senior years, she says, because her uncle wants her to focus on her ACTs and SATs. "There's probably a one in a million chance that you'll get a scholarship to college through volleyball," he tells her. What does she say in reply? "I just sit there and listen."

There is no readily obtainable research concerning the number of girls who want to play sports in this country but who can't because the opportunities are not available to them. There are indicators, however, such as the high dropout rate of girls in high school athletics. At least some of these girls stop playing sports because proper programs are not provided. For instance, their high school offers only three teams for girls, all varsity, and they are not proficient enough to make the cut. Or their families might not have the resources to pay for lessons or clinics. Or it is too time-consuming, impractical, or even dangerous to travel to an extensive after-school sports schedule, especially if both parents work full time. Or the expectation in the family is that they will be home to put dinner on the table and take care of younger siblings. All of these obstacles are faced by girls in the Acorn Track Club or the Ganado Starlings, but all of them have been surmounted with the help of a committed adult.

Beyond bromides about how "one person can make a difference" lies a deeper question about why the needs of girls in West

Oakland or on the Navajo reservation would be left unmet if a Darrell Hampton or a Rich Foley didn't arrive on the scene. That question involves the thousands of potential track stars or volleyball players all across the country who haven't been lucky enough to meet a strong, capable, effective coach and mentor. The difficulty with the "thousand points of light" approach is that a mere thousand is not nearly enough to go around. Our daughters' futures are too important for us to wait and hope they might chance upon inspiring coaches. "The youth sports situation is much more complicated because youth sports has traditionally been a community volunteer function at the lowest levels," says Donna Lopiano. "It has been rotary clubs, it has been parks and recreation commissions, it has been all those parents who have to run the show for youth sports."

Girls need our help to be able to grow up into strong, capable women, and providing sports opportunities is one established way we can help them. The message still hasn't sunk in. Girls can "own" sports just as boys do, and when they do so we all benefit. We have to give this truth a structure in our society, back it up with resources and commitment. When we don't accomplish this, either girls never get a chance at sports or, when they do get involved, their experience turns them away from sports altogether.

7

When Sports Fail Girls

If Your Daughter Drops Out

Caitlin Extrom's parents did everything right. They raised their daughter to enjoy sports. She started playing soccer when she was five, in a Little Kicks program in her hometown just outside of Worcester, Massachusetts. Because she stood a few inches taller than everyone else on the team, she had a physical advantage. Caitlin also had been involved in dance from a very early age, which might have had some collateral benefits out on the playing field. Rebecca Extrom and her husband, Kenneth, were encouraging but not pushy. They took direction from their daughter. She liked Little Kicks ("it's basically just a whole lot of little kids running around kicking the ball," Caitlin says). So they signed her up for the next level, PeeWee League, for "under-eights." This was when Rebecca first got involved in coaching. Caitlin

163

continued playing in town and club leagues on teams coached by her mother, until she turned fifteen and entered high school. Then, to the consternation of her parents, she dropped sports altogether.

Caitlin Extrom is above average insofar as her opportunities to play, the extraordinary degree of her parental support, and her advanced skill level. But as a girl who reaches a certain age and stops playing sports, she is all too typical. Across the country, across income demographics and racial and ethnic divides, girls of all different backgrounds replicate Caitlin's experience with depressing regularity. It's true of teenagers in general, not just girls: in early adolescence kids seem to hit a wall and drop out of sports in droves. "Sports participation," states one study, "and the desire to participate in sports, decline sharply and steadily between ages 10 and 18," with involvement in nonschool sports programs falling from 45 percent to 26 percent in that time frame.

But the trend is especially pronounced, and especially troubling, among girls in Caitlin's age group. During this crucial time, girls not only are less likely to participate in sports but are more likely to become sedentary, inactive, avoiding physical activity altogether. This is the age when couch potatoes are born, along with problems with obesity and health that can have lifelong consequences. The trend is growing worse. A study by the Centers for Disease Control and Prevention in Atlanta found that by the senior year of high school, only a quarter of all girls exercise vigorously on a regular basis, compared with half of all boys. Fitness surveys have shown that the percentage of kids involved in vigorous exercise dropped from two-thirds to one-third in the years between 1984 and 1990. Only 20 percent of the nation's girls have daily physical education, and only one state, Illinois, requires it by law. Gym class, health clubs, pickup games—all are increasingly unpopular with high school girls. Despite the well-publicized boom in girls' sports, regular physical activity is an endangered activity among a majority of our daughters.

In the middle-class enclave of central Massachusetts where Caitlin lives, participation in sports and other extra-curricular activities is probably higher than in other parts of the country. Soccer leagues and dance studios abound. At the same time she stopped playing soccer, Caitlin Extrom also dropped dance from her life. From a fourteen-year-old who played one or two full-length games of soccer per week and who went to eight or nine dance classes every week, she has become a fifteen-year-old who "sleeps a lot." She still takes vocal lessons and while not specifically committing to soccer or dance in the future says that stopping these activities is a "temporary" thing. "I'm out of shape. I get sick more when I'm not exercising much," Caitlin admits. "I'm kind of bored right now." At times she will dance on her own, pushing the furniture against the wall in the spacious family room her parents built as a "quasi-dance studio." "I'll just turn up the radio and break out," Caitlin says. She has two older brothers, both of whom were involved in sports, although not to the consistent degree of Caitlin's involvement in soccer.

Caitlin Extrom is such a confident, self-possessed young woman that it is difficult to assign her to a group that has failed, at physical activity or anything else. Certainly, she seems none the worse for dropping out of soccer. At her family's home on a wooded plot along a backcountry road, she speaks openly with her mother about her recent decisions to stop soccer and dance. She wears a tie-dyed T-shirt and jeans, her blond hair styled long and straight, parted in the middle. Her mother is an attractive, vigorous woman who seems genuinely puzzled about the turn away from sports her daughter's life has taken, but there is a warm camaraderie between them, and Caitlin unabashedly names her mom when asked if she has any heroes in her life.

"All of my life I've done some form of exercise," Rebecca Extrom says. "I learned how to cross-country ski when I was pregnant with my second child. I started running before my third child came along. I've always been a person that has loved physical activity. It goes back to the days when I was horseback riding. Being outside is my preference. I guess it has to do with loving nature and being out in it." At the same time, she says, "I've never pressured my kids into doing a sport. I felt that by example—by putting on my running gear and heading outdoors for a run in the middle of winter—it says to them I put value on being active."

Rebecca Extrom grew up in a "basketball family" in the same central Massachusetts area in which she now lives. She and her husband, a software designer, were "lifelong Celtic fans" whose enthusiasm for professional basketball waned with Larry Bird's retirement from the team. Around that time they began coaching Caitlin's soccer teams, both as a couple and individually. Soccer in the Worcester area is a fall and spring sport, with the fall supposedly reserved for learning fundamentals, and the spring designated for more competitive play. The club and town leagues Caitlin played on changed affiliations frequently, falling under the aegis of AYSO one year, another youth soccer organization the next. The Extroms progressed through the years with their daughter on under-ten, under-eleven, and finally a full-strength, eleven-player under-twelve team.

From the beginning, Caitlin had a "good foot," a strong kicking ability. Her father used to challenge her, saying he'd give Caitlin $20 if she could kick a ball from the road in front of their house, a good thirty yards away, and break one of their windows. "I actually did try quite a few times," Caitlin laughs. "But I never made it." "One thing that Caitlin always had to her advantage was that she could go left or right," Rebecca says. "She was very strong on her left foot, which with girls in soccer is very uncommon. So her being able to go down the left side of the field using her left foot, she was a very strong offensive weapon."

Rebecca and Caitlin exhibit a new style of mother-daughter relationship, born of the sports boom, a coach-athlete interchange that is appreciably more active than the chauffeur-rider relationship of the cliché soccer mom. As a coach Rebecca expressly designed plays to take advantage of the capabilities of her daughter, including one that used Caitlin's strong left foot, "where the inside halfback [Caitlin] takes the ball out the left side and basically runs it up and then across toward the goal."

A daughter who loved a sport and was good at it. Parents who set sterling examples, got involved, used sports as a way to bring the family together. It is difficult to determine a single overarching reason why Caitlin decided to stop playing soccer after ten years. As a freshman in high school, the first time a school soccer program was available to her, "I was nervous," she confesses, "but definitely looking forward" to playing on the school team. After a few months, however, she made the decision to quit. She recalls breaking the news to her mother in the car on the way home from practice. The conversation took a long time to resolve itself.

"Basically," Caitlin says, "everywhere we went she'd bring it up."

"You would be pretty emotional about it," Rebecca says to her daughter. "When we'd talk you'd be crying."

"She didn't understand," Caitlin recalls, "and she was really unwilling to let me give it up." Was she worried about disappointing her parents if she stopped playing? Caitlin looks at her mother. "No offense," she says, "but not really, Mom. Not at all."

"I think she made up her mind before she told us," Rebecca says. Caitlin talks generally in terms of her high school junior varsity practices being "difficult" and "extremely painful" for her. She had not worked out during the summer and was out of shape. She felt herself out of synch with the style of play, not getting along with her new junior varsity coach, a woman straight out of college, who had been an excellent Division I player. "She expected us to do the exact thing that she did," Caitlin says, "and it didn't make any sense to me." Her mother speaks a little wistfully of future possibilities. "I think she may go back and do it. She talks a little bit about wanting to try something next year. I just think as a freshman she's a little overwhelmed by everything, and rather than try it, she hung back." At another time she ascribes her daughter's leaving soccer to Caitlin's "burning out" on sports after playing soccer since she was five. She talks about how her daughter's decision has changed her own life. "It was a hard time for me," says Rebecca, "because every season since she was five, I was on a soccer field every weekend—October, November." She stares out at the bleak fall landscape. "I really missed seeing her play."

There are a host of reasons why girls leave athletics. The basis for their dropping out, or even the rates of cessation, are woefully understudied. The broad-brush picture is fairly clear: 62 percent of girls at ages six to seven are playing organized sports, but by age sixteen that number has dropped to 30 percent and falls again to 18 percent in college. During high school, girls are six times as likely as boys to quit sports. Are we somehow failing our daughters by providing the wrong kind of athletic experience? Are girls leaving organized sports altogether, or merely dropping out of one sport to sample different athletic offerings? Is it inevitable, as some people believe, that as girls reach puberty they are going to become more interested in other activities, in boys, in dating, and thus lose interest in athletics? Or is the dichotomy between homecoming queen and star athlete a total anachronism? (Christie Cooke, for example, managed both.) What about continuing sports after graduation? Two out of three women age twenty to forty are involved in some form of exercise or weight-reduction program, but adult men are much more likely to be involved in recreational team sports. How can we deliver a broader, more inclusive athletic experience?

The present body of academic research does not offer clear-cut answers to these questions. As girls from all over the country spoke in interviews conducted for this book, several themes emerged. A persistent one is that as girls get older, the trend toward elitism in school and club programs becomes more pronounced. "Isn't there a program for girls who want to play just for the heck of it?" Rebecca Extrom asks. As a society, we fail to provide activities for young people, girls and boys both, who might not be varsity material but who nonetheless have the right to the full measure of benefits that playing sports can provide.

Another theme repeatedly sounded was that as often as girls drop out of sports, sports can fail girls. Temple University's Carole Oglesby maintains that sports participation can have manifold benefits, provided all the elements are right. "But if you can imagine a coach berating and belittling somebody who doesn't perform up to expectations, it's possible to see that there can be a sports situation that is going to devastate a girl. That's not the norm, thank heaven, but it is important to acknowledge that coaching and context can make an enormous difference."

For the great majority of girls, involvement in athletics is overwhelmingly a beneficial, even lifesaving experience. But there are also real dangers that can poison that experience and turn sports into a hurtful, harmful aspect of young girls' lives. Dropping out becomes a question of self-preservation.

Megan Nelson was always a restless, active kid. "You were always moving," her mother, Jan Nelson, tells her about her infancy. "Wherever the action was, that's where you'd want to be." Nelson grew up to be an athlete, a standout in cross-country, basketball, and soccer at St. Xavier, a Catholic high school in Appleton, Wisconsin. As her mother and she sat on a couch to be interviewed, Megan's hands were constantly in motion, gesticulating, folding and re-folding. Jan stroked a small white dog as Megan recounted how athletics had focused her, calmed her, saved her—and made her suffer. Running, she says, "keeps me regulated, keeps me off more medicine, so I don't have to take so much." Now fifteen, Megan, like so many children diagnosed with attention deficit disorder, or ADD, takes a medication to alleviate some of the syndrome's symptoms. "I would feel like bouncing off the wall if I didn't have anything to do." Her mother remembers her playing in a tee-ball league in first grade. Jan was startled to see her daughter turning cartwheels at second base during a lull in the action.

Emotionally, sports has been a blessing, an "uplifter," as her mother puts it. Nelson's athletic life has been a series of dreams fulfilled. When she was in fifth grade, she told Jan that she couldn't wait until she could play high school basketball. She was one of twenty-five freshmen who tried out for spring soccer and one of five who made varsity. In that same year she went to the state championships in cross-country. Her father, Curt, practices with her, while her mother, says Nelson, "makes sure I'm good," giving her vitamins, healthy meals, and good old-fashioned nurturing. "I would never quit sports," Nelson says. It represents something of a pressure valve for her, helping her burn off adolescent frustrations. "When I'm angry, I go and I run or I kick the soccer ball." Betraying a ubiquitous pressure on adolescent girls, Nelson also says working out allows her to avoid putting on weight. "I would be seriously fat if I didn't run."

But for all the bright side of Nelson's involvement in athletics, her story demonstrates that it can have a risk, too, particularly for driven personalities who derive a lot of satisfaction from their achievements and who are willing to go through a lot of discomfort, even pain, to compete. In November 1996, three days before she was to leave for the state cross-country meet, Nelson felt a sharp pain in her right calf. Thinking it was merely a muscle cramp, she immediately stopped and rested, but the pain persisted. She saw a doctor, who advised her not to go to the meet. "I didn't listen, because I was a freshman going to state— just like, yah! I couldn't give up the opportunity." The race was torture. She did poorly, but she didn't quit. She ran past an ambulance that had picked up a runner with an injury who had dropped out in front of her. "I said, 'No, I don't want that happening to me. I'm not looking like a fool.' " She literally limped to the finish line.

A physical therapist who saw Megan soon after the race speculated that she "may have Mary Decker's injury," referring to one of Megan's sports heroes, the runner Mary Decker Slaney. The comment somehow got lost in the shuffle, and Nelson and her family embarked on a year-long quest for answers, seeing orthopedic surgeons, neurologists, psychiatrists, rehabilitation specialists, and physical therapists. The girl who loved to move kept moving. She realized her dream of playing high school basketball, impressing the varsity coach even as a freshman. But now her leg was hurting even as she walked to school. She saw five doctors. "I cried at every one," she says. One physician suggested she join the swim team. Megan snapped. "I screamed at her, 'We don't even have a swim team!' My school doesn't have a pool." All the advice she was getting was the same: get some rest. Gently prodded by her parents, she made the momentous decision to drop out of basketball. The coach said he would hold a spot on the team for her for when she recovered.

She didn't. She rested for three months, until soccer season rolled around. She was climbing the walls. The pain was still there, but so was the team—she had made varsity, one of only five freshmen to do so, the only freshman starter. She played through the injury and finished out the season: "I think I got used to the pain." Sports were helping her socially. Girl athletes weren't automatically granted status at St. Xavier the way boy athletes were, but at least belonging to a team gave her a foothold in the complex hierarchies of high school. Megan could count off the differences in the way the boy athletes at her school were treated. They got pep rallies, a fan bus, prayer services before games, a bigger locker room. The school laundered the boys' uniforms while the girls had to wash their own. The double standard was glaringly apparent, but if Nelson could play through the pain, she was not about to let the lack of a pep rally get to her. As a freshman, she lettered in cross-country and soccer and got an academic letter also.

That summer, her family hired a personal trainer who helped Nelson keep a diary of her workouts. As she increased her mileage, the pain in her legs increased. At first it forced her to stop after three miles, then after two, and finally after one. She would sing to herself as she ran, always the same song, Paul Simon's "Cecilia," and always only the chorus. "I'm down on my knees / I'm begging you please / To come home." Over and over. At sixteen, she had her philosophy already defined: "Quitters never win, and winners never quit." Once her father had to pull her off a cross-country course. She begged to continue even though she had been dragging her leg behind her like the Mariner's albatross.

Megan happened across an ad in the local newspaper announcing the arrival in town of an orthopedic surgeon relocated from Alabama. "After my first visit, he sat me down and told me that he would never give up until he found out what was going on, because something was not right," she recalls. It was a tremendous relief to hear, after a year of being told she was imagining her ailment, that all she needed was rest. The doctor finally diagnosed compartment syndrome, an extremely painful problem in which the muscles grow too quickly for the sheathing that covers them. It was Mary Decker's injury after all, and there was an established surgical treatment available. But Nelson won't be able to play basketball anytime soon.

There could not be a more unlikely candidate for a sports dropout than Megan Nelson. She herself balks at the phrase "dropping out," feeling as if it hits too close to the idea of quitting. But the risk of injury is a real element in the sports equation for all athletes, and young girls are not immune. In balance, high levels of physical activity pose little risk to the health of girls and offer manifold benefits, but at the elite levels at which Megan Nelson trained, there are three interrelated health threats that female athletes must guard against. Referred to by sports medicine professionals as the "female athlete triad," the three are eating disorders, osteoporosis, and amenorrhea. With adolescent girls, intense athletic training can drop body fat levels low enough to interfere with menarche or disrupt regular menstrual periods. Amenorrhea, in turn, is associated with compromised bone mineral density and the development of osteoporosis in later life. Athletic participation can normally bring increased bone mass by increasing weight-bearing activities, and thus for many girls playing sports is actually a hedge against developing osteoporosis as they age. Once training becomes intensive enough that the young athlete experiences amenorrhea or oligomenorrhea (irregular periods), however, those benefits may be canceled out. The picture is further complicated by the fact that amenorrhea might actually have the beneficial effect of lowering a girl's risk of developing certain estrogen-related cancers.

When injuries do strike young athletes, they are almost always associated with muscles and bones, while the positive effects of athletic activity generally accrue to an individual's cardiovascular system. The way in which school sports programs are organized can sometimes actually increase risk of injuries by grouping young athletes by age rather than skill level, thus putting smaller, less physically able children on the same field as bigger, more mature players. Through educational programs that stress proper physical conditioning and warm-up exercises, many musculoskeletal injuries can be avoided. Parents and coaches also need to be made aware of appropriate training levels and rates of specialization to limit the negative effects of overtraining and early specialization.

The relationship between participation in athletics and eating disorders is equally complicated. An undue focus on body composition in the "appearance" or endurance sports—for example gymnastics, figure skating, distance running—might contribute to higher incidence in female athletes of bulimia, anorexia or what are labeled NOS (for "not otherwise specified") eating disorders. Levels of disordered eating have been found in almost two-thirds of the female athletes surveyed in 1996 by an NCAA research team, with clinical disorders found in a full 10 percent. These are significantly higher numbers than are found in the general population.

174

Tiffany Cohen-Adams isn't a swimmer anymore, but she'll always be an Olympic gold medalist. A recent high school graduate when she won the 400- and 800-yard freestyle events at the 1984 Los Angeles Games, breaking Olympic and American records, Tiffany Cohen went on to become a jewel in the crown at the University of Texas-Austin, the best female long-distance swimmer at the premier swimming school in the country. She was eighteen. Her achievement was something she had trained for, hungered for, almost since the time she had started swimming at age eight. By the time she was in high school she was training thirty to thirty-five hours a week. Her life was structured around chlorine.

Her family, too, was swept along in Tiffany's wake. They had been living in Westchester, a Los Angeles suburb, but they were casting about for something better. "Better," for the Cohens, meant better for their daughter's swimming career. When the coach of the Mission Viejo Matadors, a top competitive club located in southern Orange County, recruited the then thirteen-year-old Tiffany, they were set to pull up stakes. Tiffany moved to Mission Viejo so she could start training with the Matadors right away, and her family followed a year later. There were other reasons for the move—it made sense for her father's career, and the school system was good—but the Matadors' national reputation was the real draw. Cohen loved to swim, she loved to win, she felt good about her athlete's body. "As a teenager I always felt really positive, really good about having a strong, lean physique," she says. When she was fifteen, she won her first national championship. "That's when we started thinking about a gold medal," she recalls.

Three years after the Los Angeles Olympics, Tiffany Cohen crashed. She suffered repeated physical collapses. She found herself too weak to make it through even the easiest practice.

Thoughts of suicide haunted her. Finally, in the fall of her senior year, with the 1988 Olympics looming, she stunned the swimming world by publicly resigning from the Austin swim team. She left school. A year later, she checked into a clinic for treatment of bulimia. The scandal broke nationally when the *Austin American Statesman* revealed that over an eight-month period, twelve members—10 percent—of the Austin swim team had been diagnosed with serious eating disorders. The media blamed "arbitrary assignment of ideal weights" by coach Richard Quick.

The fall of Tiffany Cohen was not as sudden as it seemed. The genesis lay in the little-explored matrix of highly competitive sports programs, family dynamics, coach-athlete relationships, and the overwhelming societal pressures that are sometimes placed on teenage girls. Cohen was a casualty of a world that was supposed to counteract our culture's unhealthy obsession with thinness, to replace the anorexic model ideal with the healthy, robust physique of the female athlete. But the world of athletics offers its own menu of weight-related pressures, and there is danger in replacing skin-and-bones ideal with that of the athletic "hard body." Writer Joan Jacobs Brumberg: "Our national infatuation with 'hard bodies,' combined with the idea that bodies are perfectible, heightens the pressure on adolescents and complicates the business of adjusting to a new, sexually maturing body. . . . The fitness craze can aggravate adolescent self-consciousness and make girls desperately unhappy (if not neurotic) about their own bodies, particularly if it is combined with unrealistic expectations drawn from air-brushed and retouched photographs in advertising, and the seductive camera angles and body doubles so common in television and movies." Many experts believe that a young woman going through adolescence and an intense level of athletic competition at the same time is doubly vulnerable to eating disorders.

In addition, the personality of the elite athlete and the anorexic/bulimic personality appear to have much in common. It is a chicken-or-egg question: do sports create eating disorders, or do they simply attract girls who are prone to them? The fact remains that Tiffany Cohen is not alone. The NCAA study established that elite female athletes suffer from full-blown eating disorders at a rate twice that of the general population. It seems a cruel irony. The lifeline tossed out to girls turns into an entangling, dangerous web.

Research and discussion of the problem have grown, especially after several highly publicized cases drew attention to the connection among eating disorders, weight loss, and sports: the death in 1994 of U.S. gymnast Christy Henrich, who at the time of her death weighed only 60 pounds, a series of collegiate wrestling deaths in 1997, and the death from heart failure of twenty-two-year-old Boston Ballet dancer Heidi Guenther in the summer of 1997. But when Tiffany Cohen began training for the Olympics at the beginning of the 1980s, the athletic community as a whole had yet to confront this dynamic.

Her transformation from a girl who "felt really positive" about her body into a young woman who was taking laxatives and inducing vomiting to control her weight might have had its beginnings in childhood. At Mission Viejo, a lot of attention was paid to weight. For starters, the girls were weighed daily. The coaches had the body fat percentage of each team member measured at the beginning of each season by the sophisticated immersion method, whereby the athlete is placed on a scale and lowered into a pool—a very public way to highlight what is, for teenage girls, the already supersensitive issue of weight. "They're actually called body composition tests," Cohen-Adams says of the measurements, "but we called them 'fat tests.'" If the swimmers had a body fat ratio higher than 20 percent, they were deemed members of "the Blub Club." There were also more subtle messages. Cohen-Adams remembers the Matadors coach going down the aisle of the airplane as the team traveled to a meet, gathering the desserts off the athletes' trays one after another. "The girls would just hand them in," she recalls. "But a lot of times they would sneak along little treats for themselves."

The measure of Tiffany Cohen's driven personality can be taken by her reaction to her gold medal performance at the 1984 Olympics. It should have been a high point in her life. But she was saddled with a sense of failure even at the height of her triumph, a sense that she should have done more. A pair of gold medals wasn't good enough, breaking an Olympic and an American record wasn't good enough. Her goal had been to set world records, and she hadn't. "I didn't see myself as accomplished as maybe some people might have seen me," she recalls. But she couldn't talk about it. She had witnessed the media reaction to a swimmer who had been seen pounding his fist on the pavement in frustration at not making a world record, and she realized how "ungracious" her feelings would appear to others. "I just stuffed my feelings," she says. Even years later, in therapy, her feeling of failure after her gold medal performance was one of the things she found most difficult to discuss.

Cohen's problems with bulimia began in earnest just after the Olympics, in her freshman year of college. She began to look in the mirror and see a fat person. "In Texas," she says, "the culture's a little bit different. There's this southern belle image. . . . I wanted to have a different body for personal things, social things. [I was interested in] conforming to an ideal image that I saw down there." She met her ex-boyfriend's petite new girlfriend and tortured herself with comparisons. A few comments by her coach at Austin still ring in her ears. Weighing 142 pounds at the Olympics had "felt wonderful in the water," but the coach wanted her to get down to 134. "Just think how much better you could have done if you were down to 134," her coach told her. A weight gain in the first year of college is so well recognized that the added pounds are referred to as the "freshman ten," and they can be due to a combination of stress-induced snacking, starchy cafeteria food, late-night pizza parties, the "four meals a day" consumed by kids suddenly making their own choices about diet. Like many of her peers, Cohen gained weight. When she happened to hurt her shoulder during a practice, her coach told her that she could have avoided the injury if she hadn't "been pulling so much weight." "That was really devastating," Cohen-Adams recalls.

She was already "flirting with bingeing and purging." Three or four times a week, she would have what she called "bad days." She would tell herself, "Well, I've ruined it now, so I might as well just go ahead and eat all I want, and then I can get rid of it." The coach's comment about her weight triggered a level of food obsession she hadn't experienced before, whereby she became "concerned with every little morsel I put in my mouth." Cohen hit the weight her coach asked her to, but she found she couldn't hold it there. Ironically, her new regimen had an adverse effect on her performance; she was routinely turning in times that were slower than her Olympic year performances. She was taking in only 1,200 to 1,500 calories a day, "turkey and fat-free yogurt," and that caloric level is not sufficient for someone training twenty-five hours a week. She would call home, and her mother would ask, "How's your weight? Well, how come you haven't lost it?" She never exhibited the skeletal image of the anorexic; throughout the whole ordeal, her weight fluctuated by only five or so pounds.

But by her junior year, the roller-coaster ride began to take its toll. "I collapsed in the shower. I couldn't make it through the

easiest workouts. I'd wake up in the morning and just roll over—
I couldn't get out of bed. I'd miss classes. I was suicidal and
depressed, spitting up blood, afraid for my life.'' She had read
about anorexia/bulimia in Psych 101 and knew it was possible to
tear a hole in her esophagus from repeated vomiting. ''I knew
what I was doing to myself and I was very scared,'' she says. She
tried different methods of weight control that were other variations of self-destructive behaviors: smoking cigarettes, marathon
walks, binge drinking. She had persistent anxiety about something that would seem more in keeping with an adolescent going
to the beach than a highly talented Olympic swimmer: whether
she would look decent in a bathing suit at the next Olympic
games. The worst part, for Cohen, was performing so badly. In
the fall of 1987, she competed for the last time. She realized she
had swum the same time ten years earlier. ''It took a little while
for the negative effect of the eating disorder to hit, but when it
did, it did completely. I think I was very overwhelmed. It felt like
I had lost total control,'' she recalls.

Cohen dropped out of school but still believed she could
lick the problem on her own. ''It was like I was trying to win a
gold medal for my recovery.'' She gave up swimming completely
(''I couldn't stand it at the time''). Eventually, she realized that it
was going to be a long battle. Weak and feeling close to mental
collapse, her biochemical balances severely disrupted, she was
hospitalized for nine weeks in the fall of 1988. The Olympics had
come and gone—she couldn't even watch them. Tiffany Cohen
was battling for her life. In an odd bit of irony, the rigor of her
sports training, the exact thing which triggered her disease, also
helped heal her. She credits the ''three D's'' of being an athlete—dedication, determination, and discipline—with helping
her recovery. She says she has now been ''purge-free'' for eight
years.

Several sports are strongly linked in the public's mind with eating disorders. Joan Ryan's *Little Girls in Pretty Boxes* painted a heartrending picture of the problems in gymnastics and figure skating, both sports that emphasize physical appearance. Writing in the mid-nineties (before the advent of the WNBA, among other developments), Ryan stresses how certain sports reinforce cultural expectations of feminine "delicacy" that can contribute to eating disorders:

> Gymnasts, like figure skaters, are "acceptable" female athletes who are brave but not macho, muscled but not bulky, competitive but still vulnerable. Most parents looking for sporting role models for their daughters find few from which to choose, as there still are no successful professional baseball, softball, soccer or basketball leagues for women. Among available role models, [gymnast] Shannon Miller is a more comfortable choice for many parents than large and powerful women like Martina Navratilova and Jackie Joyner-Kersee, because gymnasts play into a parent's fantasy about their daughters. They are pink satin sashes and Maryjanes. Daddy's girls. In a modern sports world grappling with the changing roles of women, from the front offices to the playing fields, gymnasts are beacons of feminine simplicity and innocence.

The emphasis on weight and body fat control are spreading to all sports, as competition becomes more fierce and coaching strategies more extreme. Dr. Margo Maine, a Connecticut psychiatrist and author who specializes in eating disorders and who gives workshops at colleges and high schools for coaches, cites volleyball as one example of a changing expectation about body type: "Even though there's been no connection established between low weight, body shape, and [performance in] volleyball, volleyball coaches have really begun looking at weight and body fat." Maine says she recognizes "the positive value in sports" for girls and cites studies that show that participating in athletics can enhance body image. But the pendulum can swing all too easily the other way.

"A sports team becomes a subculture for kids," Maine says. "It can either be a wonderful, healthy subculture, or not. If there are a couple kids who are struggling with this, and you have a coach who isn't giving the right messages, you will have a very serious problem." In her book *Father Hunger,* Maine posits a relationship between eating disorders and the complex distancing that can occur between fathers and daughters during adolescence whereby "the symptoms [of the disorder] are really a response to the depression [a girl] feels about the loss of connection with her dad." Young athletes undergoing this process of separation can be particularly vulnerable to the coach as an authority figure. It has been shown that girls also tend to internalize criticism to a greater degree than boys do, so that a coach's criticism (such as the coach's comment to Tiffany Cohen linking her injury to weight) can exacerbate an athlete's problems with self-esteem. Loaded on top of this are the general social pressures that all girls feel, the background barrage of media images of Barbie-doll figures and fashion waifs.

Maine believes it is possible that the athletic personality might lend itself to disordered eating patterns. "Kids are drawn to sports who want to do well, they want to please other people, they want to push themselves," she says. "A lot of the things that make a great athlete are also ingredients of a great eating disorder. You work through pain, you keep on setting your standards high, you're never satisfied with yourself, you're never good enough."

The high incidence of athletes with eating disorders on Cohen-Adams's University of Texas-Austin swim team was national news in 1989. Coach Richard Quick moved on, but once again there was evidence of eating disorders at his new program.

Cohen-Adams refuses to blame him, saying that he was a good coach, doing what he thought was right at the time. She also spares her parents, who, she says, were "devastated" by her illness. Her story has what she terms a "happy ending." She went back to college and received a degree in psychiatry, is the mother of two children, and speaks frequently on the issue of athletes and eating disorders. After years of not being able to bring herself to watch the Olympic Games on television, she sat through the 1996 Atlanta games. During the time she was pregnant with her second child, she began swimming again. "It was wonderful," she says. "Some days I didn't want to do it, but as I got in I always felt really good, and I realized, 'God, this feels great in my joints, and bones, and muscles.' I just kind of recaptured the love that I had for the sport."

When Tiffany Cohen-Adams was in college, the prevalence of eating disorders among athletes was largely unrecognized and chronically underaddressed. Her case helped increase the visibility of the problem, a process that has continued through the nineties. Wider recognition has in turn resulted in increased efforts at prevention. Activist Priscilla Bolin seeks to prevent eating disorders among young female athletes with an education and intervention program designed to be used at the high school and college levels. Bolin comes from a sports background (her mother was a basketball player in college and her father was a coach), and she is recovering from clinical bulimia herself. She describes the Austin swim team case as a "watershed" in generating her own interest in the special problems of the elite female athlete. She worked briefly with Tiffany Cohen-Adams and her teammates and used their experiences in developing a working model at the University of Tennessee for a program that gives young women the resources to deal with what Bolin calls "blocks to performance."

The goal of Bolin's work is to address subclinical eating disorders before they develop into full-blown syndromes. "The performance is the last thing to go," she says, noting that many girls are deep into severe phases of bulimia (more common among athletes than anorexia) and still competing. Eating disorders among elite athletes are getting more prevalent, she believes, in part because the stakes are getting higher. "On this level," says Bolin, "there is so much attached to winning, there are a lot of economic advantages, so young women are willing to often do anything to win, because their scholarship is tied to it. When you have your financial future attached to the sport, you're really at high risk, and you would go to any lengths to do what you have to do."

Along with Maine and other experts, Bolin believes that the personality of the high-achieving athlete has much in common with the addictive-compulsive personality type. Both personalities exhibit such traits as perfectionism, willingness to please, willingness "to move through pain and don't let anybody know," a high desire to comply with the expectations of others. "So when I was looking at this, I thought, well, here we have what it takes to win, which are also the things that make you go over the line into problems. So what can we do to help these women not cross over the line?" It is not, she stresses, so much that sports causes the problems, but that for many young female athletes "the seeds are already there. Then you put them in an environment that's like a petri dish where it all comes together and starts growing."

Bolin works with an entire athletic department—coaches, athletes, even the families and boyfriends of the athletes. She concentrates on removing from the sports environment triggers that can cause eating disorders, including coaches' comments, weigh-ins, cafeteria food choices, and "the myths that permeate the athletic culture," specifically the relationship between body fat and performance. "Women are all different body shapes and sizes," Bolin says, "and they perform better at different body shapes and sizes in athletics. You can't just go by a cookie cutter ideal-weight chart." There is something that parents can do at home, long before their daughters go to college, or even to high school. Mothers and fathers, says Bolin, must try to understand better the psychology of girls, the vast majority of whom, she maintains, play sports not primarily to win but to have fun. Parents who are perfectionists place undue pressure on young female athletes to succeed at all costs. We must show our daughters that while it is desirable as a female to engage in strenuous athletic competition, what we value most is who they are inside, regardless of their performance, shape, weight, or size.

Ann Maxwell and her friend Linda Kraft (not their real names), a girl the same age from her Dallas neighborhood, were saving up for ten-speed bikes the summer after their sophomore year in high school. Maxwell had started running track in junior high and had steadily progressed. Now she was performing five events, including sprints and the shot put. Her coach, she says, "told me I had talent, that I could really go places." Even though she suffered from asthma, Kraft signed on the team, too, running the 880. The girls' high school track team was a "thrown-together program, with leftover equipment," and the coaches were two math instructors who had been pressed into service, one of them acting as the boys' track coach also. Coach Stewart "paid a lot of attention to me," says Maxwell, and it felt good. He was in his early thirties, almost exactly twice her age. Her strict Catholic upbringing had fostered an eagerness in Maxwell to please others, and by her own account she was "probably behind everybody else" in terms of social and sexual sophistication. When Stewart told her she could do more events, Maxwell began doing the high jump, and "he pressed me into the 440, which is pretty grueling—you're hurting at the end."

The two girls, both sixteen, put in a lot of effort that year and they were proud of their work. That summer Stewart would be serving as director of the summer school. He offered them both positions in his office, doing light typing. Kraft and Maxwell were happy that they could put the extra money they would earn toward their new bikes. They would show up at 7:30 in the morning, work in the office until midafternoon, and then immediately break to train. Over the summer, Stewart decided that Maxwell should be a hurdler. He stretched a string across the track for her to jump. "The first thing I did was fall flat on my face," she recalls. She now had seven events to compete in. At the encouragement of the coach, Maxwell began staying late to practice. Kraft stayed, too.

Basically the girls were spending their whole day with Stewart. Maxwell liked him and felt he was doing a good job teaching her to jump hurdles. But their relationship changed. Maxwell recalls that the coach began "hanging around in back of my chair while I was typing." One day she strained her back in practice. "Let's go in the training room," said Stewart. "I'll see if I can massage the kink out." It did not seem strange or untoward at the time; Maxwell knew that he did the same for the guys. But this time the massage turned sexual. She says she will always remember Stewart's words to her that afternoon: "You've got some kind of magic."

That was the beginning. She never told anyone about it—not Kraft, not her parents, not even her confessor at church—but throughout the summer, athlete and coach spent many evenings and lunch hours "sneaking into the coach's office, making out." It never went any further than that, although Maxwell recalls being "smitten." She felt as though what she was doing was of her own volition. "I was attracted to him; I was completely confused," she says. One time, Stewart had her over to babysit his children, and she recalls feeling mortified at having to make small talk with his wife.

Part of her had always been uneasy with the arrangement, and she eventually wrote Stewart a note, telling him, "this isn't right, no more." She doesn't recall feeling especially traumatized. There were no fireworks or recriminations. "He just sort of stepped back," she says. He was still supportive of her as an athlete and continued to coach her. But in her senior year, as she prepared to graduate, Maxwell was getting her yearbook signed and stopped by his office. She recalls vividly the woman, just a few years older than she was then, perched on the edge of Stewart's desk, "with knee-high boots and long blond hair." She was a former student, he told her. The realization suddenly hit her that this was a pattern for Stewart and an abuse of power. "Oh," she remembers thinking to herself, "this guy does this all the time." Even then, however, she didn't feel angry. She felt "guilty in not coming forth to say that [Stewart] shouldn't be doing this, not in his position. He took advantage of a naive sixteen-year-old girl."

Ann Maxwell is now an adult with two children of her own. An accomplished writer and energetic producer for television and movies, she is also still an athlete; she runs and plays softball and tennis and works out in her home weight room. She does not count the incident with Stewart as a defining moment in her life. But she still burns when she thinks of the wide-eyed aspiring athlete she was, and she realizes how enraged she would be if this happened to one of her own children.

In a sense, Maxwell was fortunate. Unlike many girls who are seduced by unscrupulous coaches, she was able to get out of the relationship before serious damage was done to her psyche.

While the professional literature decries "the lack of systemic research" into coach-athlete sexual harassment, anecdotal evidence points to a very real problem. It's a problem compounded by the shame of the victims. The writer and athlete Mariah Burton Nelson is an outspoken advocate for women in sports, but it took years before she spoke publicly about a relationship with a high school coach that started when she was fourteen. From a kiss goodnight, the coach escalated their intimacy until they were "parking for hours in a deserted lot" near Nelson's home. "I was scared, excited, flattered, and in love." Like Ann Maxwell, Nelson characterized herself as a "willing participant" in the relationship. Only later did she recognize that the affair was a "terrible abuse of trust" on the coach's part. "I've become convinced," Nelson says, "that sexual relationships between coaches and female athletes, regardless of the gender of the coach, and regardless of whether the athlete is in high school or college, are always an abuse of trust, and always wrong."

There are times when such relationships can scar the athlete forever. Linda Van Housen, a California runner now in her thirties, had a sexual relationship with her track club coach, Mike Ipsen, that lasted for more than a decade, beginning with a statutory rape when she was thirteen. Ipsen so dominated and manipulated her that she turned against her family and became his surrogate daughter, moving in with his family and engaging in fantasies of becoming his wife. It took her years to confront the reality of what had happened. As an adult, and after other victims came forward, she successfully sued her former coach and was awarded a settlement of $1.1 million (she collected only a small amount). Even after his actions were revealed, Ipsen continued to coach teenage girls.

·　·　·　·

Lucy Andrews planned to attend a major public university on Long Island, where her two brothers matriculated before her—and where she intended to join the swim team. "When I told my older brothers about it, they warned me off. They said the girls on the swim team didn't have the best reputation—they were . . . 'pretty rough.' So I never went out [to join the team]." Although Andrews never came right out and talked about it, the implication was clear. The "taint" of lesbianism still hangs over girls' athletics.

Temple University's Carole Oglesby says that in connection with female athletes, the subject of sexual orientation "always comes up, always." She tells a story of doing motivational consulting with a high school girls' team in Philadelphia. When Oglesby met the team members for the first time, she planned a simple get-to-know-you session, expecting "the most superficial conversation." Instead she was hit with a comment that impressed her anew with how deep is the problem of stereotyping the female athlete as gay. "My first question was, 'So what is it like being a woman athlete here at so-and-so high school?' The first words out of this woman's mouth were, 'Well, they call us dykes all the time.' I was just astounded. That was one of maybe ten negative things they said, but it was actually the first thing at the top of their list."

If your daughter enters sports, sooner or later she will encounter this virulent brand of homophobia. Throughout the history of women in sports, stereotypes have been manipulated to limit or negate female athletic achievement. The female athlete is labeled "unladylike," mannish, muscle-bound, "trying to be a man." In recent decades these characterizations have gathered themselves together under the umbrella of antigay sentiment to produce a whole host of homophobic stereotypes. Certain sports, even certain college programs and teams, are whispered to have a high number of gay women involved, and athletics in general are imagined by many to attract a higher percentage of lesbians than other fields of endeavor.

At the University of Texas in the early nineties (just after the swim team eating disorder scandal), there was a flurry of local newspaper reports about the reputation of the basketball team there. One player remembered hearing rumors during the recruitment process. "People were saying, 'They're all a bunch of dykes up there.' " A high school star said that many people "believe that [Texas] is a lesbian team." As if to contrast their programs with that of Texas, coaches at Baylor and Penn State came out publicly against lesbian athletes. Every high school player recruited by the Texas coach received an anonymous mailing of the newspaper account of the rumors of lesbianism attached to the team.

The way parents react to these stereotypes can mean the difference in whether their daughters enjoy sports, continue to play sports, and consider sports a positive part of their lives. The discrimination and stereotyping can crop up early, with remarks over a particular girl being a "tomboy." In one survey, 8 out of 10 female executives in Fortune 500 companies labeled themselves as tomboys growing up, so this might not be an insult after all, but a predictor of future success. Jody Conradt, the basketball coach at Texas during the time of the lesbianism rumors, addressed parents' fears by citing "diversity" as one of her goals in putting together a team. "When our society learns to embrace diversity," Conradt said, "we'll be a lot better society. I would hope that everybody who is a member of [the Texas team] is made to feel welcome." It is important to divorce the question of gay female athletes from wider moral debates and instead see the damaging stereotype of the "dyke jock" as simply one more weapon in the arsenal of those who would deny girls their rightful place on the playing field.

Such negative factors as injury, eating disorders, harassment and abuse by coaches, and homophobia are risks present in almost every organized physical activity. Some of these elements are specific to sports, and some exist in the world at large but take their own form within the athletic arena. It would be a mistake to think that because so many girls flourish in athletic programs, these programs are free of the dangers in society as a whole. Equally, it would be wrong to downplay the pitfalls to girls' development that are specific to sports.

In the euphoria surrounding women athletes in general, stories such as those of Linda Van Housen or Tiffany Cohen-Adams bring to bear a sobering dose of reality. Sports involvement can raise girls' self-esteem tremendously, but it can also hurt girls who are vulnerable—and it can do both at the same time. When asked what sports had done for her emotionally, Megan Nelson immediately launches into an enthusiastic list, her mother beaming beside her on the couch. ("I feel happy, like I have something to look forward to in life, and goals to accomplish.") When asked what playing sports had given her physically, she says simply, "It hurts."

Whatever the contradictions here, Nelson says she would "never quit sports"—even after being hobbled by them. She embodies the terrific passion and determination of many young female athletes. They may be fantastic competitors, but they're still kids. They want badly to participate and don't necessarily possess the life experience or judgment to avoid possible perils. As adults, our responsibility, once having invited our daughters onto the playing field, is to ensure that their experiences there are as safe and healthy as possible.

8

Going to Extremes

Your Daughter and Nontraditional Sports

"Football," chorused a group of eighth grade girls when asked which sports they liked to play the most. They were just starting out in Manhattan's Ivy League program, which every week hosts a mean game of all-girl flag football on an asphalt playground in Greenwich Village. Caitlin Extrom says much the same thing, "I love football," adding that she prefers coed teams. "I can be aggressive with the boys, and they won't get hurt as much if I knock them down." Kate Morrel, the young soccer standout from Indiana, played football with the boys at recess in grade school and dreamed of becoming an NFL quarterback. Sixth-grade baseballer Lucy Morgenstern brings her foam football to school every day for coed games at lunchtime. WNBA star and head coach Nancy Lieberman-Cline remembers playing football and baseball before she played basketball. "I *loved* football," reminisces Greenville Y mother Patsy Hunt. "I wasn't so crazy about what we called powder puff football, where you take the little flags out of the pocket—I liked contact football." Many athletes talked about playing in neighborhood pickup games of football—sometimes touch, sometimes tackle or "semitackle," as Extrom describes it. "I like football because you get to bounce the person out of the way," says thirteen-year-old Yuris, one of the Ivy League eighth graders.

The common perception still holds that women and girls don't play contact sports, especially football. The truth is more complicated. There are, for example, hundreds of women's flag football leagues all over the country, with an annual tournament in Key West attended each year by thousands of women who do indeed play football. Girls from varying backgrounds display a striking enthusiasm for, and calm ownership of, games from which females have been traditionally excluded. If there is a message going out that some sports are boys-only, many girls aren't getting it. Once the genie is out of the lamp, it's difficult to put it back in. Once we tell our daughters that they can do anything, we have to be prepared for them to take us up on it.

On October 18, 1997, twenty-year-old Liz Heaston became the first woman to play in a regulation NCAA college football game, when she successfully made two point-after kicks in Willamette University's 27–0 win over Linfield College (in 1995 and 1996, Joyce Mungari had played linebacker for the two-year Contra Costa Junior College). Heaston was a starter on the Salem, Oregon, university's championship soccer team. She was still in her soccer uniform, coming back from a match, when she was enlisted to go in for injured Willamette kicker Gordon Thomson. In a subsequent game she missed two extra points, Thomson got healthy, and Heaston rejoined her soccer teammates. But Heaston and Mungari won't be the last females in cleats and helmets.

In the 1996–97 season there were 753 girls on seventy high school football rosters all over the country. One of them was Megan Dougherty, a defensive tackle for the Hawthorne High School team in New Jersey. "I've always loved all the energy out there," she told a reporter. "When I signed up, I was told by some of the boys, 'Girl, you don't belong here.' " But after weeks of practice and several games, "someone from another team asked me if I was the halftime joke. By then I was accepted by my team and a bunch of guys ran him down the field."

In her book *Men Will Be Boys*, which explores how women relate to the culture of football, sportswriter Sally Jenkins tells the story of Jessica Henderson, daughter of NFL general counsel Harold Henderson. Although her father had to do a little arm-twisting to get her into the local Pop Warner league, Jessica turned out to be a star running back, scoring a touchdown on a 65-yard punt return the first time she touched the ball and leading her team in rushing touchdowns and tackles. Her team members voted her captain. Although Jessica Henderson later quit football for soccer, her sister Kim went on to a game perhaps even rougher than football, playing scrum half for the Princeton women's rugby team. "You'd be in the mud, tackling," Jenkins quotes Kim Henderson about her rugby career, "and four hours later in an evening gown with your hair upswept. And you'd think, 'Man, I can do anything.' "

Back in the late eighties and early nineties, when girls first broke into high school football, the first wave typically had a rough time of it. Beth Galsley played nose guard and wide receiver for her Annandale, New Jersey, high school team. "I got constant abuse, even death threats," Galsley told reporters, "but I kept at it because I knew I was right." Equally troubling is the celebrated and more recent case of Heather Sue Mercer, who by rights should have beaten Easton onto the field as the first woman to play college football. A placekicker whose skills helped her high school team win a state football championship, Mercer enrolled at Duke University in 1994. She was first told she was on the team and kicked a 28-yard winning field goal in the annual intrasquad game. But throughout her years at Duke she was never allowed to suit up for games, sit on the bench, or practice with the full team. Even though the athletic department asked that she do interviews as the first female on a Division I team, Coach Fred Goldsmith told her to sit in the stands with her boyfriend during games. When Mercer called her coach to ask why she had not been invited to begin practice with the other players, Goldsmith responded by asking why she was interested in football and not beauty pageants. Finally, he told her there was no place for her on the team. Mercer brought a Title IX suit against the university, filing a separate civil claim for fraud, negligent misrepresentation, and breach of contract. "Placekicking is not about the size of your leg or whether you're male or female or you weigh 200 pounds," Mercer told an interviewer. "It's whether you can get the ball through the uprights with accuracy and consistency. Girls can do that."

Women have also stepped inside another heretofore male-only preserve—the boxing ring. Women have always boxed, in some cultures more than others. Captain Cook professed shock when, during his voyages in the South Seas, he saw women boxing. In the American West, fights between females were often staged for their voyeuristic value, as in the topless woman brawlers of the 1800s. In 1993, however, a Washington state boxer named Dallas Malloy successfully sued the U.S. Amateur Boxing Federation for the right to compete in title fights. Malloy was sixteen years old when she began her suit. "Dallas pioneered the movement, but in the last two or three years it's really taken off,'' says Shilpa Baker of the USABF. "It's a great way to exercise, and for women particularly, a great form of self-defense." Women's boxing is still unrecognized by the International Olympic Committee.

Millions of viewers watched the pay-per-view fight of Christy Martin, a.k.a. the Coal Miner's Daughter, versus Deirdre Gogarty, as the undercard of the Mike Tyson–Frank Bruno WBC heavyweight fight on March 16, 1996, in Las Vegas. Martin, who grew up athletic, as a catcher in Little League and a college basketball forward, won a unanimous six-round decision. She commands $100,000 per fight, making her easily the highest paid female boxer. Tom Humphries wrote about the Martin-Gogarty fight in the *Irish Times:* "It took five, maybe 10 seconds for the beery, testosterone-charged crowd in the MGM Garden to realize they weren't watching a novelty act. . . . The mixture of ferocity and serious boxing skills left the most chauvinistic ticket holders gape-mouthed." But not silent. Columnist Bill Gallo expressed an opinion typical of many sports writers: "Women are too precious and tender a commodity to have their faces butchered and bashed as they make utter fools of themselves."

Girls who play contact sports often wind up playing with or against their male peers. Some do it by design, to challenge boys-only rules. Most do so either because there are no programs for girls in their chosen sports or because they are simply seeking the most rigorous level of competition. It would be wrong to underestimate the risks of matching girls against boys, who by high school are generally heavier, taller, and stronger. The result can be a parent's nightmare—a crowd of 200-pound bodies bearing down, all aiming to crush their daughter. In 1994, claiming that she had not been adequately warned of the possibility of injury, the first girl to play high school football in Carroll County, Maryland, filed suit after she lost her spleen and half her pancreas as the result of an injury incurred during her team's initial practice scrimmage. The court ruled against her, stating that her injury was the result of a "voluntary encounter with a known danger."

Punishing "combat sports" such as football, rugby, and boxing lie at the margins of the world of women's athletics. George Orwell labelled such activities "war minus the shooting." They might give pause to many parents who otherwise advocate equal access to all sports programs. Christy Martin herself has said that she wouldn't want her own daughter to enter boxing. But we seem to have raised a generation of fearless daughters. They do what they want to do, setting their own goals and agendas, not waiting for the encouragement of parents or other adults. *They* are leading *us*. If we can't understand their choice of sports, we should appreciate the huge amount of determination it takes for them to proceed against all tradition and expectation. Simply because they want to play a game—"equal opportunity fun" is how one girl put it—our athletic daughters are creating a more open, more equitable future.

"Most kids move out of their house because they hate their parents," says nineteen-year-old snowboarding pro Kyla Duffy. "I moved out of my house when I was sixteen because I wanted to go snowboarding. And my parents have always been supportive of everything I've done."

Duffy has been touring behind the sponsorship of snowboard equipment companies and winter apparel firms since she started in the sport at age thirteen. She has supported herself doing it ("It's the best job in the world," she says), dropped out of high school to do it (she took a University of Nebraska correspondence course for the last two years of high school and graduated with a high enough GPA to allow her to "go to any college I want"), and says she will continue touring and competing "until it starts hurting really, really bad." That time might not be far in the future. Duffy has broken "a lot of bones, all of them, lots of fingers and toes, ankles—got the knee surgery—elbow, wrist, bones in my hands." At nineteen, she already feels pain in her knees when she walks down stairs. Asked if she was ever tempted to quit, she responds, "Every day!" Each morning as she's stretching out the kinks, Duffy says, she asks herself if she really wants to continue snowboarding. "But then my head gets a little clearer and I go, 'Of course I want to do this! I don't want to get a job!' " Is it the soreness that makes her want to quit? "That," she says dryly, "and the possibility that I could fatally hurt myself."

Kyla Duffy uses words like "rad," "stoked," and "burly" a lot. There is an orange tint to her hair and she paints her fingernails blue. She jokes repeatedly about not wanting ever to work at a nine-to-five job. She has taken her place in an alternative culture that adopts a deceptively casual stance toward ambition and endeavor. In conversation, Duffy customarily undercuts her devotion to the sport ("I really hate the snow") touts her "laziness," and makes light of her determination ("I come home and sit in front of my TV"). But season after season she endures injuries that could bench a football fullback and shows up faithfully on contest days in freezing weather at 6 A.M.

Snowboarding was among the first of what have come to be called "X sports," or extreme sports. It is a rather ragtag realm, intentionally loosely defined and ever morphing. X sports receive most of their exposure from biannual coverage of "X-Games" on the ESPN cable network. The label plays nicely off "Generation X," and the letter "X" itself has become something of a generational brand name. The assortment of X sports ranges from relatively familiar activities such as skateboarding to improvised competitions such as shovel racing, injury-defying variations such as snow biking, and unlikely combination sports such as mountaineering/paragliding. All the X sports share a defiance of mainstream athletic conventions and an air of studied vagabond cool. As well as a need for speed.

"We belong to the adrenaline generation," twenty-eight-year-old defending champion snowboarder Todd Richards told the *New York Times* at the 1998 Winter X Games. "When I grew up on the East Coast, you were either someone who played sports or you were one of the nerds who didn't. But I just never fit into either group, so I went out and found something new." At the 1998 Winter Olympics in Nagano, snowboarders openly chafed against what they perceived as the overly restrictive atmosphere of the games. They complained about having to wear national team uniforms, about performing under the aegis of the World Ski Federation. Some of the top world-class boarders sat out of the games to protest the mainstreaming of the sport. Finally, Canadian snowboarder Ross Rebagliati had his gold medal briefly taken away and then given back, in a controversy over testing positive for marijuana (he had only slightly elevated levels of blood indicators and claimed it was the result of breathing second-hand smoke at going-away parties for the Olympics).

Behind in-line skating, snowboarding is the fastest growing sport in the country, and half the new boards are being sold to women. Snowboarding appears to be subverting a few of the traditional expectations about female athletes. Kyla Duffy and other riders still report sexism on the slopes—the safest routes down a hill, for example, are designated "chick lines." Kyla says, "Some guys look at you and go, 'Eew, what a weird girl. She's burly. Yuck, I wouldn't want to go out with her.' And then there are other guys: 'Yeah, girls doin' it! It's the raddest thing in the world!' " The borders between the sexes are less strictly patrolled among Gen-Xers—Nirvana icon Kurt Cobain used to go onstage in a dress, for example, and polls show an increasing acceptance of gay rights among the young.

Simply by virtue of their age, Duffy and her friends are more likely to "trash gender," as the T-shirt says. They generally decline the feminist label ("I don't consider myself a feminist by any means," says Duffy), but they also refuse to be stopped by gender restrictions. Snowboarder superstar Tina Basich recalls male attitudes in the early days of the sport. "They said, 'No girls allowed,' and we were like, 'Oh, we're for sure doing it now.' " All the "board sports" are heavily identified with the under-thirty generation, and female participation is growing in all of them. An estimated 1 million of the 4.7 million snowboards in this country are female. Surfing is seeing similar numbers— 250,000 women out of 1.75 million surfers nationwide—with the sales of women's products rising by 10 to 15 percent each year.

Duffy says she encounters more of the boys-only mentality in skateboarding, less in snowboarding. "But there is the factor that no matter how much they push themselves, the girls will never be as good as the guys—not at all," she says. "And this is coming from a girl." Boys and girls who snowboard share an outsider status, and there's a sense they love tweaking the noses of the middle class. "Society looks at you and says, 'Why aren't you in your ballet class? What are you doing? Why do you want to walk around and get bruises all over your legs?' And you know why we do it? 'Cause we love it!"

Kyla Duffy grew up in Absecon, New Jersey, far from snow country, on the Jersey shore. Her father owns a civil engineering firm. Her mother was at one time a professional figure skater, but quit to raise a family. Duffy recalls vividly how, as a toddler, she quite literally followed in her mother's footsteps. "I started out sitting on my mom's foot and getting ice-skated around the rink," Kyla says. "I could barely walk then, but my Mom was teaching ice skating at the time." Her mother is still athletic and, says Kyla, even more adventurous than her daughter—she recently took up skydiving at age fifty. Before she was a snowboarder, Duffy competed as a gymnast and also did ballet, tap dancing, tennis, swimming, and horseback riding when she was young. "You name the sport, I've done it," she says.

Her parents, says Kyla, have supported her in every one of her pursuits except one. "All my life my parents told me that I'm not an artist. 'Kyla, you can't draw.' And I know I can't, I'm terrible. But if they hadn't ever said anything like that, I would never have known I couldn't. I think that applies to a lot of things. If parents tell their kids that they can't do it, then that's going to be stuck in their heads for life, and they're not going to try it, and if they do try it they're going to fail. So it's important to always tell your kids 'You can.' "

Her first sponsor "discovered" her at age thirteen, while she was experimenting with snowboard acrobatics on a trampoline. "I think I had blue hair then," Kyla recalls. Six years later, she is one of the few female snowboarding professionals. In the last year, there's been a shakeout in the ranks, as sponsors thin the number of girls they are underwriting in order to concentrate on just a few names, but Duffy is more zealous than many about pursuing sponsors, collecting cool gear manufacturers like charms on a bracelet. Her career has taken Kyla Duffy all over the world. She has just returned, for example, from a photo shoot in New Zealand via an all-girls skateboarding "jam" in San Diego.

When she manages a break from the road, she lives in Vermont, where her "college boy" boyfriend Pat publishes a snowboard zine called *Journeyman, Son of E.I.*, from "another snowboarding magazine called *East Infection*." Pat and Kyla like to tour amusement parks together and, as she says, "do roller coasters." They've been known to drive across the country in pursuit of a good ride (Duffy is terrified of air travel, especially—"just a stupid prejudice from hearing old men talk"—on planes with female pilots). Golf is another pastime, her "summer sport," she says. "I have a lot of free time. In the winter I'm very, very busy, but in summer I can do what I want, pretty much." She is a devotee of self-help books, which her father sends her in quantity, and starts her day on competition mornings by repeating "I'm the greatest" in front of her mirror ten times. "It really works," Kyla says. She knows her career has a natural shelf life, and after that her goals are apple-pie ordinary. "I'd be happy just sitting at home cooking, cleaning, and watching the kids," she says. "Whoever thought of liberation was an imbecile."

At the same time, when asked how girls are different today than they were in her mother's generation, she replies, "I think they're more dangerous." Though like many female snowboarders (and like many female athletes in general), she admits to differences in the current skill levels of male and female riders, the gap is narrowing. "Women train harder than the men," she says. "There are girls now that are doing flips and 720° spins." She says the skate jam in San Diego, the first ever only for girls, was amazing. "Everybody was so happy, and everybody felt the same way: 'This is great, we're doin' it for the girls.' "

The Lost Girls have stormed Neverland, where, after all, girls can fly as well as boys. The Peter Pan quality of the snowboarder's life does not escape Kyla Duffy. "I think about it sometimes," she says. "I tell myself, 'I want to live a normal life. I want to go to college.' Then I think, 'What am I saying? I want to go to Japan!' "

· · · ·

Krista Ford is the strongest woman in the world. "Strong," measured by how much weight a person can squat, bench-press, and deadlift. "Strong," as in how fast she can push a 400-pound bobsled over a 30-meter track. Ford won the World Power Lifting Championship in 1996 and 1997, and she is currently number one "brake"—the hindmost position, the strong woman's spot—on the U.S.A. Women's Bobsled Team. Both bobsledding and power lifting rank as nontraditional sports for women, and Ford is the first black woman bobsledder in U.S. history, only the second black woman ever in the sport. Women had been banished from Olympic bobsledding in 1940, reassembling into a national team only in 1992.

The American public may know more about the sport since the popularity of the mid-1980s movie about the unlikely story of the Jamaican national bobsled team, *Cool Runnings*. There are two kinds of bobsledding, with two- and four-person sleds. Both types are conducted at breakneck, 80-mile-an-hour-plus speeds. The course consists of little more than a steep, speed-slick gutter of ice. Bobsled races are often won or lost on the initial push, the first five seconds when the brake and the driver struggle to get the ponderous, overgrown children's sled going. This is where Ford excels, on the push, where she began breaking world records the first time she attempted it.

It is only by fluke that Ford is a bobsledder, only as a consequence of her activities in another sport where women are not heavily represented, power lifting. She got into lifting by way of bodybuilding, and the two disciplines are often confused. Bodybuilding is all about sculpting muscles for definition and bulk. Ford competed in bodybuilding contests from 1985 to 1989, when she came to realize that she hungered for a sport that was less subjective, less political, less contingent on the whim of a judge. Power lifting is clear-cut, "either you can lift the weight or you can't,'' as Ford says. She began lifting in 1990, and it quickly took over her life.

What does it take for a woman to achieve in these areas, disciplines where a female's presence is still startling, even decades after the women's bodybuilding competitions first gained popularity? In Krista Ford's case, at least, it took a great deal of pain. Not just pain in the sense of strenuous exertion during workouts, but emotional deprivation and deep-felt insecurities in childhood. Ford's experience suggests that a severe assault on the emotions—such as a psychological trauma in childhood—can trigger an equally extreme response as an attempt at compensation. It is as if Krista Ford was saying, I was frightened by my vulnerability during childhood, therefore I will respond by becoming the strongest woman in the world.

Ford was raised "poor as my little butt could be" on the east side, the "black side," of Indianapolis, which in those days, the late seventies, was still largely a racially segregated town. From a very early age, she felt somehow different from the other members of her family in ways she couldn't express, even to herself. Her older sister, Stacey, was a "brain, her nose always in a book," while Krista was an active child and a "tomboy," always running outside, always playing with the neighborhood kids. Her parents were nonathletic and "very boring." One day when Krista was five, she found herself alone with her mother in her grandmother's warm, spare kitchen down the street from their house. She summoned her courage and tried to penetrate the mist that had hung over her early years. "Mommy," said Krista, "I've got to ask you a question. Why is my nose different from yours? Why am I so light-skinned? Why are you all darker than I am?" Her mother was silent for a moment, then told her. "This is the reason. You're adopted. What that means is that your mother, who looks like you, is not with you. So we took you." Another silence.

Krista said nothing more, but rose to her feet and left the room. Today she claims the moment was not upsetting so much as "confusing," saying that her mother answered her question. But the reply was not really a satisfactory answer. What she did not and perhaps could not give, and what was probably the thing the five-year-old Krista most needed to hear, was why her birth parents had given her up for adoption and why her adoptive parents had taken her in. "I didn't know what to think," she says. "But I knew she had answered what I had asked her and that now I had to figure some things out. I didn't ask her any more questions. I understood, but I didn't understand why." This uncertainty troubled Krista for years, through the primary grades and up through high school. "There's always a question in an adopted person's mind: Who am I? So I'm constantly on this quest in life, trying to figure out who I am."

Sports became her answer. "It's been my mother, my father, my sister, my brother," Ford says. "It's been my family, my sports have." Throughout her life, whenever she faced a situation that was stressful or alien to her, Krista found refuge in the gym or on the field. She began challenging herself in successive sports, first track and field in high school, progressing later to bodybuilding and power lifting. She had "billions of questions": Who had named her? Why was she given up? Why did she have the temperament that she did? Why did she think the way she did? Where did her athletic talent come from? Her adoptive parents couldn't answer her. Sports were, she says, "my way of finding out who Krista really is."

Ford sensed—it ultimately didn't matter if it was real or not—that her mother favored Stacey, her natural child, in subtle but hurtful ways. The household became more and more strained during Krista's last years of high school as mother and adopted daughter had become increasingly uncomfortable with

each other, and the day after her graduation, her mother uncere-
moniously asked her to leave their home. Ford moved in with a
cousin in California, started a bodybuilding regime, and embarked on a four-year quest through the adoption bureaucracy,
finally finding the mother who had given her up for adoption
living in Franklin, Massachusetts. The reunion, Ford remembers,
"was picture-perfect. You couldn't have made it better. You know
when they have those meetings on *Sally Jesse Raphael* or *Oprah,*
people are in the airport with the camera, the whole deal? That's
what happened. I was on cloud sixty, because I finally got to see
this woman that I had been thinking about, crying about, going
through all these changes all my life."

At that first moment of meeting in Logan Airport in Boston,
all the uncertainty that Krista had felt since she was five years old,
symbolized in her early questions about her appearance, melted
away. The stranger who put her arms around Krista had her very
same chin, her nose, her smile. Her mother was white, of Italian
descent; Krista's father, her mother told her, is African American. For a week, mother and daughter bonded. They shared con-
fidences. Then, in a cruel replay of her original abandonment,
Ford's birth mother abruptly withdrew. She handed her daughter a nine-page single-spaced letter "that's like a chapter in a
book," Ford says. She told Ford she wanted to have nothing
more to do with her. "She went so far as to say that I needed to
stop fantasizing about this so-called mother that I had."

Successive blows, successive shocks: her confusion over her
adopted status; her adoptive mother casting her out; trying to
make sense of her biracial identity; the embrace of her birth
mother changing suddenly into yet another rejection. Ford
makes the connection herself, between the shattered state of her
ego during this period and the fact that, only months after her
trip to Boston, she won her first power lifting trophy. "I met my

mother in May of 1989," she says. "I won my first power lifting contest in July of the same year. I thought I would never experience rejection in my life as bad as that. Lifting weights was my outlet before I ever met my mother, because I felt alone. My sports have always been my refuge, and my salvation."

Extreme pain sometimes requires extreme measures in response. Perhaps some other child might sail through similar experiences without permanent emotional scars, but speaking with Krista Ford, one feels the impact of all the hurt and betrayal she has withstood. By definition, extreme sports, nontraditional sports, offer participants a more extreme experience. For someone who feels the way Krista Ford does, an extreme experience may be the only kind that will suffice.

The laughter and shrieks of young girls having a good time echo down the stairwell from the third-floor gymnasium of the Father English Community Center in Paterson, New Jersey. There are sixteen girls present, ages eight to twelve, all from the impoverished core-city precincts of this decaying factory city. The gym has sheets of plywood nailed over the windows. "It's being redone," explains Pablo Rivera, the after-school director at Father English. He stands beside a pair of mats in the center of the room, where coach Chris Cuffari demonstrates a wrestling takedown on a slender, dark-haired woman who wears shorts and a T-shirt that reads, "Wild Women Make a Difference: There Is No Excuse for Domestic Violence." Cuffari is a solidly built former All-American from Trenton State who heads the wrestling program at the New Jersey Athletic Club. As the girls watch, he hits the young woman just above the knees, pushing her backward and then down. She slams to the mat, and the girls laugh and scream. "You have to drive, drive, drive," Cuffari tells the group.

The woman gets back on her feet and retrieves her glasses

from Rivera. She is Nancy Fingerhood, a twenty-seven-year-old graduate student from nearby Fairleigh Dickinson University, founder of the program that brought Cuffari and the novice wrestlers together. GAINS (Girls Achieving in Nontraditional Sports) seeks to introduce girls not only to wrestling but to football, baseball (hardball), roller hockey, and karate. "I picked the sports that involve physical aggressiveness, contact," Fingerhood explains. "People have this stereotype of what girls want to do and what they should do. People just don't think that girls want to have physical contact or they're good at it. People underestimate how much girls want to feel strong, or women want to feel strong. I guess they just think we want to feel pretty or something."

The girls gathered on the mat are pretty, but they're also dangerous, or learning to be, in a way that Kyla Duffy would appreciate. "You keep reaching in like an eighty-year-old man," Cuffari calls to the group. "I want you to bend your knees!" All sixteen girls assume the closest approximation to a wrestling crouch they can manage, lunging forard at the end of a crab walk across the mat. "Here, wait," Cuffari says. "Nancy!" Fingerhood gives her glasses back to Rivera and steps out once more to be Cuffari's guinea pig. Crouch, lunge, slam! She goes down laughing. "All right, we're going to partner up!" Cuffari says. The girls grab for their best friends, which leads to some unlikely match-ups—a husky five-footer opposed by a slight 55-incher.

This is the first of six wrestling clinics that Cuffari will coach as part of the GAINS program. He owns a private wrestling academy in Fairfield, New Jersey, where he teaches kids age seven through college, and he regularly takes wrestlers to Russia for competitions. he is not new to coaching girls—Vicky Zuma, the national girls champion, trained with him. Fingerhood pays him only a nominal fee for his services. Cuffari represents the high caliber of coaching she seeks for her program. The fact that the girls are learning from a real wrestling coach upstairs does not go unnoticed by the kids in the after-school program downstairs. "Some of the boys get jealous because the program isn't for them," Fingerhood says. "I tell them, 'Well, you can play football at your school' or 'You have other ways to do it.' " The previous year, when Fingerhood had East Side High varsity coach Donald Davis oversee a five-week football clinic, the Father English boys could only look on in envy. "I heard one of the boys say, 'I want to be a girl so I can play football.' Imagine hearing that!" The girls "feel that they're getting something the boys aren't getting, and that makes them feel good about themselves."

Fingerhood was inspired to start GAINS after returning from a Worldteach job in Thailand and reading authors such as Mary Pipher and Naomi Wolfe on girls and self-esteem. The books sparked a memory of growing up. "I remembered how I got these subtle messages that I shouldn't be doing certain things, and although I was a feminist from when I was seventeen, I still had this kind of helpless feeling, like guys can put things together, they can fix things. I would let guys carry my luggage. I know it sounds trivial, but I wanted to be able to do more things for myself." The idea of girls in contact sports, she says, "breaks a lot of barriers. It's almost like a revolution." Fingerhood appreciates the huge numbers of girls pouring into soccer and softball programs across the country. "But I think we need to move even further than that and break some more ground. The sports I'm choosing are very aggressive, physical sports, and girls have always been told not to do things like that. Sports like that make you into an assertive person who feels competent with your body and what you're capable of."

Fingerhood grew up in Fairlawn, New Jersey, swimming, roller skating—doing the "typical kid things." She was never on a team, thinking herself "too incompetent to play sports." Her parents, she says, didn't really encourage athletic participation, for either herself or her older sister. Her first real sports experience came after college, when she started playing pickup games of roller hockey with a boyfriend and his friends. "I started noticing on TV that there wasn't much sports coverage for women," Fingerhood says, "and for some reason it just started annoying me. I thought, Well, what do women do when they want to play something like hockey and there's no women around to play with? You have to play with the guys. Which is fine, but sometimes the guys don't respect you right away, or in some sports unless you outskill them incredibly, it's really hard to play with the size difference." When in June 1996 she offered a hockey clinic at the Boys and Girls Club in Clifton, New Jersey, and forty-seven girls turned out, she knew she was onto something. She put together a proposal and began casting around for financing and a home for what was to become the GAINS program.

No one bit. Company after company, foundation after foundation turned her down. She found herself in a catch-22 situation—she couldn't get funding without a venue, and couldn't get a venue without funding. She went to the Board of Education in Paterson, to YMCAs in the area, to national organizations. At one program, the director at first said she was interested and then called a few days later to back out. "I asked her why, and she said, 'I don't want to give these girls hope. I don't want to raise their expectations that they'll ever be able to actually play these sports.' I said, 'Well, I used to play piano, but I never really expected to be playing Carnegie Hall. Can't they just do it for fun?' " She spent months trying to find someone to support the program, and many times considered giving up. "I said to myself, 'Why don't I just quit this whole crusade and do something for myself, because nobody else seems to care.' But as soon as I would say that to myself, 'no one else seems to care,' I'd go, 'that's right—so I have to.' "

While wrestling in an all-girls after-school program is one thing, coed matches at the high school level have generated storms of controversy. Can girls survive boys' supposedly superior strength? Is it seemly or wise to allow girls to get pinned by boys—or vice versa? Consider the story of Abielle Schwartzberg, a college student who started wrestling in high school. She chose to go to California State University at Bakersfield precisely because of its established varsity-level wrestling program for girls. She had been recruited to play college softball, but Schwartzberg chose the mat over the diamond. "This is on the rise so quickly," she told a reporter. "We're pioneers of the sport. I don't think many other women can say that." Female wrestling is in fact popular in other countries, particularly Canada, France, Russia, Japan, and Sweden. Proponents hope to have it on the Olympic slate by the year 2000. But in America, in the late 1990s, girls' wrestling upsets long-standing cultural norms.

Abielle Schwartzberg reports that she first encountered what she labels "totally absurd" fears about male-female contact on the mat while wrestling in high school. A competitor, she feels, is "just another body." The sport of wrestling "is not late night with the lights dimmed. You're banging heads." But the trepidation of adults raised in a different era persists, along with the notion that girls on a varsity wrestling team are stealing spots that rightfully belong to boys. At the college level, the strength and skill levels of men and women are too far apart for them to compete fairly, so Schwartzberg mostly wrestles her female teammates in exhibition matches. Watching Schwartzberg wrestle conveys some of the pure power of which girls in sports are capable, in the sense of both physical power and the strength of an image to destroy previously conceived notions. At one point, as

Schwartzberg and teammate Seba Clemente square off in an exhibition match, Schwartzberg is straining to avoid a pin, her left
arm braced against the mat, every muscle arched. In freeze-
frame, Schwartzberg seems the physical embodiment of an ideal
that is as ancient as Atalanta, the Greek demigoddess raised by a
bear.

The story of how Schwartzberg got to wrestle at Bakersfield
offers a window into the entry of girls into sports that have traditionally been for boys only. Her coach, T. J. Kerr, who is also
president of the National Association of Wrestling Coaches, felt
his all-male program was under pressure from Title IX restrictions. He knew he had until 1998 to satisfy a court-enforced
agreement with the National Organization for Women which
specified that in all colleges of the California state university system, enrollment in and spending on men's and women's sports
programs must mirror the gender ratio of the student body as a
whole. Kerr didn't want to see his Division I program cut. He
decided to actively recruit women. College administrators nixed
the idea, so Kerr performed a breakout maneuver. He formed a
coed off-campus wrestling club and recruited interested girls
through the physical education classes he taught. Eventually,
pressure from female wrestlers forced the administration at Bakersfield to open the varsity team to women.

The experiment did not run smoothly. Five of the ten men
who lost varsity slots to women filed grievances against the university, claiming reverse discrimination. But for Abielle Schwartzberg and the six other female team members, it has been a success: "Not only do you get in great shape," said Schwartzberg
about wrestling, "it's great for your self-esteem—and for self-
defense."

Across the country, in December 1996, the Texas Wrestling
Officials Association voted to disband rather than officiate at

mixed-gender matches. "Hell will freeze over before I officiate girls being brutalized by guys," vowed John Rizutti, president of the association. "What in heaven's name are parents teaching these girls where they want to jump in the ring with brutes?" Rizutti claimed that if the officials had to referee coed matches, they would be legally liable if the girl was hurt—or if she were to misconstrue an official's action in a rough-and-tumble match. "Many times we have to grab wrestlers when they fall off the mat or get too physical," Rizutti said. "We have no protection against some sexual harassment charges if some girl is offended by the way we touch her." Two of the Texas wrestlers, Melony Monahan and Courtney Barnett, along with their mothers, filed a discrimination suit against the association. "It's just a good ol' boys club," said Texas wrestler Ashley King, seventeen, a second-degree karate brown belt who wants to become a Marine Corps officer. "They just don't want to be told what to do. Texas is stuck in the twenties, anyway."

Parents, young athletes, and coaches across the country are increasingly encountering issues that arise when girls try to break into sports formerly played by boys only. As in other contact sports, the numbers are still small: only about a thousand girls wrestle at the high school level. Most of them compete on boys' teams, since there are too few to make up girls' teams. No matter how far we've come in terms of the equity of the sexes, a girl competing with a boy is still a jarring image for many people—especially if she wins. It's inevitable, as girls become more practiced, that they will beat boys. Recently, for example, twelve-year-old Teresa Gordon-Dick won the national Greco-Roman championship in the 100-pound weight class, the first female to take the gold in a coed final. "What you have to understand is that many of the boys Teresa wrestled against were undefeated," says her father, Edward Dick. "And one of the most interesting things to watch was these boys react, because for them to lose to her was obviously very difficult.''

This brings up the thorny question of whether participation in mixed-gender contact sports is healthy for the boys involved. ''I worried that if I won, I would be accused of beating up a girl,'' wrote Mark Oppenheimer in a *New York Times* op ed piece about his experience as a freshman wrestler at a Connecticut prep school. ''If I lost, I would be mocked until the day of graduation.'' Parents fear that if they let their son enter competition in which he is beat by a girl, it will harm him for life. They ignore the possibility of another kind of lesson: that girls are equal players in sports as in other domains.

We are almost certainly going to debate these questions for some time, because they touch on deeply felt ideas about ''proper'' behavior for the sexes. Although professional ballplayers become parents with the usual regularity, a great deal was made in the press of WNBA sensation Sheryl Swoopes's first baby. It's as if people needed the image of her as a nurturer, a mother, to neutralize her aggressiveness on the court. It remains threatening to encounter natural aggression in a female—of any age. Listen to eleven-year-old ice hockey player Lily Strauss Matathia on why she likes her sport: ''I can take out all my anger on people, smash 'em into the boards and stuff. Believe me, I'm going to start smashing when we play.''

But shouldn't our culture de-emphasize violence for all children? Shouldn't we downplay ''smashing'' (or—choose your sport—checking, blocking, administering clean hits, right or left jabs, and so on) in favor of cooperation and team spirit? Or are there lessons in contact sports and rigorous competition (even if it is violent) that girls can learn nowhere else in our society? And are these lessons critical to success in other previously male-dominated venues: the military, the street, the corridors of political power?

It heralds a brave new world when the USA Women's Ice Hockey Team receives such favorable exposure at the Nagano Olympics. This is not just a measure of the progress of women into every field of endeavor, although that is welcome, of course. But the entry of women into an activity such as hockey, with its high component of roughness, its odd combination of grace and violence, teaches us that women are capable of things simply not held possible a generation or even a decade ago. At the Amos Tuck School of Business at Dartmouth, one of the top three graduate schools for business in the nation, half of the female graduate students play on the Mighty Tucks, a recreational hockey team. According to one MBA player, the games "combine teamwork with competitiveness"—vital lessons for these future corporate stars. Can more women on the ice translate into more women in the boardroom? Can sports become a vehicle for social change?

Behind these questions is a larger issue that is a subject of hot debate within the women's sports community. Will the male-dominated sports world influence the female participants in it, contaminating them, as it were, with a culture of violence, domination, and aggression? The FBI has established, for example, that football players are involved in sexual assault cases at a higher rate than the general populace. From 1995 to 1997, there were an average of 100 formal criminal complaints per year of physical or sexual assault on women by professional and college athletes. Bill Redmond, the father of a female athlete raped by a football player at the University of Nebraska, formed the National Coalition Against Violent Athletes to combat this trend. Do female athletes really want to enter what is essentially a club that discriminates against them? Or can the spirit of competitiveness found in sports somehow benefit women and girls?

Put more simply, will sports change girls or will girls change sports? There are some ominous signs. Steroid use is rising among female athletes, starting at a younger age, with as many as 175,000 high school girls taking the illicit performance-enhancing drugs. As the amount of scholarship money available to female athletes increases, the economic stakes are raised. Abuses such as steroid use, competitive stress, overuse injuries, and overtraining, common in the world of male sports, are already crossing over to the world of female athletes. But most experts believe that for the majority of girls involved in athletics, the positive overwhelmingly outweighs the negative. "Playing sports teaches boys what they *must* be; it teaches girls what they *can* be," says Don McPherson, a former college All-American and pro football player who is national director of a program called Mentors and Violence Prevention at the Center for the Study of Sport in Society at Northeastern University. The weight of expectations we place on our sons can be stressful and deleterious, in other words, while the challenges we put to our daughters can bring out the best in them. This presents a precise flip of the traditional view of sports as right for boys and wrong for girls.

Nancy Fingerhood would agree. She sees mental health benefits for girls in sports that require some physical bulk, decrying the body image problems that sometimes afflict girls in "sports where it's good to be small," like figure skating or gymnastics. Instead, she points out, "with certain sports, like rugby or hockey, bigger is better." Fingerhood wants to create a new physical ideal for adolescent girls, a different vision of a "good body." "Girls' bodies are often seen as attractive or sexy, but what about useful? Men are always using their bodies. They're productive. I want girls to know that their bodies can be useful as well."

To people who claim the number of girls desiring the rougher sports is too small to warrant moving ahead, she says, "If you get the girls early enough playing these sports, then they'll think it's normal and natural, and then you can have girls' teams, because you'll have a big enough base. A lot of girls are doing it on their own, despite what everybody else is doing." She agrees that it might be a long time before that happens. She says the girls she works with probably don't understand the long-term benefits of having fun wrestling or playing football. She recalls when one of the girls came up to her and asked her, "Why do you do this for us?" She answered, "I want you to know that you can do anything the boys can do. I don't want you ever to think that there's something that you can't do out there." The girls of GAINS, she hopes, will remember wrestling and playing hockey and football as they get older. "If they feel like somebody's trying to limit them, maybe they can think back to this experience and say, 'Hey—I got to play on a football team when I was ten years old. Nothing's impossible.' "

Fingerhood wants to take GAINS national. She envisions chapters all over the country. Her "big dream" is a female-only Olympics, "competitive, not political," she emphasizes, where athletes would face off in games like rugby and football, raising money for charity. (Her dream is not that far-fetched. In spring 1999, the Women's Sports Foundation will inaugurate the Women's Global Challenge, an international gathering with top amateur and pro athletes competing in eight sports.) "I'm just this average, ordinary person who did this. I think if other women who care about girls can do something like this, start a program like this in their town, imagine if that happened

throughout this whole country. It would really make a difference."

Over the past few years, the sight of young female athletes playing soccer, softball, and basketball has become so widespread as
to be familiar. If we imagine the sports landscape as a concentric
target, then competitive team sports have now joined such
stalwarts as gymnastics and tennis in the bull's-eye. Many parents
now feel comfortable encouraging their daughters to participate
in these sports, but they become increasingly uneasy as we head
to the outermost borders of the athletic world, into realms previously closed to women.

But there are good reasons why our daughters are attracted
to games like football, rugby, and hockey, to activities such as
snowboarding, windsailing, in-line skating. For one thing, the
nonconforming, rebellious part of their natures at this age makes
them want to test limits and renders the odd and extreme more
attractive. Kate Greathead's mother directed her daughter
toward tennis, which she thought had merits as a "social" sport.
Her daughter, meanwhile, was more attracted to the "loneliness
of the long-distance runner." We can't always predict, and we
can't always control the choices our daughters make, in sports as
in other realms.

To limit girls' choices is to limit the lessons they'll take away
from their experiences. Lynn Hill is one of the world's top rock
climbers, the first person to free-climb the nose of El Capitan in
Yosemite in one day. "Climbing," she says, "can teach females
things about themselves that aren't generally stressed by society—such as perseverance, problem solving, and self-confidence.
Climbing is a matter of capitalizing on one's own particular
strengths and realizing that there is usually a solution for anything, however insurmountable it may seem at the moment."

The sports landscape is changing rapidly. There are now more snowboards sold every year, for example, than conventional Alpine skis, a circumstance no one could have imagined ten or even five years ago—and more than half the boards are sold to women and girls. Parents who think they are staying current by encouraging their daughter to play in the local soccer league might be surprised to hear she wants to take up paragliding. Many new and nontraditional sports involve elements of risk and thus are attractive to eager fledglings ready to test their wings. With the proper caveats over safety, however, the explosion of possibilities in the world of athletics can only be good for our daughters. More sports means a better chance a particular girl will find her "fit" and adopt one to which she can dedicate herself. It's a brave new world of sports out there, and our daughters are discovering it for themselves. It's a good thing, even if it feels a little dangerous at times, that our daughters have more choices in their lives than their mothers did.

9

What Parents Can Do

The taboo against girls playing sports today has been largely dismantled. According to the best-regarded study of parents, kids, and sports, 87 percent of parents believe athletic participation is as important for girls as it is for boys. But no deeply ingrained prejudice can be eradicated in a generation. There are still stubborn vestiges from the days when sports were for boys only. It is up to you to limit their impact on your daughter.

The first place to begin is by examining your preconceptions, attitudes, and expectations about sports for kids. Such an examination should be grounded in your own experience, so some self-reflection is necessary. Did you play sports in high school? Were you a Little League standout? Or were you a child who was "not good at sports," for whom the playing field was a scene of embarrassment and anxiety? Before we ask what sports can mean to our children, we have to establish what they mean to us.

Of course, this is different for everyone, and usually much different for men and women and for people of different generations. If you are a woman who grew up in the fifties or sixties, there is a chance that your own sports experience was somewhat limited or even nonexistent. While that might drive you to get your daughter involved, you might unconsciously minimize or restrict your daughter's sports involvement, because that was the way it was done during your day. As a man of the same generation, your experience of sports might have been as a football star or a bench warmer—and your approach to sports for your daughter might be colored accordingly. You may be so intent on duplicating your positive sports experiences that you fail to leave room for her personality. Or you might fall into the trap of "reliving" your own youth through your daughter, making her perform where you did not, for example, pushing her to win the big game where you failed.

Assemble a mental catalog of your athletic experiences so that you can assess positives and negatives, and gauge how the circumstances have changed since then. Recalling your own childhood helps you keep some perspective on what your daughter is capable of at her age, and may prevent you from judging her by what you as an adult can do now. This is a good starting point to reassess your feelings about athletics for girls and women in general. Your attitudes represent the ground zero of your daughter's life, the starting point for her explosion of learning, of becoming.

Make it a habit to share with your daughter examples of successful female athletes. These can range from the softball player next door to superstars in the media. It can be as simple as pointing out a picture of Jamila Wideman in a magazine or tuning in to the Olympics when women's events are being televised. Actively seek out images, stories, videos, and games that portray female athletes in a positive light. Call your daughter's attention to those instances of female athleticism that you might happen to see, from a Friday evening WNBA game to a girl playing goalie in a pickup soccer game on your hometown playing field. Of course, this could mean you have to educate yourself in the rudiments of sports and the current crop of female stars.

The national media might not help out much with this, and may actually undercut attempts to convey a positive image of women in sports. "Men-centric" sports coverage frequently stereotypes female athletes, trivializing or marginalizing their achievements. Research shows that sports commentators tend to describe female and male athletes differently: women are often talked about in terms of their appearance or desirability, while men are described according to their physical skills or playing techniques. In photos, male athletes are pictured in action, while female athletes tend to be posed or on the sidelines. Parents need to search out those shows and publications which present sports coverage in an evenhanded manner. *USA Today* has been a pioneer in print media for its attention to female athletes, and *Sports Illustrated for Kids* features a relatively good representation of women.

Often ignored in the national press is the phenomenon of local sports heroes, stars that hometown fans follow throughout their careers. Local papers know readers care about these athletes, so they cover their stories. It's a pantheon that includes girls as well as boys. High school senior basketball standout Jackie Stiles of Claflin, Kansas, already has autograph-seekers who dog her footsteps before games. Her legendary exploits include a sophomore year when she broke the wrist of her shooting arm.

Playing with a cast on her right arm, she learned to shoot with her left hand, and still managed to average over 23 points per game. Cindy Blodgett of the University of Maine Black Bears was the leading scorer in NCAA Division I women's basketball for a record three years in a row. "She is the most beloved figure in the state," says author and fan Tabitha King. "She represents the things that Mainers value most—work ethic and character." Fans trade tales of Cindy getting frostbite from shooting outside in below-zero temperatures, or of her practicing dribbling while riding a bike. "Cindymania" supports a clothing and souvenir line, the proceeds from which ($1 million over four years) go to a women's scholarship fund. Stiles and Blodgett are only two of the many regional female sports heroes all across America who may not be nationally known but who are beloved legends in their own towns, counties, or states. Following the career of one of these hometown heroes can be an exciting way to make sports real for our daughters.

Our daughters need us as active partners in their sports participation all through childhood. They need us in the stands, as spectators. C. C. Ryan is a sixteen-year-old sprinter from Chicago, an avid participant in the Chicago program A Sporting Chance. "It means so much to me to have my mom and dad there, even though my mom's voice is so quiet: 'I know you can do it, dear' as I run by, while my dad is going wild."

They need our interest in their games—and not just a vague question about who won. They need a sense from us that we believe in them. Eleven-year-old Lizzie Cook is an example of a child who has had a lot of blessings in life. Her family divides its time between New York City and a summer home in Connecticut; her father is a lawyer and her mother an accomplished journalist. But when asked to reflect on the highlights of her young athletic career, she singled out not expensive tennis lessons or a molybdenum racquet but a word of praise from her father. She recalled the pride she had felt at the end of the previous summer, during which she had worked hard on her tennis game, upon hearing her father turn to her mother and say, "She's going to be the next Martina."

We need to get out on the baseball diamonds with our daughters, onto the tennis courts and soccer fields. Lizzie talked about preferring to play with her dad over her coach. "My dad is really really good, so that's helped me to play tennis," she said. "He hits the ball so hard that I have to just smack it right back. And it's hard—it hurts your wrist when he hits it. When my teacher in Central Park hits it, it's not as hard, so it's easier but it's not fun. I'm so used to hard balls, but every Monday I just get little, easy balls, and I'm more used to having big, hard, strong, tough balls over the net. She does not hit the ball hard."

SPORTS AND THE PRESCHOOLER, AGES 0–5

Here are some ways to help your preschool daughter get off on the right foot with sports:

- Be active in sports yourself.
- Make fitness part of your family's everyday life.
- Encourage your daughter to play with boys and in mixed-gender groups.
- Point out examples of female athletes and athletic achievement.
- Teach basic sports skills in a relaxed, fun atmosphere.

The primary way to influence even very young children in their response to sports is to show yourself as a role model. This is not to say that we all must be weekend warriors on the softball field (or the basketball court, the hockey rink, and so on)—or even be in any way sports-minded. "As a family we are the far-thest thing away from being sports fanatics," says Kate Greathead's mother, Christina Pennoyer. "Her father and I never played in school, and we don't even watch sports on televi-sion." The vital thing in Greathead's family is the general sup-port she receives for her endeavors.

But if you do play sports, the likelihood of your daughter playing is increased. One survey found that 70 percent of girls who participate in athletics have at least one parent who also plays sports. But there are a host of ways you can be involved without putting on the sweats yourself—as a coach, as a referee, as a fan, as the team chauffeur. Remember that as a parent you represent a crucial element of your daughter's participation in sports. *The Wilson Report: Moms, Dads, Daughters, and Sports* indi-cated that 44 percent of girl athletes list "parental involvement" as the factor that gave them the most encouragement in their athletic activities.

There are many ways to integrate sports into your family's day-to-day rhythms. We need to limit sedentary activities such as television watching, video game playing, and computer time. Ex-ercise can be an attractive alternative to these largely isolating pursuits if we make it a social, not a solitary, activity. Taking walks or bike rides together helps establish fitness as a way of life. Re-wards or gifts of sporting equipment lends athletic activities value in children's eyes. How about a child-sized basketball this Christ-mas rather than yet another doll? Framing and displaying photos of your daughter's sports activity shows how much you value it.

There does appear to be one factor that is even more impor-tant than parental involvement in determining the future of your daughter's role in sports—her choice of childhood playmates. According to the *Miller Lite Report on Women in Sports,* those girls who play in childhood with boys or in mixed-gender groups are far more likely to participate and attain leadership positions in organized sports at all levels, from grade school to college, as well as continue to be involved in athletics as adults. One of your responsibilities as a parent, then, is to ensure that your daughter has a variety of playmates.

Because of disparities in the way we treat toddler and pre-school girls and boys, the statistical likelihood is that by the time she reaches kindergarten a girl will be a year or two behind her male peers in development of skills such as overhand throwing, kicking a ball, and hitting with a bat. These skills are essential not only to playing but to enjoying a sport. As a parent, you can do much to eliminate this developmental gap. "Playing catch" must be a fundamental part of your daughter's childhood, just as it is for many boys. That said, it is crucial to communicate these basic sports skills in as relaxed a way as possible. Your daughter should enjoy learning to throw a ball with you—it shouldn't be an oner-ous task to be "checked off" when she has mastered it. Even though children can be enlisted as pupils for intensive, concen-trated, rote-style "training," in the long run such an approach can backfire. The association of sports with stress and anxiety can be with her all her life and may eventually lead to her dropping out of sports altogether.

Kids have told researchers that having fun is their primary reason for playing sports. In one study by the Youth Sports Insti-tute, "winning" wasn't even in the top three, or the top five—for girls, it came in twelfth, behind being with friends, learning new skills, and getting exercise. Try to put yourself in your daughter's frame of mind. What sports means to a child—especially a pre-school child—is something very different than what sports means to most adults. For some in the adult world, the essence of sports is winning and losing. In the world of the young child, the es-sense of sports is play.

It is impossible to overemphasize this distinction when talking about what kinds of sports activities are suitable for very young children. Generally, anything overly competitive, anything that smacks of a contest or a race only increases anxiety levels of young children. The question to ask your preschool daughter when she returns from playing kickball is not "Who won?" but "Did you have fun?" Even in the professional leagues, it has become something of a sports cliché: "I'm going to keep on playing until it isn't fun anymore." Those athletes who are most successful at pro sports—Michael Jordan is the supreme example—always seem to keep an element of fun in their play.

One way to keep it fun is to keep it positive. John Wooden was one of the most successful college basketball coaches of all time, leading his UCLA team to numerous national championships. His coaching philosophy is one of overwhelming positive reinforcement. When a team of psychologists analyzed Wooden's instructions to his team, they found that an astonishing 94 percent of Wooden's comments had some positive element—either outright praise, expressions of optimism, or encouragement. Only 6 percent were negative, an those always involved descriptions of specific player actions, not criticism of the player as an individual. If this is true of a successful college coach, dealing with relatively mature players able to take criticism, how much more should it apply to those working with preschoolers?

Helping your daughter choose a sport should fall within these same general guidelines. The first thing to understand is that there is no special reason to push your preschool daughter into an organized sports program at all. If she is learning to throw overhand, to kick a ball, to swim or skate on her own, with support and encouragement from you, then she is progressing well and has no need for a structured sports environment. If she voices a desire to join a program, however, and if in assessing her

227

needs and development you conclude it is a good idea, then it is essential to research not only the general philosophies of programs, but the attitudes of her prospective coaches as well. Several national organizations have clearly articulated rules that encourage equal playing time and fair play. But a program is only as good as the people in it. Meet and speak with the coach and try to determine if his or her philosophy matches yours. Better yet, become a coach or an assistant coach yourself, and make sure the kids have a positive experience.

SPORTS AND THE PRE-ADOLESCENT, AGES 5–13

As you continue working to keep her sports experience relaxed and stress-free, to stay involved yourself and to point out positive female athlete role models, here are some additional ways to help your elementary school daughter get involved and stay involved in sports:

- Make it a practice to ensure that girl and boy athletes receive equal support.
- Search out sports programs that emphasize growth, learning and the positive value of fun.
- Attend and take interest in her games and practices.
- Choose coed or single-sex programs according to what kind of environment your daughter might be comfortable with, and what will contribute most positively to her learning and growth.

If your daughter has not participated in sports by the time she is ten years old, there is only a 1 in 10 chance she will still be active athletically at age twenty-five. In order to gain the lifelong benefits that playing sports provides, in other words, your daughter should begin to get involved in athletics during grade school.

If during her preschool years she has developed the basic skills necessary to feel confident on the playing field, your daughter will be better prepared during this crucial period of her life. If she hasn't, help her in the basics now.

You can also help your daughter by thoroughly investigating the opportunities for her to play sports in your area. What you are looking for is programs which give girls an equal chance in all aspects of the athletic experience. Even though we have made great strides in the last two decades welcoming our daughters onto the playing field, there are always places where the pace of change hasn't caught up with the organizers. You should steer clear of programs that fail to recognize these basic truths: during grade school, ages five through thirteen, girls and boys are on an equal footing physically, they are equally avid as competitors, and they largely accept the principle of coed athletics.

As the parent of a young daughter, you need to be aware of the need for equal treatment and make others aware of it, too. Sometimes the hurtful attitudes of adults can be aimed directly at girl athletes. One father was stricken to hear boos and hisses of other team parents as his daughter—the only girl in the league—came up to bat. Usually differences in how girls are treated are more subtle. They get less playing time or are played at different positions or in a different manner than are boys. You need to ask hard questions. Do the coaches allow sexist comments ("You're playing like a bunch of girls!") or do they coddle or make special exceptions for the female players? Sometimes you have to dig a little to get at the real situation on your daughter's team. Wisconsin runner Megan Nelson's mother, Jan, expressed surprise when Megan recited a litany of discriminations that the girl athletes endured at her school. "This is the first time I'm hearing any of this," Jan Nelson marveled. Megan responded: "Why mention it? It's not like they were going to do anything about it."

You don't have to go overboard with this, or become the Carrie Nation of the basketball court. Gentle reminders and private conversations can sometimes accomplish things that all the sideline screaming in the world won't. Encourage your school administrators to give equal support to girls and boys (it's not only a good idea, it's the law). Talk to your daughter's coaches before the season starts. This is a golden time in children's lives, and luckily it is also a time when boys and girls are more or less equal physically, because the transformations of maturity have not yet taken place. It is a time when we can lay the foundation for equal treatment later, not only on the playing field, but in all fields of endeavor. This is as much for our sons as for our daughters. When he's played alongside girls and learned to respect their contributions to the team, a boy will be much less likely to grow up with a restrictive idea of women's capabilities in the world.

It is during this period, the grade school years, that competition begins to dominate the environment of youth sports. It is too early. Once again, the reason girls and boys of this age play sports—the overwhelmingly important, number one reason for them—is to have fun. When you search out a program or a team for your daughter, look for one that de-emphasizes winning in favor of learning and growth. Author and sports psychologist Rick Wolff tells a story about a young boy who caught the attention of his coach during a Pop Warner football game by actually skipping back to the line of scrimmage from the huddle. Of course, this went against everything the coach held dear about the rough and tumble nature of football. He was about to castigate the boy when he realized that here was the essence of kids at play. The boy was simply enjoying himself. The coach bit his tongue and let the moment pass.

A good, informal way to gauge if a youth sports program is fulfilling its primary mission—giving kids a chance to have fun— is simply to stand at the edge of the playing field and listen. Is the mood tense, full of recriminations and screaming? Is there a lot of verbal abuse of the opponent? Do the players, coaches, or parents of the players use obscenities? Or rather, is the air filled with the sound of children laughing, shouting, having a good time? That sound is instantly recognizable from any pickup game which children organize themselves. Why should the games adults put together sound any different? We need more informal leagues, teams on which everyone is welcome, more alternatives to the kind of youth sports teams where the kids are treated simply as miniature versions of adults.

The arguments for and against coed play during this age period won't be resolved anytime soon. Luckily, there is a pretty simple guide for you as a parent—ask your daughter what she thinks. There are some girls who won't be satisfied with anything less than the most rigorous, most physically demanding level of play, and this is often found in a mixed-gender league. Other girls want the freedom to explore their game at their own pace. Your daughter's opinion might not be your only guide—she may not know if she would be happier on a coed or single-sex team— and it is up to you to investigate the offerings in your area until you come up with a satisfactory match.

THE TEEN YEARS

During adolescence your daughter needs the physical, psychological, and social benefits that being involved in sports can provide.

Here are some ways to help your high school age daughter get the most out of her athletic participation:

- Make sure your daughter's school is in compliance with Title IX and ask for changes if its not.
- Resist "professionalism" and overemphasis on winning.
- Be aware of the dangers of overtraining.
- Watch for signs of disordered eating.
- Guard against verbal, emotional, and sexual abuse of young athletes.
- Help your daughter investigate future opportunities in organized sports: college scholarships, intramural play, employment possibilities such as coaching, sports medicine, or media.

Our daughters need us for support in an adult world that may not welcome them as female athletes. That means continuing to monitor your school system to see that it treats boy and girl athletes the same. Naomi Fritson and her husband Dean Casper are just about as Middle American as you can get—they're rhubarb farmers in south central Nebraska. Fritson noticed that her two sons had more opportunity to play varsity sports in high school than her daughter, Sarah. She embarked on a four-year quest to start a girls' varsity softball program, starting club teams, raising funds, and eventually going to court to force her school district to recognize the value of girls' sports. "How can I expect my daughter to believe she can be whatever she wants to be when I go to school and hear, 'No, you can't'?" Fritson asks. Her campaign succeeded—just in time to see her daughter leave high school for college. We need to examine the selection of sports at our schools, the provision of equipment, scheduling, assignment of coaches, facilities, even publicity. When the girls' team is forced to play on second-rate fields that are not adequately groomed, unequal facilities become a health issue, since bad field conditions can be dangerous.

Has your daughter announced that she's "just not good at sports"? Has she dropped out of an athletic program, avoided physical education classes at school, become sedentary? In these cases, remember that your daughter has not failed at sports but that sports has failed your daughter. Every person—certainly every child—has the right to the pure physical joy of movement. Your school sports program might have developed unfortunate elitist tendencies—only superjocks need apply. The "professional" model of athletics is filtering down from the major leagues to colleges and universities and to our nation's high schools and even to middle and grade schools. We need to resist it and to continue to insist that there be ample opportunity for kids to play sports "just for the fun of it."

Choosing not to continue with sports is a major decision in a young girl's life, but it is important to keep it in perspective. Sometimes dropping out is really just "stopping out," a much-needed interval of reassessment, recuperation, and change. "I was burned out," recalls star high school gymnast Elizabeth Mc-Nabb, who quit at age sixteen. "I recognized it. I was getting a lot of pressure to get to the Olympics. My parents were pushing me, my coaches were pushing me, although my parents were doing it in a good way. I just didn't like it anymore. Those days, I would cry at the gym. I was afraid to do things. I was afraid to fail." She concentrated on track and racquetball, expecting never to go back to gymnastics. On a tour of the facilities after she entered Arizona State University, she happened into the gymnastics room. A flood of memories came back, and McNabb found them surprisingly positive. Joining the university's gymnastics team as a walk-on, she gained a full scholarship the following semester.

For parents concerned about the dangers of overtraining, it

may be an odd form of reassurance to learn that girl and boy athletes are equal in one respect—they have roughly an equal chance of sustaining a sports-related injury. Girls, in other words, are no more fragile than boys.

"There's no such thing as a 'good' injury for a boy or a girl," writes Dr. Lyle Micheli, president of the American College of Sports Medicine. "But the fact that 'sex-specific' injuries are a rarity puts to bed outdated and erroneous concerns about women and sports." Breast injuries, long an obsessive concern of many people wishing to "protect" females from the rigors of the playing field, turn out to be among the rarest injuries in sports. In the 1987–88 season, a survey of 318,000 female high school athletes and 379,000 male high school athletes indicated that each group had 23 percent of players sidelined at least once in the past year by an injury.

The "play with pain" ideal prevalent in the male sports world has its inevitable counterpart among female athletes. Gymnast Kerri Strug's celebrated sprained-ankle vault in the 1996 Olympics conveyed a stirring image of toughness and tenacity, but it also sent a potentially dangerous message to the country's coaches and athletes.

Some problems are specifically associated with girls who train rigorously. Many involve disruptions in menstruation, of concern primarily because amenorrhea (lack of periods) has been linked to loss of bone mass and to osteoporosis in later life. At low levels of body fat—15 to 20 percent—menstrual periods may become sporadic or disappear altogether for months or even years. In addition, there are clinical indications that the hormonal changes associated with amenorrhea are also linked with disordered eating patterns. Clearly, for the athlete whose periods have been disrupted, there is need for medical vigilance, but there have been no long-term implications for reproductive health. In fact, a group of elite Olympic athletes, interviewed years after their participation in the games, reported relatively fewer birth complications and easier labors than a control group of less active women.

For all high school athletes, a pre-participation medical check is essential. Parents should not rely on schools to decide if their child is physically fit for sports, since a recent study found that screening questionnaires are often incomplete or inadequate.

Eating disorders, especially bulimia, plague female athletes at rates somewhat higher than typical for the general populace. There are numerous red flags for which parents can watch. Bulimics often cannot conceal the signs of binge eating and purging: frequent use of the bathroom after meals, fluctuations in weight, bloodshot eyes, swollen glands, swollen extremities, discolored teeth, and feelings of depression, guilt, or shame about eating. Warning signs for anorexia include sudden weight loss or weight gain (fluctuation of more than 15 percent of ideal body weight), an obsession with weighing oneself, preoccupation with food and dieting, loss of hair, and obsessive exercising. Parents need to know which athletes are most susceptible to eating disorders—in sports which emphasize smallness, thinness, or low weight, in activities where an athlete is most likely to display her body in a form-fitting leotard or swimsuit. Elevated levels of eating disorders may be found in sports such as gymnastics, figure skating, swimming, diving, distance running, cheerleading, and bodybuilding.

Eating disorders can be fatal if left untreated. The Renfrew Center has published advice for parents of children who exhibit some of the warning signs for disordered eating. Parents are advised to communicate their desire to help, to seek professional help for their child as soon as possible, and to learn all they can about the problem. "Be prepared to hear her deny that there is a problem," states one Renfrew publication for parents. "People often experience eating disorders as shameful, embarrassing, hard to acknowledge." Be patient, refuse to get caught up in battles of will, and examine your own prejudices about weight. Don't agree to keep her disorder a secret, and don't try to solve the problem on your own. Avoid comments about her appearance, about "good" and "bad" foods, about dieting and nutrition—talking about these subjects might only contribute to her compulsion.

The middle school and high school years are among the most rewarding for the student athlete, but there are risks associated with participating in organized athletic programs about which every parent should be aware. Carefully monitor your daughter's relationship with her coaches. Parents are naturally cautious about the closeness that can develop between an athlete and her coach, but usually this intimacy is healthy, allowing your daughter to move out from the protected circle of the family and yet still remain secure. In rare cases, the relationship between a coach and an athlete may turn abusive. There is no reason for coaches to dominate, manipulate, verbally harass, or physically abuse their charges. Parents need to know where the line is drawn and to confront the coach who crosses it. This can be done in person—although not just before a game, and preferably in private—or, if the seriousness of the case warrants it, brought to a higher authority such as an athletic director, principal, or board of education member.

Carole Oglesby of Temple University identifies "two paths" in dealing with the stereotypes and bias that still beset all female athletes. The first path is our attempts to reform the world our daughters enter. "In the school setting and in the family setting, we can establish rules for what's going to be said to each other,"

236

Oglesby says. "We can make sure that the boys don't ridicule or call the girls on the team 'dykes.' There should be one set of standards that everybody should stick to." But Oglesby recognizes the limitations of this approach. "You are not going to keep every comment from hitting your daughter. Somebody is going to do something—maybe a lot of somebodies. They'll hang out of a car window on the street and yell something. It will happen." Because we can't possibly control every element of our children's lives, Oglesby recommends a second path in conjunction with the first, something she calls "drown-proofing"—ensuring that our daughters become secure and confident individuals. "The more that the parents can push for psychological health in every way they think of, the better. If I am very secure about myself, and secure about everything about me that has to do with my identity and sexuality, if that security is solid, then it will not be shaken by a comment."

Throughout the period of your daughter's involvement in sports, it is a good idea to discuss with her various scenarios for the future. One reason for this is to avoid becoming preoccupied with the gold medal/national championship fantasy. Whether or not your daughter qualifies for the elite sector of high school or college sports, don't let her face the future as a closed door. Encourage her to realize she can enjoy sports for her whole life. Explore career options such as coaching, sports medicine, or media jobs so that she can continue to be involved in the sport she loves even after her involvement in school athletics is over.

The best approach to sports participation grows out of the best approach to parenting: a partnership, a give-and-take between parent and daughter, athlete and coach, body and mind. Today we send our daughters into a dizzying, often destructive world. Sports can make all the difference in how she negotiates her path through that world. "When a girl is raised in such a way that she feels entitled to her rightful part in sports," says Carole Oglesby, "then she is not going to settle for anything else. It's like having the right to vote. I cannot imagine what it would take for women to feel that they should lose the right to vote. Women and girls need to feel that way about sport, about exercise and staying active, about the control of their own bodies."

The evidence points to a simple fact: playing sports helps our daughters grow into healthy, strong women. As parents, as educators, as members of the human community, we need to recognize that this fact carries with it a responsibility. We need to make athletics an integral part of our daughters' childhood, so that their ownership of it is something they take for granted, like air or sunlight. We need to stitch it into the fabric of their lives.

Do You Have a Story About Girls in Sports?

We are interested in anecdotes, life stories, reports of bias, exemplary programs, or instances of exciting achievements by young female athletes.

Communicate with us via our e-mail address: athleticdaughters@yahoo.com or by writing to:

Raising Our Athletic Daughters
P.O. Box 8606
Tarrytown, NY 10591

Appendix

Resources and Further Reading

Resources

The following national organizations offer sports programs for girls.

American Youth Soccer Organization (AYSO)
5403 West 138 Street
Hawthorne, CA 90250
310–643–6455
The premier soccer program for kids (and the source of one of the country's most popular bumper stickers). Rules encourage skill development and equal playing time.

Girls Incorporated
30 East 33 Street
New York, NY 10016
212–689–3700
The Girls Incorporated motto is "Helping girls become strong, smart, and bold." The large sports component features different initiatives at each of their locations throughout the country, but most share a "Sporting Chance" curriculum: "Stepping Stones" for girls age six to eight, "Bridges" for ages nine to eleven, and "Sports Unlimited" for ages twelve to fourteen.

Girl Scouts of the USA
420 Fifth Avenue
New York, NY 10018
212–852–5732
The Girl Scouts calls its program "GirlSports," and it emphasizes basic skills for girls age 5 to 8. Also hosts an annual national sports event and "Sports Days" throughout the summer.

Little League
P.O. Box 3485
Williamsport, PA 17701
717–326–1921
Still the biggest sports organization for America's children.

P.L.A.Y.
One Bowerman Drive
Beaverton, OR 97005
503–671–6499
A public service arm of Nike, Inc., that trains high-school-age coaches in a wide variety of sports, among other programs.

PONY Girls Softball
P.O. Box 225
Washington, PA 15301–0225
412–225–1060
PONY stands for "Protect Our Nation's Youth." Functions as the governing body for girls' softball leagues nationwide.

Soccer in the Streets
149 South McDonough
Suite 270
Jonesboro, GA 30236
770–477–0354
A national program that uses soccer in an urban setting not only as a physical activity but to teach a wide range of social skills.

Starlings Volleyball
1723 Aldergate Road
Encinitas, CA 92024
619–944–9013
Working to provide an alternative for children who do not have access to the club system, which is where most colleges recruit their players. Urban and rural components.

START SMART
National Alliance for Youth Sports
2050 Vista Parkway
West Palm Beach, FL 33411
561–684–1141
Gets very young kids off on the right foot—developing basic skills that will allow them to enjoy sports at every period of their lives.

Teenie Tennis
P.O. Box 2285
Redmond, WA 98073–2285
206–881–1446
Using a variety of stratagems and teaching methods, the program helps bring game skills to even very young players.

WOMBATS: Women's Mountain Biking and Tea Society
Box 757
Fairfax, CA 94978
415–459–0980
There's probably only one thing they're totally serious about: crossing the finish line first.

YWCA of the USA
726 Broadway
New York, NY 10003
212–614–285
The national basketball and volleyball effort in conjunction with Nike, "Health and Sports Advocay," provides start-up costs for sports programs and is the centerpiece of a serious drive to get more girls involved in sports.

The following are some of the numerous regional organizations that provide sports programs for area girls.

Acorn Oscar Bailey Track Club
805 Filbert Street
Oakland, CA 94607
510–891–9833
An inspiring story as well as a nationally recognized source of world-class track stars.

Girls Achieving in Nontraditional Sports (GAINS)
4–18 John Street
Fair Lawn, NY 07410
201–836–5752
Dedicated to the proposition that the whole concept of "girls' sports" is a fallacy. Exposes girls to such nontraditional sports as wrestling and football.

Girlsports International
275 S. Monroe Court
Louisville, CO 80027
303–664–0724
Brings girls together across socio-economic, ethnic, and national divisions to play sports and travel.

The Peter Westbrook Foundation
G.P.O. Box 7554
New York, NY 10116
212–459–4538
A program that helps children from disadvantaged communities become champion fencers and positive role models.

Real Options for City Kids (ROCK)
400 Montgomery Street
Suite 805
San Francisco, CA 94104
415–434–1331
Volunteer mentors provide sports instruction to high-risk elementary-school-age kids in San Francisco's multi-ethnic Visitación Valley neighborhood.

A Sporting Chance Foundation
6650 North Artesian
Chicago, IL 60606
773–381–1707
Provides sports and fitness activities to enhance girls' self-esteem, leadership, team-building skills, and academic excellence. Clinics, "Sporting Chance Day," a sports and leadership camp, equipment program, coach training. Free resource guide and other publications available.

Sportsbridge
965 Mission Street
Suite 220
San Francisco, CA 94103
415–778–8390
Matches mentors to individual athletes with excellent results.

Sports4Kids
520 Third Street, Suite 202
Oakland, CA 94607
510–893–4180
High school mentor coaches and other volunteers offer skills-based sports in elementary schools at recess.

Wendy Hilliard Foundation
792 Columbus Ave., Suite 17T
New York, NY 10025
212–721–3256
Provides free classes in rhythmic gymnastics for inner city youth.

Women's Soccer Resource Center
P.O. Box 3905
San Rafael, CA 94912
415–454–7627
Recycles soccer gears and conducts an annual soccer camp for girls, as well as serving as a clearinghouse of soccer coaching talent.

The following can provide information and/or research about health, physical activity and sports for girls and women, coaching, and sports careers

Amateur Athletic Union (AAU)
c/o The Walt Disney World Resort
P.O. Box 10,000
Lake Buena Vista, FL 32830–1000
407–934–7200
Motto: "Sports for all forever." Sponsors Junior Olympic Games, the AAU Sports Program, and, in conjunction with Walt Disney World Sports, hosts the AAU national championships.

Black Women in Sport Foundation
P.O. Box 2610
Philadelphia, PA 19130
215–763–6609
Its purpose is to increase the opportunities available to African-American females in the area of sports. Sponsors an annual conference and mentoring workshops, as well as a program called "Sports through Reading," an educational initiative.

Children's Trust Fund
444 Lafayette Road North
St. Paul, MN 55155–3839
612–296–KIDS
Provides a resource packet entitled "Keeping Youth Sports Safe and Fun," which includes a bibliography of good books about sports for kids.

Melpomene Institute
1010 University Avenue
St. Paul, MN 55104
651–642–1951
Advocacy and research organization focusing on the link between girls and women's health and fitness. Offers information packets, books, and videos to

the public on subjects such as "Girls, Physical Activity & Self-Esteem," "Body Image," and "Eating Disorders."

National Association for Girls & Women in Sport
1900 Associate Drive
Reston, VA 22091
703–476–3450
800–321–0789
The leading organization for equity issues in sports; instrumental in educating the public on Title IX legislation. Offers publications such as "Title IX Toolbox," to measure schools' compliance with the law; and "The High School Athlete: Her Personal Journal." Sponsors the annual National Girls & Women in Sports Day in early February.

National Collegiate Athletic Association (NCAA)
6201 College Blvd.
Overland Park, KS 66221–2422
913–339–1906
The governing body for collegiate sports.

National Federation of State High School Associations
11724 NW Plaza Circle
P.O. Box 20626
Kansas City, MO 64195–0626
816–464–5400
Collects national high school sports participation statistics; produces rule books and other instructional materials on high school sports programs.

National Women's Law Center
1616 P Street NW
Washington, D.C. 20036
Functions as one of the premier national resources for Title IX legal issues.

Tucker Center for Research on Girls and Women in Sport
University of Minnesota
203 Cooke Hall
1900 University Ave. S.E.
Minneapolis, MN 55455
612–625–7327
An interdisciplinary research center that studies many related aspects of women and sports, and offers copies of the president's council report, "Physical Activity and Lives of Girls."

United States Olympic Committee
One Olympic Plaza
Colorado Springs, CO 80909
719–578–4833
Offers information for kids aspiring to the elite levels of athletics.

Women's Sports Foundation
Eisenhower Park
East Meadow, NY 11554
516–542–4700
Founded by Billie Jean King, it has evolved into an effective umbrella organization and a powerful advocacy force for female athletes nationwide. Sponsors an annual summit, important funding initiatives in partnership with corporations, training and travel grants, and the forthcoming Women's Global Challenge sports event.

Further Reading: A Selective Source List

Books

Best, Raphaela. *We've All Got Scars: What Boys and Girls Learn in Elementary School* (Bloomington: Indiana U. Press, 1993).

Bissinger, H. G. *Friday Night Lights: A Town, a Team, and a Dream* (New York: Addison-Wesley Publishing, 1990).

Black, David R., Ed. *Eating Disorders Among Athletes*(Reston, VA: American Alliance for Health, Physical Education, Recreation and Dance, 1991).

Blais, Madeleine. *In These Girls, Hope Is a Muscle* (New York: The Atlantic Monthly Press, 1995).

Brumberg, Joan Jacobs. *The Body Project: An Intimate History of American Girls* (New York: Random House, 1998).

Cahn, Susan. *Coming on Strong: Gender and Sexuality in Twentieth-Century Women's Sport* (New York: The Free Press, 1994).

Chambers, Marcia. *The Unplayable Lie: The Untold Story of Women and Discrimination in American Golf* (New York: Pocket Books, 1995).

Corbett, Sara. *Venus to the Hoop: A Gold Medal Year in Women's Basketball* (New York: Doubleday, 1997).

Crisfield, Deborah. *Winning Soccer for Girls* (New York: Facts on File, 1996).

Debold, Elizabeth, Marie Wilson, and Idelissa Malare. *Mother Daughter Revolution* (New York: Bantam, 1993).

Eagle, Dr. Carol, and Carol Colman. *All That She Can Be: Helping Your Daughter Achieve Her Full Potential and Maintain Her Self-Esteem During the Critical Years of Adolescence* (New York: Simon & Schuster, 1993).

Festle, Mary Jo. *Playing Nice: Politics and Apologies in Women's Sports* (New York: Columbia University Press, 1996).

Fine, Gary Alan. *With the Boys: Little League Baseball and Preadolescent Culture* (Chicago: University of Chicago Press, 1987).

Gadeberg, Jeanette. *Raising Strong Daughters* (Minneapolis, MN: Fairview Press, 1995).

Geist, William. *Little League Confidential* (New York: MacMillan, 1992).

Gilligan, Carol. *In a Different Voice: Psychological Theory and Women's Development* (Cambridge, MA: Harvard University Press, 1982).

Gilligan, Carol, Nona Lyons, and Trudy Hammer. *Making Connections: The Relational Worlds of Adolescent Girls at Emma Willard School* (Cambridge, MA: Harvard University Press, 1990).

Gilligan, Carol, and Lyn Mikel Brown. *Meeting at the Crossroads: Women's Psychology and Girls' Development* (Cambridge, MA: Harvard University Press, 1992).

Guttmann, Allen. *Women's Sports: A History* (New York: Columbia University Press, 1991).

Hastings, Penny, and Todd D. Caven. *How to Win a Sports Scholarship* (Los Angeles: First Base Sports, Inc., 1995).

Hoferek, Mary J. *Going Forth: Women's Leadership Issues in Higher Education and Physical Education* (Princeton, NJ: Princeton Book Company, 1996).

Holliman, Susan Chappell, ed. *Eating Disorders and Athletes: A Handbook for Coaches* (Dubuque, IA: Kendall/Hunt Publishing Company, 1991).

Jenkins, Sally. *Men Will Be Boys* (New York: Doubleday, 1996).

Johnson, Susan E. *When Women Played Hardball* (Seattle: Seal Press, 1994).

King, Billie Jean, with Cynthia Starr. *We Have Come a Long Way: The Story of Women's Tennis* (New York: McGraw Hill, 1988).

Layden, Joe. *Women in Sports: the Complete Book on the World's Greatest Female Athletes* (Los Angeles: General Publishing Group, 1997).

Lieberman-Cline, Nancy, and Robin Roberts. *Basketball for Women: Becoming a Complete Player* (Champaign, IL: Human Kinetics, 1995).

Lobo, RuthAnn, and Rebecca Lobo. *The Home Team: Of Mothers, Daughters & American Champions.* (New York: Kodansha, 1996).

Mann, Judy. *The Difference: Discovering the Hidden Ways We Silence Girls, Finding Alternatives That Can Give Them a Voice*(New York: Warner Books, 1994).

Messner, Michael A. *Power at Play: Sports and the Problem of Masculinity* (Boston: Beacon Press, 1992).

Navratilova, Martina, with George Vecsey. *Martina* (New York: Alfred A. Knopf, 1985).

Nelson, Mariah Burton. *Are We Winning Yet?: How Women Are Changing Sports and Sports Are Changing Women* (New York: Random House, 1991).

Nelson, Mariah Burton. *Embracing Victory: Life Lessons in Competition and Compassion* (New York: William Morrow, 1998).

Nelson, Mariah Burton. *The Stronger Women Get, the More Men Like Football: Sexism and the American Culture of Sports* (New York: Harcourt Brace & Company, 1994).

Nyad, Diana. *Other Shores* (New York: Random House, 1978).

Oglesby, Carole A., with Doreen L. Greenberg, Ruth Louise Hall, Karen L. Hill, Frances Johnston, and Sheila Easterby Ridley. *Encyclopedia of Women and Sport in America* (Phoenix: Oryx Press, 1998).

Pipher, Mary. *Reviving Ophelia: Saving the Selves of Adolescent Girls* (New York: Ballantine Books, 1995).

Reece, Gabrielle. *Big Girl in the Middle* (New York: Crown, 1997).

Riley, Dawn. *Taking the Helm* (Boston: Little, Brown and Co., 1995).

Ryan, Joan. *Little Girls in Pretty Boxes: The Making and Breaking of Elite Gymnasts and Figure Skaters* (New York: Doubleday, 1995).

Sabo, Don, and Michael Messner. *Sex, Violence and Power in Sports: Rethinking Masculinity* (Freedom, CA: The Crossing Press, 1994).

Sadker, Myra, and David Sadker. *Failing at Fairness: How Schools Cheat Girls* (New York: Touchstone, 1994).

Salter, David F. *Crashing the Old Boys' Network: The Tragedies and Triumphs of Girls and Women in Sports* (Westport, CT: Praeger, 1996).

Summitt, Pat, with Sally Jenkins. *Reach for the Summit: The Definite Dozen System for Succeeding at Whatever You Do* (New York: Broadway Books, 1998).

Thompson, Ron A., and Roberta Trattner-Sherman. *Helping Athletes With Eating Disorders* (Champaign, IL: Human Kinetics Publishers, 1992).

Whitney, Marceil. *Teenie Tennis: A Love Game* (Redmond, WA: ATS Publishing, 1991).

Willard, Frances. *A Wheel Within a Wheel* (Bedford, MA: Applewood Books, 1997).

Wolff, Rick. *Good Sports: The Concerned Parent's Guide to Little League and Other Competitive Youth Sports* (New York: Dell, 1993).

Zaharias, Mildred Babe Didrikson. *This Life I've Led: My Autobiography* (New York: A. S. Barnes, 1995).

Reports

A Call to Action: Shortchanging Girls, Shortchanging America (Washington: American Association of University Women, 1991).

Mitchell, Carolyn B., and Stephen F. Austin, coordinating and contributing editors. *Gender Equity Through Physical Education and Sport* (Reston, VA: American Alliance for Health, Physical Education, Recreation and Dance).

New World Decisions, Ltd., in cooperation with the Women's Sports Foundation. *Miller Lite Report on Women in Sports* (December, 1985).

Poinsett, Alex. *The Role of Sports in Youth Development: Report of a Meeting Convened by Carnegie Corporation of New York* (New York: Carnegie Corporation, 1996).

The President's Council on Physical Fitness and Sports, under the direction of The Tucker Center for Research on Girls & Women in Sport, University of Minnesota. *Physical Activity & Sport in the Lives of Girls: Physical & Mental Health Dimensions From an Interdisciplinary Approach* (Department of Health and Human Services, 1997).

Sabo, D., K. Miller, M. Farrell, G. Barnes, and M. Melnick. *The Women's Sports Foundation Report: Sport and Teen Pregnancy* (East Meadow, NY: Women's Sports Foundation, 1998).

Schoen, Cathy, and Karen Davis, Karen Scott Collins, Linda Greenberg, Catherine DesRoches, and Melinda Abrams. *The Commonwealth Fund Survey of the Health of Adolescent Girls* (New York: The Commonwealth Fund, November 1997).

Wilson Sporting Goods Co., in cooperation with the Women's Sports Foundation. *The Wilson Report: Moms, Dads, Daughters and Sports* (June 7, 1988).

The Women's Sports Foundation Gender Equity Report Card: A Survey of Athletic Opportunity in American Higher Education (East Meadow, NY: Women's Sports Foundation, 1997).

Publications for Parents

Daughters: A Newsletter for Parents of Girls Ages Eight to Eighteen (1808 Ashwood Avenue, Nashville, TN 37212–5012. Phone: 800–829–1088).

New Moon Publishing: For Adults Who Care About Girls. New Moon Publishing, P.O. Box 3587, Duluth, MN 55803–3587. Subscription information: 218–728–5507.

Books for Children and Youth

Barber, Barbara E. *Allie's Basketball Team* (New York: Lee & Low Books, 1996).
   Boating, Yaw Adabio. *Miss John*(New York: Chelsea House Publishers, 1994).
Charbonnet, Gabrielle. "American Gold Gymnasts" series: *Competition Fever; Balancing Act; Split Decision; The Bully Coach* (New York: A Skylark Book, Bantam, 1996).
Christopher, Matt. *Red-Hot Hightops* (Boston: Little, Brown and Co., 1987).
Christopher, Matt. *Supercharged Infield* (New York: Little, Brown and Co., 1985).
Crisaldi, Kathryn. *Baseball Ballerina* (New York: Random House, 1992).
Davis, Gibbs. *Christy's Magic Glove* (New York: A Skylark Book, Bantam, 1992).
Davis, Gibbs. *Katie Kicks Off* (New York: A Skylark Book, Bantam, 1994).
Goldstein, Margaret J., and Jennifer Larson. *Jackie Joyner-Kersee: Superwoman* (Minneapolis: Lerner Publications Company, 1994).
Haigh, Sheila. *The Little Gymnast* (New York: Apple Paperbacks, Scholastic, 1962).
Herman, Hank. *Super Hoops: In Your Face!* (New York: Bantam, 1996).
Knudson, R. R. *Zanbanger* (New York: Harper & Row, 1977).
Knudson, R. R. *Zanboomer* (New York: Harper & Row, 1978).
Kovalski, Maryann. *Take Me Out to the Ballgame* (New York: Scholastic, 1992).
Krull, Kathleen. *Wilma Unlimited* (New York: Harcourt Brace, 1996).

Levy, Elizabeth. *Something Queer at the Ballpark* (New York: A Young Yearling Book, Dell Publishing, 1975).

Levy, Marilyn. *Run for Your Life.* (New York: Houghton Mifflin, 1996).

Lord, Bette Bao. *In the Year of the Boar and Jackie Robinson* (New York: Harper Trophy, 1984).

Marney, Dean. *Dirty Socks Don't Win Games* (New York: Scholastic, Apple, 1992).

Minters, Frances. *Cinder-Elly* (New York: Viking, 1994).

Moore, Elaine. *Who Let Girls in the Boys' Locker Room?* (Rainbow Bridge, 1994).

Morissette, Mikki. *Jennifer Capriati* (Boston: Sports Illustrated for Kids, Little, Brown and Co., 1991).

Parish, Peggy. *Play Ball, Amelia Bedelia* (New York: Harper Trophy, 1972).

Pascal, Francine. "Team Sweet Valley" series: *Win One for Sandra* (New York: Bantam, 1996).

Pinkney, Brian. *JoJo's Flying Side Kick* (New York: Simon & Schuster Books for Young Readers, 1995).

Plantos, Ted. *Heather Hits Her First Home Run* (Windsor, Ontario: Black Moss Press, 1989).

Proboz, Kathilyn. *The Girls Strike Back: The Making of the Pink Parrots* (Waltham, MA: Sports Illustrated for Kids, Time, Inc., Little, Brown and Co., 1990).

Snyder, Zilpha Keatley. *Cat Running* (New York: Delacorte Press, 1994).

Suzanne, Jamie. *Standing Out* (New York: Bantam-Skylark, 1988).

Willard, Nancy. *The Highest Hit* (New York: Harcourt Brace Jovanovich Publishers, 1978).

Wyeth, Sharon. "American Gold Swimmers" series: *The Winning Stroke; The Human Shark; Splash Party; In Deep Water* (New York: Skylark Books, 1996).

Acknowledgments

It is customary to save the best for last, but in this case we would like to thank Betsy Lerner, our editor and good friend, right up front for her contributions to the genesis, vision, research, and writing of this book. It would not exist without her.

We could not have proceeded without the help of all the families who generously invited us into their lives. The sports professionals we spoke with provided proof positive that committed, energetic individuals can make all the difference in girls' sports experience. The people behind the organizations that are supporting girls in sports gave generously of their time and insights.

Kim Witherspoon represented the project with a deft hand. We would also like to thank her staff at Witherspoon Associates.

Our families, as always, were a great help. Thanks especially to Medith and Thomas Phillips, who provided contacts and research. Acton and Eloise Reavill were always there with interest and enthusiasm. Alesha Kientzler was a great help with research.

Steve and Betty Zimmerman kept their respective clipping services going at top speed for the duration of this project and also offered generous amounts of logistical support. Sandra Morrel helped make a crucial contact. Peter and Andy Zimmerman put in many hours' service to the cause (they also serve who babysit and wait), as did Suzanne Levine and Alexa Duncan. Lisa Senauke and James Carrington put us up during our research in the Bay Area. Many other friends put up with us during the long haul. Thanks always to Felice Schwartz, an energetic sportswoman, whose life was an inspiration.

Finally, Maud Reavill provided a constant source of good humor and joy. She has taught us what a privilege it is to raise a child, especially one with a good arm.

Jean Zimmerman is the author of *Tailspin: Women at War in the Wake of Tailhook* (1995) and coauthor with Felice Schwartz of *Breaking with Tradition: Women and Work, the New Facts of Life* (1992). Gil Reavill is a travel writer and journalist. They are married and live in Westchester County with their daughter.